Kuwabara Takeo, born in 1904, is professor
emeritus of Kyoto University and member of
the Science Council of Japan. Katō Hidetoshi
is professor of sociology at Gakushuin University and research fellow at East-West Communication Institute, East-West Center. Kano
Tsutomu and Patricia Murray are translators
at the Center for Social Science Communication, Tokyo.

# Japan and Western Civilization

# Japan and Western Civilization
## Essays on Comparative Culture

Kuwabara Takeo

Edited by
**Katō Hidetoshi**
Translated by
Kano Tsutomu and Patricia Murray

UNIVERSITY OF TOKYO PRESS

Translation supported by a grant-in-aid from the Ministry of Education,
Science and Culture

© University of Tokyo Press, 1983
UTPN 3095-87468-5149
ISBN 0-86008-338-1
Printed in Japan

# Contents

Preface      vii

Editor's Introduction      xi

1. The Social Effect of Art      3
2. Seven Beauties and the Modernization of Rural Tastes      27
3. Tradition Versus Modernization      39
4. The Classics in Contemporary Japan      65
5. Another Look at Japanese Culture      75
6. Europe and Japan      85
7. Cooperative Research in the Humanities      97
8. Japan and European Civilization      115
9. The Meiji Revolution and Nationalism      155
10. Japan's Third Opening      175
11. The Secondary Art of Modern Haiku      187

# Preface

ALTHOUGH everything I have ever written has been in Japanese and for Japanese readers, I always hoped for the opportunity to be able to reach foreign readers as well. Aside from a few essays translated into European languages and published in such journals as *Diogenes*, however, that hope remained unfulfilled. So when the University of Tokyo Press came to me with an offer to publish a volume of my essays in English, I was delighted to accept. The majority of the essays were to be selected from a collection published in 1974 entitled *Yoroppa bunmei to Nihon* (Japan and Western Civilization, Asahi Shinbun). The remainder may be found in another collection published in 1972 by Bungei Shunjū, *Dentō to kindai* (Tradition and Modernization). Professor Katō Hidetoshi of Gakushuin University kindly agreed to select the essays and write the introduction.

I have no idea how people outside Japan will react to the ideas expressed in these essays—the immediate task is to translate them into an idiomatic style accessible to English readers. I have always resisted the self-centered absorption of many Japanese with the concerns of their own country; this volume represents the opportunity to test the ideal of universality I have always sought in my own writing before an international readership, and it is an opportunity for which I am most grateful.

Inspired by the pacifist ideals embodied by Unesco, in 1947 my colleagues and I at Tōhoku University in Sendai began a movement urging cooperation with Unesco, despite the fact that Japan had not yet become a member. The achievement of world peace is certainly not as easy as we then so naively thought; in fact, it has grown more and more difficult. Back then we were very ignorant of world affairs, but we were filled with confidence and, above all, optimism. Today we are in urgent need of such optimism, and the confidence that humankind has the power to avert catastrophe. The indispensable precondition for achieving this goal, I believe, is mutual understanding among the peoples of the world based on unbiased, well-informed perceptions of each other. I will be content if this book can contribute to such an understanding by offering some insights into Japan and the Japanese.

The essays in this volume, save for the last, are arranged in chronological order. It is not necessary to read them in order, but I believe the reader will find it helpful to be aware of the year in which each was originally published. The essays were not intended as commentaries on current affairs, but the issues and events of the times are inevitably reflected therein. They are not concerned with explaining the essence of Japanese culture, but rather to present the perspectives of one intellectual whose thinking progressed through several ideological phases. Professor Katō has provided a lucid and insightful commentary on the background of each essay and its overall significance in the development of my thinking; I hope the reader will thus begin with the introduction.

The introduction is so thorough that there is little I need add, except for a brief comment on the final essay, "The Secondary Art of Modern Haiku," which I especially asked be included in this collection. Even in times when Japan has come under severest attack from other countries, haiku alone is never criticized. The popularity of haiku is not confined to Japan alone but is now quite international. People write haiku in their own vernacular in countries around the world. It should not be overlooked, nonetheless, that there were Japanese intellectuals in the early postwar period who dared to be so "un-Japanese" as to criticize this literary "pride" of the Japanese people. I wrote this essay not long after Japan's defeat in World War II at a time when I was a radical modernist. Today, at a time when poetry as a literary genre is in decline everywhere in the world, it is significant that Japan's literature of short verse is thriving as never before. Perhaps the popularity of haiku is a phenomenon

characteristic of mass culture, which if subjected to proper study, might lead to a better appreciation of the essential character of Japanese culture.

With regard to European history, I have learned a great deal from the works of Professor Geoffrey Barraclough. Recalling the pleasant and stimulating conversations we had on many occasions in Paris, Tsukuba, and Kyoto, I must again acknowledge my profound debt to this great scholar.

The publication of this volume would not have been possible without the goodwill and cooperation of many. The Japanese Ministry of Education provided a grant to cover the cost of translation, offering the much-needed initial impetus for the project. Professor Katō Hidetoshi wrote a brilliant and penetrating—and at times much too flattering—introduction. The excellent translation was prepared under the supervision of Kano Tsutomu by Patricia Murray with the assistance of Lynne E. Riggs and Takechi Manabu. Tada Hitoshi and the staff of the University of Tokyo Press planned the publication and supervised the successive steps leading to its completion. To all of these I would like to express my most sincere gratitude and appreciation.

Kyoto                                   Kuwabara Takeo
August 1983

# Editor's Introduction

BORN in 1904, the son of the eminent sinologist Kuwabara Jitsuzō, Professor Kuwabara Takeo majored in French literature at Kyoto University, from which he graduated in 1928. After spending some postgraduate years in France, he began his teaching career at Osaka Higher School and Tōhoku University (1943) and was appointed professor at the Research Institute for Humanistic Studies, attached to Kyoto University, in 1948. In 1955, he was elected Director of the Institute and demonstrated flexible and progressive administrative capabilities.

His early scholastic efforts were devoted to modern French literature, including the translation of works of such authors as Stendhal and Alain, and he has been a leading figure in the Japan Association for French Literature and other French studies organizations. But he has never considered himself only a French specialist. He has been, and remains, not only a man of literature in its broadest sense but also a man whose interests cover all aspects of human affairs.

Kuwabara has never been content to be an armchair scholar. He is essentially a positivist who speaks out of his own solid experience. He gives unconditional priority to firsthand observations and experiences over secondary information sources, such as books, although he is widely read in such fields as primate studies, fine arts, Chinese classics, cultural anthropology, world history, and behavioral psychology, to mention only a few.

Kuwabara's wide range of interest, and his positivistic attitude, come partly from his background as an alpinist and explorer. As a child, he loved climbing the mountains surrounding the city of

Kyoto; while a student at Kyoto University, he joined a mountaineering club; and his activities as an alpinist continued even
in his mid-fifties, when he led a Japanese team that set out to
conquer the peak of Chogolisa in the Himalayan range. This
adventurous mind made him an extensive traveler, and he
visited parts of the world from England to Bhutan, and from
China to the United States. For him, his direct observations
were the fundamental keys to understanding the different cultures of the globe. In this volume, the reader will discover many
episodes based on Kuwabara's own experiences, and the way
he quotes these episodes is surprisingly keen, appropriate, and
persuasive. This pragmatic approach to the subject is one of the
major characteristics of his literary style.

When Kuwabara Takeo took a chair at Kyoto University in
1948, his talent as an interdisciplinary intellectual came fully
into its own. Since the Research Institute for Humanistic Studies
was a place where research scholars had no teaching obligations,
Kuwabara was able to demonstrate his leadership in assembling
and integrating scholars of various expertise. His administrative
philosopy and practice are well described in essay seven of this
volume. As a matter of fact, he was innovative enough to put psychologists, historians, philosophers, economists, and anthropologists together to work on particular subjects, breaking through
the walls of tightly compartmentalized academic disciplines.
When he started this new interdisciplinary project team concept,
many observers especially university people, were either skepti-
cal or cynical about this adventurous experiment. They believed
that the scholars would feel much happier and more comfortable
in their own segregated compartments, not mixed up with
"aliens." How, they asked, could an atomic scientist work with
a philosopher whose major interest was ancient Chinese Taoism?
In spite of the skepticism and cynicism, the project team proved
to be very successful, and the research scholars involved thrived
on the stimulation of different disciplines. Once, when a psy-
choanalyst made a presentation on the relationship between an
individual's physical type and temperament, he proposed to have
everyone in the team photographed in the nude to prove a hypothesis. Naturally, historians, philosophers, and linguists alike
were embarrassed and even scared. But Kuwabara liked the idea,

and he volunteered to be the first person to have his picture taken. Reluctantly, the others followed suit, and in the end they were fascinated not only by the outcome of this unique experiment but also by the light it shed on psychosomatic theories.

Episodes of this nature are numerous. What made possible this miraculous interaction among scholars of different disciplines was the firm and warm-hearted initiative and leadership of Kuwabara. Through a series of such exchanges of ideas and experiments, the team under his administration became interdisciplinary in the academic sense, and, more importantly, each individual participant became an interdisciplinary person, like Kuwabara himself. This group of researchers was later labeled the neo-Kyoto School (Shin Kyoto Gakuha) by both academicians and journalists who regaided in with respect and admiration.

Kuwabara's approach to academic affairs was revolutionary in many respects. His recruitment of research staff, for example, was radically democratic in the sense that any vacancy was announced nationwide and a research scholar to fill that vacancy was selected by means of fair competition, including written examinations on foreign language, history, philosophy, and so forth. This method, again invented by Kuwabara, was beyond the imagination of the majority of Japanese university professors, because for them, faculty "inbreeding," hiring faculty usually from among graduates of the same university, had been taken as a matter of natural and customary course for any person in the university ladder system. Of course, there were many academics who were critical of the inbreeding system, but nobody was brave enough to put his ideas into practice.

Indeed, one of the major factors which made the birth of the neo-Kyoto School possible was this free recruitment system initiated by Kuwabara. The tradition was inherited by his successors, and in the spring of 1983, for the first time in the history of Japanese national universities, the Research Institute for Humanistic Studies recruited a young British scholar as a full-fledged associate professor. Kuwabara's philosophy and practice of personnel recruitment had now expanded across national boundaries. These liberal arrangements—in the organization of interdisciplinary project teams and in recruitment procedures—were

Kuwabara's great contribution not only to the Research Institute but also to Japanese academic circles at large. His innovative ideas and administrative success, coupled with his energetic writing, established him as one of the best-known scholars, authors, and critics in Japan. In 1951, he was elected to the Science Council of Japan (Gakujutsu Kaigi), and eventually he was appointed vice-president of that academic body.

His activities on the international scene also have been extraordinarily wide-ranging. He attended numerous international conferences, including many Unesco meetings, as a Japanese delegate, and he is currently the vice-president of the National Federation of Unesco Associations of Japan. Also, as an active member of the Japan P.E.N. Club, he took the initiative in organizing the International P.E.N. Conference in Kyoto in 1974. The writings in this volume include papers he delivered at the East-West Center, Honolulu (essay nine) and the General Assembly of the International Council for Philosophy and Humanitistic Sciences, Ann Arbor, Michigan (essay four).

Looking back over his long career, it is easy to see that Kuwabara has been cosmpoplitan in the best sense of the term; with his appreciation of the diverse cultures of the world he adjusts himself comfortably to any culture he visits. He can sit with eminent scholars and artists in sophisticated restaurants in New York or Paris and discuss intellectual subjects, but at the same time he is happy to spend hours with the peasants in a mountain village of Bhutan. One day he may chair an academic conference, and the next day he may drink beer in a small town bar and chat with whoever is sitting next to him. He is thus an anthropologist in the best sense, and he may be much better than most of those who consider themselves anthropologists.

In 1967, he applied for a Ministry of Education grant to do anthropological field research on western Europe, specifically France and England. For most anthropologists, field research means conducting interviews and collecting indigenous artifacts in "primitive" cultures, and to most Japanese scholars, western Europe is considered a place for making respectful visits to learn from its advanced technologies, philosophies, and fine arts. In this context, nobody ever thought of an anthropological study of western Europe. But in Kuwabara's framework, any culture in the world is appropriate as an object of study from a humanistic and unbiased viewpoint. He received the grant, and several younger researchers, including myself, were organized to conduct field research in Europe, living in small towns and rural villages. The project was a successful one, and the end result of this exploration encouraged him to write two of the essays in this volume, essays six and eight.

Moreover, the expedition to Europe set a good precedent both for the Ministry of Education and for the scholars who had thoughts similar to Kuwabara's. Field research funds to study advanced countries are now taken for granted by the ministry, but it should be remembered that the venture was initiated by this imaginative individual.

As is obvious given the background described above, Kuwabara's name is well known not only in intellectual circles in Japan, but also among the general reading public. His literary style is relaxed and persuasive. Above all, he has been extremely conscientious about writing in plain, basic Japanese, especially when he writes for popular magazines or when he gives speeches to general audiences. Yet he has kept a sophisticated approach and critical attitude to the subjects under discussion. The readers of this volume will discover these characteristics of his style on each and every page.

Essay eleven of this book, which was written in 1946, the year following Japan's surrender to the Allied Forces, marked his debut as a brave new literary critic. As an assistant professor of forty years of age, he posed a radical question about haiku, the seventeen-syllable Japanese poetical form, which for its very simplicity has attracted the deep interest of literary people around the world. This artistic genre had been well established since the eighteenth century and was followed by many poets, and nobody had ever criticized the literary form itself. In other words, haiku had been sacrosanct among Japanese intellectuals until Kuwabara wrote a critical review of the genre. What he tried to point out in his epoch-making essay was that there was no practical and realistic basis for those who were known as haiku masters to claim themselves as professional artists. In order to prove his point, the author gave an interesting experimental quiz, so to speak, to a number of people: he asked whether they could recognize professionally created haiku among the fifteen poems by both masters and total amateurs placed in random order The outcome of this small experiment was shocking; nobody could see the difference between the haiku composed by professionals and those by amateurs. Thus the author attacked the myth attached to haiku and rated this poetical genre as a quasi-art. When his findings were published, the whole Japanese literary and scholarly world was stunned, and the pros and cons made for a very hot debate on the subject. Indeed, it would be quite fair to say that this essay was the landmark by which post-war Japanese literary criticism was given a new direction and horizon.

Incidentally, a certain skepticism about the nature of haiku had existed among scientists even before Kuwabara published his criticism. Haiku composition is, mathematically speaking, simply a matter of combining of seventeen syllables out of fifty Japanese phonetic symbols (*kana*), and the simple number of such possible combinations can be calculated mathematically. But such an argument did not attract the attention of literary circles. Looking at this "mathematical theory of haiku" in 1983, when the completion of a "fifth-generation" computer is anticipated in the near future, one can see that haiku may not be able to retain its position as a creative art; the new computer can determine which combinations of seventeen phonetic symbols are *meaningful*.

The greatest contribution of this essay, however, is that the author stressed that all works of art, including haiku, are part of a given social milieu, and that arts should be interpreted against their sociocultural backgrounds. Kuwabara's concern about the arts, especially literature, in a word, has been strongly related to societies and cultures at particular historical stages of development. However, his approach is not rigid, as is the Marxist theory of "superstructure," and he remains flexible in examining the relationship between the arts and society. His major interest in this problem area has been to investigate the social function of literary work.

Essay one of this volume is a good example of this approach. He looks at the social effect of the arts, including the novel, theater, music, movies, and even popular songs. His basic questions are: what are the effects of the arts on the individuals who are exposed to them, and how can such effects be measured? As readers will see, in order to establish his unique theory, he mobilizes the findings of behavioral psychology, i.e., the stimulus-response theory which leads to attitude formation. Also, he does not neglect possible discrepancies between the "intention" of artists and the "effects" which the audience may experience. In this sense, he regards art essentially as a medium of social communication.

Toward the end of the essay, he makes clear analytical statements, looking into several factors involved in the extremely subtle and complicated processes of the social transmission and diffusion of the arts. The key factors which give "vectors" are the personality of the individual observer or listener, including the degree of adjustment flexibility, and the social conditions and context in which particular art works are appreciated. For those who are engaged in communication research, it is well proved that the "effect" study is the most difficult and ambiguous area, because one cannot isolate the effect of a particular message. Of course, in the past few decades, communication researchers have devised various methods to measure the effects of communication. For example, those engaged in marketing communication try to prove that a newspaper ad or a television commercial can motivate consumers to buy the products advertised. Despite such efforts, so far no researcher has proved the relationship between an advertisement and consumer behavior in scientific terms. Kuwabara concludes that the value of arts, and communication in general, should neither be overestimated nor underestimated as a force for change in the minds of the people as well as in society at large.

As readers will notice from this essay, Kuwabara's approach is comparative, and his quotations range from John Dewey to Li Po, from Jean Piaget to Mao Tse-tung, and from Karl Marx to Japanese popular songs. This wide range of knowledge is indicative not only of Kuwabara's style but also of the style of many Japanese intellectuals. As a matter of fact, the Japanese probably are the best informed people in the world, because major books and writings of the East and West, old and new, are all available in the Japanese language. In this sense, essay one will be a good prelude through which foreign readers can be introduced to the orchestrated intellectual atmosphere of Japan.

Essay two is an amusing essay that brings out Kuwabara's style at its best and shows him to be a scholar with a full range of intellectual curiosity. He was associated with many sociologists and anthropologists, from whom he was quick to absorb the current state of these disciplines. Naturally, he became aware of the importance of the social survey, and as a pragmatist he was fascinated by this new methodology and technique, imported from American-style sociology. He "tuned in" to social survey methodology immediately, so to speak. At the same time, he could not help but see possible dangers caused by careless social researchers, and he distrusted those sociologists and anthropologists who conducted field research for somewhat egoistic reasons, such as simply to write dissertations.

In Kuwabara's philosophy, no social research should exploit people. An interview must be a dialogue through which both parties can experience stimulation and enrich their learning. Above all, the research must be something in which people like to participate and which they can enjoy without any anxiety or hesitation. Therefore, he invented a unique tool of social research: the "beauty contest" method. Kuwabara says that when photographs of seven beautiful women were shown to them, the men who were interviewed became interested in rating the ladies, and they actually enjoyed "being studied." Some villagers even eagerly looked forward to the visit of "the professor with the pictures of beauties."

The test he conducted with the pictures, as he admits, did not have any solid scientific basis. Social "scientists" may argue that what he did with the pictures was simply to compile an impressionistic description of the tastes of randomly selected common people, and that no generalization is possible out of his quasi-research. However, when Kuwabara described this inventive research method to Harold Lasswell, the eminent political scientist showed keen interest in it. David Reisman, whom Kuwabara met in 1961, was also very much impressed by the "happy amateurism" of the Kuwabara team, including this kind of social research. The perceptive reader will immediately identify Kuwabara in Reisman's *Conversations in Japan* (New York: Basic Books,

1967), where major intellectual figures in Japan are described under pseudonyms.

Essay two is on the one hand a satire on fashionable social research and on the other the starting point from which Kuwabara's questions about modernization began. Indeed, the beauty contest survey was designed to examine the degree of modernization, though his esthetic judgment with regard to the continuum of traditional and modern faces of women may seem to be problematic. However, his findings, through this imaginative "projective method," at least succeeded in proving that different social groups had different senses of beauty, that such differences may indicate socio-cultural changes taking place in Japan, and that such changes may imply modernization processes.

Essay three can be read as a good theoretical continuation of essay two. The topic of tradition and modernization has been, as Kuwabara states at the outset, a century-old subject of discussion among Japanese intellectuals, and very often scholars and writers of Japan have been divided into traditionalists and modernists. In the late nineteenth century, this division was clearly marked. The traditionalists were, generally speaking, the people who believed that the dangers of overwhelming industrial progress were brought from the West and who resisted most things and institutions of Western origin. They respected Japanese traditions in philosophy, customs, and lifestyle. On the contrary, the modernists of the day were people who welcomed *anything* from the West. Therefore, for the old-fashioned modernists, "modernization" was synonymous with "westernization." In other words, the traditionalist vs. modernist problem in the past could be interpreted as a confrontation of the pros and cons of Western influence upon Japanese culture and society.

The social context in which Kuwabara's paper was written in 1957 was extremely complex, even confusing, because unlike "traditional" traditionalists, whose ideological inclination was more or less that of the right-wing reactionary, the "new" traditionalists of the 1950s were found to be, strangely enough, Marxists. The Japan Communist party at that time was decisively anti-American and was propagating a struggle against American imperialism. In fighting for that goal, they stressed the urgent need for the preservation of Japanese traditions, because, in their thinking, Japanese traditions were endangered by American expansionism, popularly known as "Coca Colanization." In other words, Marxists and left-wing intellectuals found themselves in an ironical situation. By definition, they were progressive and sometimes even advocated destruction of established values. But in this particular context, they imposed upon themselves an ultra-reactionary role.

It was against this background that Kuwabara felt the necessity of "intellectual traffic control." In this essay, he classifies Japanese scholars into four groups and analyzes the nature and function of each group. At the same time, he proposes six major modernization indices. For him modernization is not necessarily westernization, and though he recognizes the problems caused by exceptionally rapid sociocultural change, he assures us with confidence and factual evidence that Japan has been a modern nation-state since the latter part of the nineteenth century, when the Meiji era began. As readers will notice, this essay has a strongly political tone, but they may be able to appreciate its value if they are reminded of the ideological landscape of 1957.

What Kuwabara says to an international audience in essay four inherits the spirit of essay three and applies it on a wider, global scale. On the one hand, he characterizes Japanese culture by its strong integrating power, especially in the field of humanities, and on the other he discusses the necessity of reinterpreting the classics. His concluding statement in this paper is bold: he declares that certain elements of tradition might not be able to survive the process of internationalization of cultures and states that he would not mind if these elements disappeared. In his opinion, traditions that cannot hold their own against contemporary conditions are not worthy of being called traditions. Here again, he mentions the importance of the cultural revolution that took place in Japan in the middle of the nineteenth century. It should be noted that he defines the social change of nineteenth-century Japan as a "revolution," as opposed to its usual label of Meiji "restoration."

This thinking leads him to his analysis of contemporary Japanese culture, which is described in essay five. His major point in this essay is the fallacy of the kind of historicism that tends to make Japanese people seem inferior. His illustration of the Japanese camera industry, which he mentions at the outset, is persuasive. He says, in short, that photographic technology was invented by the French, but the high-quality cameras in today's world market are made in Japan. If one looks at cultural elements in historical reflection and investigates the origin of such elements, most of them are imports from the outside, especially from China and the West. But Kuwabara stresses that this intriguing study of origins is not important to an understanding of contemporary Japanese culture, and that it would be simply nonsense for Japanese people to have an inferiority complex vis-à-vis places of origin.

He also highly evaluates the virtue of Japanese people, both present and past, in their keen selectiveness. In his opinion, Japanese have not been imitative at all. Rather, they have been selective and flexible in the process of cultural contact, and Kuwabara even praises the "childlike spirit" of Japanese people who do not hesitate to experiment with all new things. If such new things are good, Japanese integrate them into their culture, and if not, they just disregard or discard them.

As an example of the latter, he mentions the fact that, in spite of efforts of the Christian missionaries after the sixteenth century, only a tiny minority of the Japanese people accepted Christianity. And he poses a very interesting hypothesis in saying that the fundamental factor in Japanese industrial success after the Meiji revolution was the polytheistic view of religion that was deeply rooted in the Japanese mind.

Since this lecture was delivered to a public audience, he used no academic language or references. The implication of this essay is very important, since there were, and still are, many Japanese social scientists who believe firmly in Max Weber's theory of the Protestant ethic and capitalism. For them, Christianity, more specifically Protestantism, was the necessary prerequisite and absolute condition for the rise of capitalism. Since Japan had no Christian tradition, for these scholars the logical conclusion was that Japan could not have a "pure" capitalism of the Western type. According to them, even if Japan was a capitalistic country, it had to be an immature and distorted capitalism, not authentic. On the contrary, Kuwabara explicitly states in this essay that the capitalistic industrialization and modernization of Japan was possible precisely because of the *absence* of mono-theistic religion. The essay can be read as a sharp criticism of Japanese social scientists and historians. At the same time it should be emphasized here that Kuwabara's observations and interpretations of contemporary Japan are shared by the majority of the Japanese public, who usually show more common sense than Weber-bound social scientists.

This essay proves that Kuwabara is not looking at the West as a model for Japan. For him, each culture has its own virtues and shortcomings, and he is simply giving the socio-historical facts of the West and Japan on a comparative basis. This attitude and philosophy, regrettably, are very rare among those Japanese scholars who have studied abroad: they tend to point out only the shortcomings and "immaturity" of Japanese society in comparison with the Western countries where they spent their days as students. Kuwabara, as mentioned earlier, studied in France, but he is not "Frenchified" at all. He remains a self-confident Japanese scholar, encouraging the Japanese public through his thoughts on the virtues of the Japanese people and their ancestors.

Essay six, which was read publicly in the city of Morioka in 1967, supplements essay five by providing more comparative facts on contemporary Japan and Western Europe. Some of the points and episodes in this essay are repeat those in essay five, but in this lecture, Kuwabara's observations about Western Europe are updated; the lecture was given only a few weeks after he returned from his 1967 expedition to Europe, described earlier.

He foresees, in this essay, the relative economic decline of Western Europe, in remarkable contrast to Japan's miraculous postwar economic growth. Here again, he tries his best to break the myth of the "advanced" West and "backward" Japan with a variety of illustrative episodes, mostly from his own experience. According to Kuwabara's observations, England is essentially a society based on a rigid class structure, while Japan is a fundamentally egalitarian society where everything is mobile and flexible. He also points out the indifferent, if not ignorant, perceptions and attitudes of European people concerning Japan. His observations cover even a children's book published in England: from the fact that Japan's bullet train was not listed in the pictorial book among other major high-speed trains of the world, he predicted the decline of England. For him, any culture which is not attentive to other cultures will end up in ethnocentrism and self-conceit.

Surprisingly enough, what he predicted about Japan's future in 1967 came true in the 1980s. As everybody today is well aware, Japan came to be the economic giant on the world scene, and its industrial products, such as automobiles, televisions, and computers, are threatening to outpace those of both the United States and EEC countries. Kuwabara is not an economist; but very few economists in the 1950s accurately predicted Japan's economic position of twenty years later. In this sense, he was a much better economist than most of the professional economists—if economists are those who not only analyze but also predict economic situations in long range terms. And he was right when he ironically said that the popular belief in Japanese "backwardness" was the product of a conspiracy by the guardian gods of Japan so that people would work harder in the past century to enable Japan to catch up with the West and to achieve a new identity as one of the most advanced industrial countries in the world today.

Essay seven is the transcription of a speech Kuwabara delivered in 1968 to commemorate his retirement from Kyoto University. Usually such ceremonial "farewell lectures" are extremely academic and technical, for better or worse; but Kuwabara's approach was quite different. He reviewed his own experience in organizing the unique interdisciplinary project team, and by doing so, he explicitly criticized the bureaucratic sectionalism of the Japanese university system, even mentioning the names of his opponents. He was especially critical of the majority of Japanese professors who, he said, had been enjoying monologues in their own offices instead of having dialogues with others. He pointed out the low productivity caused by the hierarchical university organization where a seniority system was dominant. Indeed, if Japanese universities had been reorganized in the way Kuwabara suggested, perhaps there would not have been the campus unrest that took place in late 1960s and early 1970s.

In the midst of presenting these serious issues, he never lost his good sense of humor or his strong persuasive power: he would admire the beauty of Marilyn Monroe or admit his relative ignorance of cybernetics. In short, his farewell address to his colleagues and students of Kyoto University was a farewell to the conservatism of Japanese academia and, at the same time, a message of encouragement to younger scholars who, being more innovative and progressive, might change the academic atmosphere.

His activities in writing and lecturing did not terminate with his retirement from Kyoto University. As a professor emeritus of the university, he continued his involvement in Japanese government agencies, and Unesco and other international organizations. He has been frequently invited as a guest speaker in both the public and private sectors. For example, essay eight is a transcription of his lectures given for the Asahi Seminar, an adult education program organized by the Asahi Shinbun.

In this lecture series, he acted as both the coordinator and main speaker on the subject of European civilization and Japan. As readers will notice in the first few pages, he presents a grand view of world history in which the age of European dominance is a relatively new, even transitory, period. Furthermore, he points out that the dominance of Europe in world history after 1500 was the product of exploitation of the people in the colonies, such as India, Africa, and parts of Asia. The era of expansion and prosperity of Europe, according to his observation, is coming to an end toward the end of the twentieth century. The metaphor he draws from Barraclough's book, of looking at contemporary Europe as an old man with false teeth, suffering from gerontological diseases and yet pretending to be young, is an excellent one.

Here he strongly emphasizes that, given the global changes over the past five centuries, Japanese people must look at the world objectively and realistically. He sees special danger in the mystification of Europe in the minds of Japanese. His opinions and interpretations, including his forecast for the future of declining Europe, may seem to be nationalistic in the sense that he stresses economic and cultural strength while pointing out the indicators of European weakness in the coming decades. But he neither speaks out of fanatic patriotism nor indulges in narcissism. He appeals to the public to see these realities not only for the Japanese national interest but also for better understanding among the nations of the world. At one point in this lecture, he refers to the increasing number of Westerners visiting Japan and points out that they come to Japan not to study haiku and other aspects of traditional Japanese culture, but to study the Japanese automobile industry. Here again, his insight has proved correct. In 1971, when this lecture was delivered, very few people either in Japan or overseas were aware of the potential power of the Japanese automobile industry. Kuwabara was warning the Japanese public of the possible future problems Japan would have to deal with in its international economic relations. In this sense, he was a brilliant futurist, too.

In the preceding essays, he often mentioned the importance of the Meiji revolution, and he finally crystallizes his ideas in essay nine. This was a paper delivered in 1973 at the East-West Center. In this paper, he clearly states that the commonly accepted term Meiji restoration is incorrect, because nothing was restored, and that the term "revolution" must be used in order to understand the nature of the drastic cultural and social change that began in 1868. He further says that the Meiji revolution was as important as its counterparts in France, Russia, England, and China, and that in many respects the Japanese revolution was even more radical than other famous revolutions. For instance, he points out that Japan abolished its hierarchy of social classes, a feat that major European countries never achieved in spite of revolutions. He also says that, though the Meiji revolution was essentially initiated by the leaders of the day, the masses of people supported their initiative. He does not think that a revolution necessarily requires a bloody confrontation between establishment and revolutionaries. He then proceeds to elaborate on the definition of modernization presented in essay three, and he pays special attention to the cultural aspects of the Meiji revolution by referring to the egalitarian educational system and the high literacy rates of the nineteenth century. He recognizes, of course, the many shortcomings and problems caused by the rapid industrialization in Japan; but basically, he gives a high rating to the revolution which made Japan a modern nation-state within only a few decades.

Interestingly enough, among other factors, Kuwabara believes that historical and geopolitical "luck" played the most important role in the success of modernization of his country. Having been an independent nation before the revolution, Japan could be receptive to Western culture in the mid-nineteenth century, in sharp contrast to the Asian societies that had been colonized by the West. Furthermore, Kuwabara says that Japan was the first nation-state to emerge out of the non-Christian world and to establish its own unique nationalism. The implication of this observation is extremely important, because it is an implicit encouragement of the new wave of nationalism in developing countries. Toward the end, he sees an important task assigned to the peoples of the advanced countries, where cosmopolitan internationalism must harmoniously exist with the new nationalism of the twentieth century. Again, some of the points given in this lecture overlap with those of other essays, but for the devoted reader, the redundancy may serve to reinforce them.

Essay ten is a summary of his presentation, on what Japan can contribute to the world, to an international symposium held under the auspices of Asahi Shinbun. Since this was an abstract, he did not go into detail, but for readers who want to grasp Kuwabara's perception of and perspectives on Japanese culture in the international context, this probably is the best reading material. He summarizes his views under eight major categories. In this summary, he emphasizes the importance of looking at Japan from a real-time, contemporary viewpoint rather than from a nostalgic, history-bound one. He says that his philosophy is essentially sociological or common sense-based, and consciously avoids discussing traditional culture, which has largely disappeared. He expresses his fear of introducing Japan to foreign countries through traditional arts, such as flower arrangement and the Nō play, because these arts merely foster the idea of Japan as exotic, further strengthening an image of Japan that is full of misunderstandings.

According to Kuwabara's observations, Japanese people no longer appreciate simplicity. If anything, their lifestyle has become overdecorative as a result of the society's affluence. In demonstrating the discrepancies between the old-fashioned popular image of Japan and present reality, Kuwabara mobilizes his imaginative power and refers to seemingly totally unrelated facts such as the growth of meat consumption among the Japanese people and their literary taste. He insists that lifestyle, i.e., culture, cannot stay unchanged where meat consumption has increased eightfold in the past thirty years. The illustration he provides in this essay is the Kuwabara style at its best.

Another important point he makes in this paper is that Japan today is a mass society of the highest quality in the world. He, of course, is not opposed to the idea of introducing this high culture to other societies, but to his way of thinking, it is more important to Japan for foreigners to be exposed to its mass culture. Otherwise, he thinks, cultural exchange and international communication about the realities on the people-to-people level cannot be achieved. In other words, he regards the mutual mystification among the peoples of the world as the largest obstacle in international communication today. He does not want the Japanese people to mystify the West and vice versa, and he believes in a common sense shared by the masses of people, not in highly sophisticated intellectual discourse, as far as intercultural exchange is concerned.

To conclude this essay, he touches on the question of the Japanese language, which most foreigners think difficult to understand. In his opinion, language is another example of mystification. If Japan tries to simplify its language, especially by minimizing the use of Chinese characters, then more people abroad would be interested in studying the language. He makes his position on this issue very clear, saying that he has consistently simplified the Japanese language in his own writings as a step toward "internationalizing" the language.

Since the late 1970s, Kuwabara has been stressing the importance of cultural power, which, he thinks, will have equal significance with military power and economic power in the future world, and the perspective on the Japanese language that he develops here probably is one of the major keys to the extent and meaning of Japanese cultural power in the twenty-first century.

As noted above, essay eleven, dealing with haiku, was the essay that firmly established Kuwabara's position in literary circles. When viewed in conjunction with the possible future of Japanese cultural power, what Kuwabara wrote in 1946 is still quite fresh

and appropriate—or even more so—in 1983. He is a man of letters in its strict sense, and has never forgotten the importance of
letters and language that are plain and simple enough to be
communicated to everybody, not only in Japan but also in the
world. As a matter of fact, according to The Japan Foundation
and other organizations, approximately one million people are
taking courses in the Japanese language throughout the world,
and the number is still growing. Could the Japanese language
possibly become one of the major international languages, along
with English, French, or Spanish, in the twenty-first century?
Surely no Englishman in the seventeenth century foresaw that
his language would in three centuries be the language that
airport control towers would use on every spot of the earth.

Professor Kuwabara's essays have the power to inspire pride
in Japan, which I share, and they impose an equally strong
sense of responsibility to put whatever strengths Japan has to
work in the interest of equality, creative interdependence, and
mutual understanding. I am honored to have had the opportunity to be editor of this fine volume and to be able to introduce an extraordinary author to readers thoughout the world.

To conclude this introduction, I wish to acknowledge the
friendly assistance of Ms. Virginia Jamieson of the Center for
Asian and Pacific Studies, University of Hawaii.

The East-West Center, Honolulu                  Katō Hidetoshi
August 1983

Japan and Western Civilization

# 1

# The Social Effect of Art

MOST people believe that in some way or another art has a definite impact on society. There are, of course, exceptions. Those who have no sense for art and regard it as being a form of entertainment and no more, for example, discount any other function. They dismiss art as a socially ineffectual mode of creativity that cannot be expected to have any social impact. And there are those who become so passionately involved that they fail to see beyond the art itself. They are convinced that good art is perfection embodied, a spiritually inspired, transcendent form. They do not wish to sully it by allowing any association with something so vulgar as society. On the whole, however, regardless of their philosophical or ideological position, people generally accept the idea that art can and does influence society.

Marxists happen to be particularly strong believers in the social influence of art. The Soviet authorities have made this very clear for decades in their blanket denunciation of Dmitri Shostakovich's music, and the work of most other modern artists, as degrading and harmful. In France, the Catholic Church takes the effect of art very seriously. It gives ratings to all commercial films according to their moral probity—or lack of it—and posts them weekly at the entrance to country churches. Goebbels, Hitler's propaganda expert, and Franco both tried to keep close reins on the art that the public had access to, as much in an effort to control its influence as to demonstrate their authority.

Originally published as "Geijutsu no shakaiteki kōka," *Gendai Shisō*, vol. 10 of Iwanami Kōza, June 1957.

The American pragmatist John Dewey, also, was outspoken in his belief in the influence of the arts: "The sum total of the effect of all reflective treatises on morals is insignificant in comparison with the influence of architecture, novels, drama, on life. . . ." Even the existentialists, although they tend to focus on the individual actor himself and do not directly address the social implications of art as such, nonetheless do not question the effectiveness of art as a positive force in society. That much is obvious in the very intensity with which these people seek to thrust their message upon others, using their creative work as a channel.

We can safely assume a wide acceptance of the social influence of art, but precisely how that influence is achieved is not at all clear. It is easy enough to learn whether or not people like a given work of art; yet to evaluate, to quantify its actual influence is another matter. To begin with, the response is extremely difficult to assess in any comprehensive, objective way, especially since most people are actively involved in society and are constantly receiving multiple stimuli. It is virtually impossible to isolate their reaction to one specific work from the aggregate response to all the artistic stimuli they are exposed to, and then scientifically calculate the influence it has. Unfortunately, the discipline best equipped to provide analytic tools, experimental psychology, has not developed enough in this area to be of much help. Various tests have been made using the polygraph and other electric devices to record the momentary reaction to films, radio programs, and so on, but no one has yet succeeded in tracing the precise effects that stimulation from a work of art had on the subsequent feelings, thoughts, or behavior of the observer. There are no empirical data, in other words, and without them we can do no more than observe that art certainly seems to have an effect on society; we cannot make an evaluation in any but the most subjective terms. One hopes that the fruit of academic and scientific endeavors will one day make it possible to lift this subject out of the realm of speculation, but for the time being, observation and intuition must suffice as a base for the comments that follow.

No matter how strong the social leverage a work of art is expected to have, or even how deeply it is rooted in a collectivistic ideology, its real effect is achieved only when it touches the subjective consciousness of the individual. Whether one is part of a large group gathered to watch a play on revolution or is enjoying a piece of sculpture alone, in private, the process is the same. In the first instance, a strong pre-existing feeling of group solidarity, and in the second, a sense of solitude, color the impact of the work on the observer, but in both cases, the effect of art ultimately operates on people as individuals. Apart from those cases when the audience is primed to stage a demonstration immediately after the play, usually, even if they have been stimulated to some degree, they leave the theater after the play and go their separate ways. (Certainly the possibility remains that some are so stirred with revolutionary fervor that later they become committed activists.) A work of art can also operate to alienate people; it may be so strongly infused with an escapist type of individualism that it makes a person withdraw into himself and turn as far away from society as he can.

Art can indeed exert a truly powerful influence, whose effect on society emerges in two stages. First, it moves the individuals—in large numbers—of which a society is composed; and second, the effect on those individuals is transferred to society, which is moved as a whole. It is tempting to assume that when the first stage is reached, the second will follow automatically, that society necessarily will be affected by something that has moved a large number of its individual members, but that is by no means always the case. The effect may stop at stage one, and the distinction is important, for strictly speaking, the social effect of art can occur only in stage two.

Such terms as "collectivism" or "individualism" can be misleading, for they are so often ideologically weighted, and they are used here only for convenience in discussion. Some artistic genres can express an ideology directly or give it tangible form, while others cannot, and so it is important not to burden all of them with the potential of creating ideological or some other form of stimulation. In creative writing, for example, the difference between the political ideology of Sartre and Tolstoy comes out clearly in their novels, but in painting, while stylistic differences in the works of Renoir and Cézanne are eminently visible, any distinction between the political ideology of the two is impossible to discern. If we wish to consider the social effect of art, particularly its potential to change society, we should first categorize the various artistic genres according to the mode of response they elicit—the way their influence operates.

## Linguistic and Non-Linguistic Arts

Let us propose two major types, A and B. An A-type work stimulates people and moves them, yet the kind of response it produces is difficult to conceptualize. It may have a strong internal impact on the individual, but its effect usually stops there. Its social influence, if any, is only fragmentary. Works of the B type, as long as they are art, have the same impact as A, but since they are transmitted through the agency of conceptual thought, their effect is retained in the consciousness as a force that can eventually influence society. The two categories, which are purely my own invention and were designed only to help clarify my thoughts, overlap somewhat, as we shall see.

The main difference between A and B effects is the involvement or non-involvement of language. A good example of the A-effect is the enthrallment one experiences listening to a symphony orchestra. Language or words are not called up in creating the excitement, which makes it impossible to analyze or verbally record the full impact of the music. To adequately convey that excitement to others in words is also very difficult, albeit not impossible, apparently, as can be deduced from the plethora of criticism today focusing on the non-linguistic arts. Critics express themselves in diverse ways, writing what seems most appropriate, but in comparing music criticism, for example, with literary criticism or scholarly reviews, one is invariably impressed with the superficial nature of the former. As for the layman, when he comments after a concert, "Oh, it was wonderful," "marvelous performance," that response is enough to convey the stimulation of the music. He verbalizes his response in interjections, not logical propositions.

That music has such an effect does not rule out comparing Bach's and Mozart's music in an essay (although it would pale beside a good comparative discussion of Stendhal and Balzac), of course, but the point is that the stimulation from music is not conducive to logical linguistic expression. It does not lend itself to being organized into the kind of conceptual frame necessary for substantial discussion, nor can it be a turning point toward social action. The excitement remains personal, locked inside the individual. The same tends to be true of dance, painting, sculpture, architecture, and the other plastic, visual arts. The fact that so many works in painting and sculpture, as well as in music, are designated by a number instead of a title most certainly reflects the recognition that these arts, unlike history or literature, are essentially non-linguistic.

We must also recognize, nevertheless, certain other effects that these "non-linguistic" arts can have. Painting and sculpture involve the graphic representation of a definite subject, which the finished work resembles to one extent or another, and so one can hardly avoid being conscious of what the subject is. Seeing a painting or piece of sculpture in terms of its subject is perfectly natural and cannot be faulted. A painting may be highly pleasing in color and design, but if it happens to be a portrait of Hitler, the association with Auschwitz and fascism would destroy its beauty for anyone who knows something about the man. It is even conceivable that the subject alone could create in the viewer a strong loathing for fascism, which is a socially directed sentiment. Listening to the music of Khachaturian might strengthen the sentiments of a Russophile, or, conversely, precisely because a person is a Russophile, he might find himself that much more deeply moved by Khachaturian's music.

In these and similar cases, however, the effect of the art is merely to reinforce a pre-existing attitude. The stimulation received does not cause the emergence of new attitudes toward society. These genres of art are incapable of generating essentially new social attitudes or ideologies. Suppose someone, deeply impressed by a concert, urges a friend to go and hear it. The act of urging is directed outside oneself, and the friend may go to the concert, but any effect the music has on him will be purely personal. The interplay between the two people represents individual, not social, behavior. It cannot be social behavior until the person consciously intends to influence society by his action. That distinction is important in culling out what are genuine social effects of art.

Given the internal, personal nature of the A type of effect, it would be easy to call it a "sensuous effect," but too often the word "sensuous" implies a value judgment that places it one step behind reason in the three-stage format of sensuous cognition → rational cognition → action. This schema is certainly not applicable to music or painting. Modern education theory owes a great deal to Rousseau, who argued that childhood is not simply part of a progression toward adulthood, but has a value and identity of its own. While there is a progression in growing up, however, the same is not true of the response to painting or music. One's response does not—and should not—move from a sensuous to an intellectual stage as he listens to Bach or contemplates a Cézanne. For that reason, I think it fair to place the A-effect in the realm of sensitivity only if the more primitive connotation of the word is excluded.

The stages of intellectual development in animals go through (1) instinct, (2) sensation (motor response), and (3) logical reason. The linguistic function develops in the transition from (2) to (3). Since the A-effect has no recourse to language, it might seem to correspond with stage (2), but that is not necessarily the case. The intellectual function of sensation, or motor response, can be observed in both chimpanzees and infants, which have the characteristic capacity to adjust their behavior in response to external phenomena, but neither evinces any ability to respond with abstract reasoning. A chimpanzee will use a nearby stick or pile up several boxes to stand on in order to get a banana that is out of reach, for example. With this faculty, as opposed to simply instinct, a creature can intuitively reorder its field of perception, but it has only a minimal grasp of past or future; its perception is geared almost entirely to the present.

The A-effect, in contrast, besides being accompanied by no such responsive behavior, clearly occurs in humans when they have reached the stage of linguistic intelligence and have established communal patterns of living in a society built upon consciousness of past, present, and future. Furthermore, as life becomes increasingly dominated by rational scientific intellect, the desire for A-type experience by no means diminishes. It actually increases, in fact, which is why it cannot possibly represent a lower stage leading up to rational intellect. While people possess linguistic intellect, often they deliberately avoid conceptualization in the desire for the kind of immediacy that can be experienced at the level of sensory intellect (motor response), or the fanciful reversion to what Swiss psychologist Jean Piaget called "egocentrism." And that desire has grown stronger as we move deeper into the machine age. It is probably such a response that Paul Valéry tried to describe in the term "intellectual animal."

Those arts that have the B type of effect are, chiefly, literature (poetry and prose), drama, film, and the other basically linguistic genres. What sets them apart is their contextual presentation of human lives. A single work may cover only a small fragment of a life, or it may describe an entire lifetime, even several generations. The time may be of any duration, and it may involve the life experiences of one or many people. To be moved by the work is to identify with the life (lives) portrayed therein. (The same kind of effect cannot be ruled out completely in the case of A-type art works, but since they do not portray life experience per se, such identification is immeasurably more difficult.) Any work that represents human life experience, moreover, invariably is built around a fixed value system, and both artistic and social values are transferred to the reader (audience) throughout that process of identification.[1]

In works of the B type, words are the medium of transmission, which means that, granting differences in degree, the experiences they convey can be related to the actual society one lives in. It is not always easy to systematize the stimuli one receives into a clear, conceptual framework, but the substance of the life experience contained in the work can be conveyed, albeit imperfectly, through words. It is a tall order to set someone chuckling with a discussion of Beethoven's 61st concerto, but I have been able to make people think or laugh in talks on Sartre's *The Wall* or the film *Teahouse of the August Moon*. No oratorical talent, of course, can substitute for the original works, but well-chosen words can stimulate the same effect. Unlike music, whose effect can never be transmitted by any means except hearing the work performed, the substance of the conceptual information contained in works of the linguistic genres can be adequately transmitted without requiring reference to the original. True art appreciation demands more than such second-hand consumption, but for our purposes, the fact that art can exert influence in this way, also, is the important point here.

## Circuitous Routes of Art's Effect

To say that art can affect society implies some kind of action that changes society, carried out by someone who has been stimulated by a work of art. But can the response to artistic stimuli lead directly to action? Let us consider some of the ramifications of this question before trying to answer it.

There was a murder last year (1956) in the Gobanchō area of Kyoto. After seeing the film "Darkness at Noon," the murderer turned himself in. In a sense, a work of art was behind the action. It could produce this effect, however, because the man was already under the psychological stress of guilt, knowing that some innocent youths had been arrested in his place. The film was catalyst for action. Music and singing are tried and true stimulants in strengthening the resolve of a group at times of war or revolution; in some cases, this kind of artistic effect actually seems to generate by itself certain kinds of group behavior. But here, too, as when a film stimulates someone already disturbed to commit violence, the art is only working on an abnormal psychological urge already present in the individuals involved.

Strictly speaking, normal and abnormal are purely relative terms, yet it is common sense that a "normal" state of mind seldom is inspired to direct action by a work of art. Generally, animals experience the phases of stimulus → emotional response → reaction (action). This pattern is all too easily extended to suggest that if the stimulus from a work of art produces a response, it will then lead to some kind of action. But here we must make a distinction. While human beings have much in common with other animals, they are extremely complex creatures. Man alone has the intelligence to create language and to build and sustain a society with historical continuity. Only man possesses art. Humans cannot be tested in the same way as laboratory animals, which produce a simple, given response to a single stimulus. Show a person some food, and chances are he will immediately start thinking unconsciously about the social conventions associated with eating; or say the word "food," and he conjures up all kinds of images besides the victuals mentioned.

The formidable array of functions possessed by human beings act most of the time to inhibit an immediate outward reaction when a person is moved emotionally. Whatever the reason, such stimulation must first be screened through the consciousness, which, as long as man is a social animal, is subjected to social constraints. In any case, we know from experience that the translation of artistic stimulation straight into action rarely occurs, if at all. If, indeed, the stimulus from art cannot become a direct impetus to action, art itself has no power to change the environment of the aficionado. How, then, *does* art operate? It cannot work change on the social (external) environment, but the experience of responding to artistic stimulation has the potential to cause internal change, and in so doing, it can regulate the way a person will act later on.

What is meant by the somewhat vague term "internal change" is a change in the way certain nerves respond. The precise mechanism by which any external stimuli, not just those from art, work on human nerves is not completely clear. I hope, however, that some day we will be able to stop speculating and identify exactly how, physiologically, the effect of art works on man. In any case, art that genuinely moves leaves a lasting impression. In a sense, it prods the formation of an "attitude." In this, art operates in the same way as the many other stimuli that influence the formation of attitudes or, perhaps more correctly, proclivities or mental inclinations. Still, a proclivity does not necessarily induce an external act that differs from one's usual behavior. More often, a given stimulus triggers a certain psychological reaction, and that may or may not produce some kind of action.

In each of us there is an intertwining network of countless such attitudes that constantly interact. Dewey referred to the internal structure of attitudes as habit (*Human Nature and Conduct*, 1922). Man, he said, is a creature of habit. He is no more a creature of reason than a creature of instinct. Clearly man is not controlled by basic drives such as instinct—although they are

present—yet man's behavior is not always rational and reflective, either. Most of us behave according to habit. It is not that
our behavior is mechanized, or controlled by inertia; rather,
even our spontaneous acts are regulated by a set of individual
habits that characterize not only our external conduct but our
internal thoughts and feelings, also. Habit is, in short, the building block for the formation of the self.

Both attitudes and habits have a lasting quality, but they can
change. The rigidity of one's habits corresponds to the in-
flexibility of his social environment. Thus, the changeability of
habits increases as society develops from one stage to the next—
it is much greater in modern societies than in feudal, for example (no doubt the emergence and growth of the concept of
freedom is closely related to this correspondence). In general,
then, the quality in a work of art that moves us operates on our
habits and changes them, indirectly influencing the way we behave, which is itself regulated by habit. Our behavior, in turn,
works to influence society. It is this somewhat circuitous, but
traceable, route by which the effects of art can exert an impact
on society.

## Social Conscience and Ideological Effect

Works of art with the A-type effect influence the individual
by causing new habits to form or by modifying old ones. This
change is not simply a matter of taste or degree. One's appreciation for Western music, for instance, may become more refined
the more one listens to it, or the desire to hear it may intensify,
but here we are talking about something else, about an imprint
that affects everything the person does. Works in music, painting, and others leave their "imprint" on the psyche, and nervous
activity involved in art appreciation increases and grows more
fluent. Our sensitivities in general are sharpened, which affects
our conceptions about not only painting and music but also
science, literature, and many other areas of artistic, linguistic, and
analytic endeavor. The effect is even harder to discern than the
influence orchestral music is said to have had on Proust's *Remem-
brance of Things Past*. It is too soon, nonetheless, to describe this
effect with any certainty. We can say little more about the com-

plex A-effect except that the attitudes which form in response to it are personal and internal, usually without social ramifications.

One could argue the other way. To stay with the example of music, it is a fact that Japanese, who before the Meiji Restoration (1868) could not even distinguish between Bach and Mozart, much less appreciate their works, today enjoy and know more about Western music than any other non-Western people. Does this not testify to the social effect of music? Not really. The steadily increasing interest in Western music among Japanese is only one facet of the process of westernization that began in the Meiji period (1868–1912), and it is a product of their identification with Western people. It could be called social change, but because the interest in Western music arose out of socially unconscious—as opposed to socially conscious—behavior, it is actually a kind of cultural change. It is an important phenomenon, of course, but cannot be taken as evidence that A-type art works affect the social consciousness of individuals.

By "social consciousness" I mean a reform-oriented attitude toward society; it is the root motivation of reformism, revolution, and other approaches to renovating society. The social effect of art is too complex a subject for thorough treatment here, and so I will confine my discussion to its influence in social reform. To judge that a work of art generates no social consciousness does not mean that it should be dismissed by anyone who believes in the need for reform. Marx observed that art is the supreme pleasure man creates for himself, and it is a major raison d'être for the society man perpetuates and continually modifies. When this wonderful gift of art cannot be shared by all, then there is a need for social reform. That it cannot be used as a lever for change in no way reduces its value. In that sense art is similar to higher mathematics. Like the French mathematician Evariste Galois, artists can certainly take part in revolutionary movements, but it is a mistake to demand that a piece of music or a painting itself be revolutionary. In Yenan, Mao Tse-tung urged writers to write, but did not seek to make the Peking Opera or the Southern School of painting into revolutionary forms. Today, with the revolution over, neither the Peking Opera nor the work of the foremost painter of the New China, Ch'i Po-shih, could be called revolutionary, regardless of the ideology of the individual artists. Such art forms do not foment revolution, but instead serve as symbols of the people's joy in achieving it. The same is true of the Russian ballet. Soviet citizens take pride in its internationally acknowledged excellence. That pride and respect and its power to move them add something to their own lives, but the ballet does not generate the social consciousness that would inspire political reform.

The arts that reproduce a form, such as painting and sculpture, can have some effect in society via the subject they portray. The portraits of Lenin and Stalin that one sees all over the Soviet Union are intended to strengthen the solidarity of the people, but I wonder if such pictures can even be called art. For the most part they are not good portraits, but seem instead to function as symbols, similar to the Stars and Stripes in America. Like the flag, they elicit an emotional, but not an artistic, response. Actually they seem to represent a form of ritual.[2]

There can be no doubt that the scenes in *Genbaku no zu* [The Hiroshima Panels] by Maruki Iri and Maruki Toshi did much to intensify public abhorrence of atomic weapons and boost the ban-the-bomb movement in Japan. But this work should be considered an exception, not a typical example of contemporary art, and certainly not a base for generalization. Then there is Picasso's masterpiece, "Guernica," painted to declare his view of the Spanish Civil War. Picasso exhibited the painting and charged a high admission fee, donating all the proceeds to the Spanish army. Thus, the way the work was used certainly had a large effect, but one cannot be so sure that by itself it generated any anti-Franco sentiment among those who saw it. More than the painting, it was the deep opposition to Franco by the world's greatest painter that inspired André Malraux, Ernest Hemingway, and others to support the government side against Franco. Rodin's "The Burghers of Calais" is resonant with the suffering of patriots, but one doubts that it had much effect on the patriotism of the French (though it might have if it had been completed in wartime). No one can say that "The Burghers" is superior to "The Kiss" or "The Thinker" because of its appeal to patriotism.

Another genre, music with lyrics, has an effect close to the B type, since it incorporates language. Actually the same can be said of comic strips, although I would not call them genuine art. In any case, while paintings by Yasui Sōtarō or Umehara Ryūzaburō do not reveal the political ideology of the artists, the cartoons of Shimizu Kon and Yokoyama Taizō do. Listening to Yvette Giroux or Japanese singers performing in foreign languages brings pleasure of its own kind, leaving an imprint that has nothing to do with the ideas the lyrics impart. Their songs could have no appreciable ideological influence. Among songs that might have such influence, however, are the moving, old-fashioned songs of Mihashi Michiya, sung in his lilting folk style. One of them goes:

> Remember that picture, Mother,
> of the Double Bridge over the Palace moat?
> How Brother longed to show you the capital.
> Even now he must be watching
> from the other world.

> Remember the story, Mother, of
> Saigō Takamori, whose great statue stands in Ueno?
> He died for his country,
> Brother gladly gave his life, too.

> Let us go to worship, Mother,
> at Yasukuni Shrine.
> How Brother longed to show you
> its stately gate.
> Let us go to meet him there,
> where he and his comrades sleep.

There are several factors at work in the effect of this song. Mihashi did not write it himself, but he sings it as though it were a part of him. And as he sings, he acquires the stature and authority of a "hero," which draws the audience to identify with him. In addition to the message itself, the effect of his performance, illuminated by several spotlights, causes the capacity audience to rise in ovation. An elderly man sitting next to me at a Mihashi concert I attended was so moved that he rose from his seat and gradually made his way toward the stage. Surely this song has an ideological effect, not the least because it embodies old, basic values. Identification is difficult when one is required to discard established values, especially for adults and old people, who have a stronger resistance to such change. But in this case, even the elderly identify. The effect is undoubtedly stronger when the performance is heard live, rather than on a recording or over the radio, and the voice of Mihashi is particularly well-suited to this genre of song. He could probably put across a revolutionary song if he tried, but the effect would undoubtedly be a lot weaker.

Of course purely A-type works have an even more indirect impact, but while they basically lack social dimensions, they can have the side-effect of raising social consciousness. Several people might form an art appreciation group, for example, and through their activities their solidarity might grow to the point of producing social consciousness. On the strength of belonging to a musical or other art-oriented group, the members might find the power to resist injustice and join together to overcome it. Just the simple fact that many working people in Japan have formed and join art groups is one indicator that Japanese society is not on the verge of revolution. On the eve of revolution in both Russia and China, there were no organizations like the Japan Workers Music Society. Because such groups usually exert a politically moderating influence, revolutionaries should not expect too much of them.

## Translation into Action

Being art, works in literature, drama, and film elicit a direct response. In that, their effect is the same as the A-type effect, but insofar as these genres are about life experience, they convey values that can affect society even more directly than the A-type. Some artists whose work is in these genres deny their social effect. Valéry wrote that "a poem should be a feast of the intellect. It can be nothing else. After the feast is over, nothing should remain, only ashes and trampled flowers." Animal intellect originally developed as the instrument of interaction with the world outside the individual. But man alone has the ability to withdraw into himself and concentrate solely on the enjoyment of symbols for their own sake. And those symbols need not be confined to music, painting, and so on, but can include even poetry, as Valéry implies.

The Russian poet Vladimir Vladimirovich Mayakovski (1893–1930) believed exactly the opposite, that poetry itself could carry a person to action. When the poet Sergei Aleksandrovich Esenin (1895–1925) committed suicide, he left a poem written in blood: "In this world death is not a stranger, but then, neither is life." To Mayakovski, the possible social reverberations of these "impassioned" lines were frightening, and he believed that no argument had the power to combat their effect. "The only means to challenge this poem—and challenge it we must—is poetry, poetry alone." With much effort he composed the poem "For Esenin," which ends, "In this world, how easy to die; how very much harder to go on living." It is a masterpiece of a poem that must have had considerable social effect. We cannot know the full extent of its impact, but at the same time we cannot read the line, "These are painful times for the writer," without sadly remembering that he himself took his own life four years later.[3]

What concerns us here, however, is not the artist's intent, but the effect of his work on people. That can run the gamut from a simple A-type effect to plunging us into despair (like the effect of Baudelaire's poetry), to buoying our optimism about life (Aragon's poetry). Costumes on stage or screen may spur a new fad in clothing, but the notable effect of the B-type arts, including literature, is the transmission, by means of identification, of the values the works are structured on. Values are not collected randomly and then systematized; rather, beginning in infancy, an entire value system is internalized through the process of identification with someone in authority, such as one's parents. A set of values, moreover, is subject to constant revision. It becomes progressively more difficult to experience this process of identification as one grows older, but even for adults a work that moves them deeply has that effect. Paul Bourget, the French novelist, summed up that impact: "When one is bitten by Stendhal, the scar never heals."

If one has empathy, he can grasp a work at the emotional level, but he experiences a less personal involvement than does one who feels sympathy. With empathy, identification can be only partial. The degree of sensitivity or identification varies widely, but in general, the capacity for sympathy declines with age until one may read *And Quiet Flows the Don* by Sholokhov and gain no more than the information that both armies killed their prisoners of war. By then, the effect is no longer artistic.

Ideally, a work of art is absorbed as a whole, but fiction and film contain many elements, and sometimes, unavoidably, only one of the elements has any effect. Still, if that effect is strong enough, it can result in new attitudes and affect all one's habits. The change in values and habits is a product of both social and esthetic effects—they are probably closely linked—but here we are concerned chiefly with the social effect, that which influences the social consciousness. At this point we should seek an actual example of a work of art that moved people enough to exert a clearly discernible effect on society.

Both Victor Hugo's *Les Misérables* and Harriet Beecher Stowe's *Uncle Tom's Cabin* are claimed by literature historians to have had an enormous influence, the first on the development of programs to help ex-convicts, and the second on the emancipation movement in America. Stowe's book, in fact, is said to have been a factor in the Civil War. There is no statistical or scientific evidence of any effect in either case, but let us nonetheless assume that something happened in society because of them and trace the process it followed.

First, B-type works, because they record human experience and bear a set of values, carry a message or promote a cause. The long and largely unhappy tale of Jean Valjean in *Les Misérables* plays out the themes of the many social contradictions of the time, the unfair way trials were conducted, and the idea that society not only has no right to destroy a man's last years but should actually offer him help. (These are only a few of the many interwoven themes but, for our purposes, the most relevant.)

Second, the above themes are transmitted to the reader by means of the identification that takes place as he is moved by the writing. By the end, the reader has a new generalized sympathy for ex-convicts and may feel an obligation to actively try to help them. Anyone who had been intimidated by an ex-convict in the past would be less inclined to develop such an attitude, but the way people change attitudes or habits also depends on personality. The enormous success of Hugo's voluminous novel indicates that the basic "personality" of his society was amenable and open to the suggestions in his themes. Yet only through the agency of politicians or opinion leaders can a given work effect concrete action.

Third, the fact itself that *Les Misérables* has been such an enormous popular success gives the problem of helping ex-convicts both moral justification and political expediency. Once that is recognized, intellectuals and politicians are free to take up the cause. Others, whose habitual attitudes have been modified or changed by the work, join in. The martyr type of personality tends to support the cause immediately, and the general public slowly follows suit, once it is clearly safe to do so without criticism. At that point the movement to help ex-convicts is on its way.

The above describes the way the effect of a work of art moves through systematic stages until it is translated into action. Of course it does not always work out that way, as progress from stage to stage depends on the personality and strength of habits in the person affected, as well as on the environment. It also depends on the stage of society and what currents are dominant at the time. Had *Les Misérables* appeared in the seventeenth century, in France or Japan, its effect probably would not have developed to the third stage. Or, approaching it the other way, this particular work simply would not have arisen out of the society of seventeenth-century France in the first place. In other words, one can look at a work purely in terms of its dominant themes, but that is not enough to explain its effect. Stendhal's *The Red and the Black* had little impact when it first came out, but forty years later it became an influential work. Countless people found it easy to identify with the main character, Julian. In a sense, he represented a basic personality type among the intelligentsia. Some works produce an immediate, some a delayed effect (like Stendhal's), but today, in the age of mass communication, the latter type of work may be deprived even of the chance to appear.

Modern Japanese literature is noted, of course, for many its

"I-novels," those introspective, highly personal and ruminative works, but it also has produced a great many works with social, even revolutionary, themes. Still, there is a notable absence of works like *Les Misérables*, or *Oliver Twist*, a novel that helped bring an end to the cruel exploitation of child labor in England, and the reason can be found in the peculiar and pervasive nature of social control in Japan that regulates the way and extent any work can affect the society. Tokutomi Roka's *Hototogisu* [The Cuckoo] (1900) brought tears to the eyes of readers with its heart-rending portrait of a tuberculosis victim, but no legislative or other action followed that might help such people. In short, social reform in Japan was not instigated from below by the people. Change was planned and implemented from the top.

The works we have mentioned so far have had comparatively specific themes and clearly defined goals, whether emancipation of slaves or help for ex-convicts. But in stories like Hans Christian Andersen's *The Little Match Girl*, the theme is the overall wretchedness of poverty, and the story constitutes an appeal for the elimination of the gap between rich and poor. Here, the effect is general. There is no call for specific action and no elements that could induce a backlash. If one were affected by the story enough to act, he could attack the problem as stated in any way suitable to his personality and social environment: spiritually through education, practically through social reform, or through revolution. Such a broad theme permits all these possibilities. Most important, however, the impact one receives changes his habits (or inclinations) and sensitizes him to the problem of poverty. As a matter of fact, it was this story that in my boyhood first opened my eyes to the shocking problem of poverty. A broad theme is more easily acceptable and less likely to invite social monitoring than a narrow one, but broad or narrow, the possibility of people translating it into action is heavily influenced by social conditions.

## Art and the Social Environment

So far we have talked about constructive, "healthy" themes, but many effective works are built on frankly negative, or ambivalent, themes. One, a film called *White Hot,* involves a young man (James Cagney) caught up in a crime racket. While his mother presses him to "Be a general!" he makes his way up to become chief of the gang. Finally, surrounded by police, he climbs atop a gasoline storage tank, and just before he blows the whole thing up, he cries out to the world, "I am a general!" This is not a healthy theme, and ostensibly an average citizen like me with basically humanistic values would hardly feel sympathy for a desperate, murderous gangster, yet the film moved me deeply. Why should a Marxist enjoy "I-novels" more than other types? Some do—and surely some Russians like gangster films. It is not just because of some social contradiction or other. There can be no pat explanation for such tastes, and in any case the theme is not directly translated into action even when one is moved by such works. *White Hot,* however, contains other elements that seem to exert an effect: the hero's determination to persevere to the end toward his goal, the precision in his work, his strategy of command, his bravery and defiance. There is no saying that my experience in seeing this film will not change or reinforce my habits or will not affect my activities as a scholar. Here, too, when the effect is very indirect, whether and how it is translated into action depends on the combined operation of individual and social factors in the process.

Literature and revolutionary movements have much the same relation. Lu Hsun claims that a poem is useless against an anti-revolutionary military clique, but a cannonball will send them running. "Some believe," he said, "that literature has tremendous revolutionary power. I have my doubts" (*Literature of the Revolutionary Age,* 1927). Mao Tse-tung has great respect for the views of Lu Hsun, and yet in his essay "Discourse on Literature and the Arts" (1942) he takes the position that literature definitely can have an effect on society, and on that basis, he calls on writers to help push the revolution. As Mao himself explains, the radical change that swept China during the years since 1927 gave literature a new role in society and created an apparent contradiction between his own position and Lu Hsun's.

"Discourse" was written at the height of the revolutionary

war. The Japan Communist party should not therefore accept Mao's position stated therein and try to apply it intact to postwar Japan. The same is true of any official pronouncements made by the Chinese Communist party (CCP) after 1945 on literature and the other arts. It would be an exercise in futility for the Japan Communist party, which holds a mere four seats in the Diet, to take the same position on the effect of art in society as the CCP, which controls all of China, and hope for any practical results. It is often overlooked that the effect of art (psychologically, at least) must move in different directions depending on the social environment. As long as they affirm the socialist revolution, Chinese or Soviet artists have to support the status quo, whereas Japanese artists would have to do exactly the opposite—work to destroy the status quo.

Actually, art in Japan today, like all genuine art, to borrow the words of Henri Lefebvre, has multiple values, is complex and rich; its practical, social, and political usefulness is only one of its many facets, so that only when specific historical conditions demand precedence of political criteria over esthetic does usefulness acquire dominant value. When the Japan Communist party leadership criticized the novelist Noma Hiroshi for his deviation from the party line, they did not consider that the solid effect of literature would be quite different in Japan from China or the U.S.S.R. (see *Zen'ei*, special issue, "Bunka mondai to Nihon Kyōsantō").

A recent example of how far our reactions to art are controlled by social conditions might be found in the Soviet film *Mother*, which is a new technicolor version of the Gorki masterpiece. Being a product of the Soviet Union, one would expect this film to have a heavily pro-U.S.S.R. or strongly revolutionary effect, but that assumption is not necessarily borne out in this case. The film happens to be structured around the old-fashioned montage theory, but the reason lies elsewhere. One of the most intense scenes shows Pavel advancing with the others on May Day holding the red flag aloft and being mowed down by the czarist troops. The effect is unexpected. As the soldiers, bayonets lowered and eyes expressionless, close in on the group of workers, finally opening fire, and the ground is covered with the limp corpses of the workers, some of us watching the film immediately saw the Red Army mowing down the people of Budapest in 1956.

Of course the scene should not be judged out of its total context; the czar's army and the Red Army are not the same, and we should not confuse historical facts, but admitting all that, the instantaneous, unconscious response is there and does not disappear. In film, images of reality impose themselves on the viewer's sensitivity, giving much wider margin than literature for a reaction different from that intended by the director (author) to emerge. In this case, if one had seen the film before the Soviet invasion of Hungary, no such hallucination would have arisen. Watching *Mother*, I did not experience any particularly anti-Soviet feelings, but the film certainly did not arouse any pro-Soviet or revolutionary sentiments, as it was undoubtedly intended to.

I have reread the original Gorki work, but to my surprise I was never so profoundly moved as when I first read it in 1932 in the Japanese translation, which had been heavily censored by the authorities. Today, one can find the full works of Marx and Engels on sale in bookshops anywhere in Japan yet there are few revolutionary currents running through this apparently tranquil society, so utterly different from Russia under the barbaric regime of the czars. It is almost impossible in Japan today to imagine in any realistic way what it would be like to be arrested and beaten merely for possession of a socialist tract. Certainly I have changed somewhat since I first read *Mother* in 1932, but what has really changed is our society.

The social effect of a work of art operates in extremely complex ways. It hinges on the individual psychology of the viewer or reader, the prevailing social conditions, and the interplay between them. Still, I believe that it is possible to arrive at a viable conclusion. My main point is that one must avoid blind acceptance of theories formulated in foreign countries, where language, traditions, and social conditions differ so markedly from ours.

Why bother with the question of the social effects of art in the first place? Basically, because man by nature seeks happiness. In a society with a strong humanistic element, we seek others' happiness as well as our own, for our own happiness is closely related to theirs. Our happiness becomes deeper, more genuine, as the whole society becomes a better place to live in. When humanism is lacking, people are concerned only with the esthetic or stimulation value of art. Its social effect, in fact, is apt to be considered threatening rather than a positive source of improvement. A society that is concerned with the beneficial effect of art on society, even if it is not already a good society, still possesses the necessary element to make it a better one. When people are truly intent upon social reform, they tend to place great hopes in the educational power of art. Their motives are the best, but more is needed. It is almost a truism that only concrete, practical action can bring concrete change. The political or intellectual leaders in a society all too often expect art to influence in a way it cannot. Not fully understanding the nature of its effect or how that effect works, they are disappointed when it does not directly inspire immediate action at times when they have turned to art for help in breaking out of the status quo. These people have the best of intentions, but they are ignorant, and there are too many who think like them.

My own study of this subject is still inadequate, but I am convinced that if more of us do not give it greater attention, we run the risk of robbing our thinking on art and its relation to politics of any substance. As I hope I have made clear, I do not suggest for a minute that even if art cannot exert direct and immediate influence on society, we should be esthetic purists and never judge art on the basis of political ideology. Under certain historical and social conditions, people inevitably regard art in terms of their political interests. The currents of any society change, and when new currents carry predominantly political interests into it, individual interests also tend to become political. At such a time it would probably be impossible to see a work only in an esthetic light, and even if one tried, he would be unable to gain any realistic understanding of it.

I am not suggesting either that we always look at art predominantly in political terms, but simply that if we want to consider the specific problem of the social effect of art, as opposed to the basic nature of art, we must observe and analyze what interests are dominant in society at the time, and then consider the particular work of art in relation to them. Having stated my case, however awkwardly, I should now try to describe the social conditions that prevail in present-day Japan and analyze the dominant interests in order to lay the base for an examination of a given work of art. I will rest content, however, having expressed some of my thoughts on the subject, and save my study of Japan's case for the future.

# Notes

1.   There are some extremely compressed forms of poetry that, like a snapshot, have no more effect than a small, A-type landscape. Film, too, although it includes dialogue or narration, has aspects that are similar to music or painting. In fact, it is the combination of A-type and B-type elements in film that give it such strong appeal. Because films are a direct reproduction of the world they are describing, they cannot be as fully controlled by their creators as can a literary work, which depends entirely on the symbolism of words. Thus, film, with its multifaceted effect, entails a much greater risk than does literature of moving the viewer (reader) in a way never intended by the creator of the work.

2.   The difference between these portraits and the truly excellent portraits Velázquez painted of rulers bears thinking about. It could not be simply lack of talent among Soviet painters; I believe the Soviet political system is also a factor. It would be interesting to know how far Velázquez's portraits of the Spanish royal family actually contributed to national unity.

3.   Mayakovski's essay "How Poetry Should Be Written" contains a discussion of the circumstances surrounding the writing of this poem. It has been translated into Japanese by Kashima Yasuo (Shi wa ikani tsukuru beki ka, Tokyo: Miraisha, 1954), but the translator fails to mention Mayakovski's suicide in his afterword. In Bungaku to wa nanika [What Is Literature?], which I wrote many years ago, I touched upon the problems in faithfully accepting the official explanation concerning his death that can be found in Russian textbooks. Certainly he experienced conflicts between anarchism and communism, but behind all that, as in his photographs, he appears to be heading toward death. Perhaps research on the man and his personality will determine the cause of his suicide some day. The Japanese Left seems not to take this essay very seriously. If they did, they might heed his warning, "Nothing is harder to create than a poem," which in effect denies the composition of poetry to amateurs. But to the contrary, our leftists are busy encouraging amateur poets and writers and exploiting them for political ends.

# 2

## Seven Beauties and
## the Modernization of Rural Tastes

THE idea of measuring changing standards of beauty (for our purposes, sex appeal may be a better word) first occurred to me in the early 1940s. I had noticed that my students registered little intellectual or visceral response to photos of well-known geisha of the Meiji era. The reason may seem obvious—that the Meiji era was well behind them and their standards had changed. But were today's femmes fatales so very different? And was this disinterest universal? I began to consider the possibilities of documenting the effects of modernization on what I will call esthetic taste by means of a survey, using still photographs. It seemed that such a survey might also yield more than just information on changing esthetic tastes or preferences in women; the instrument of photographs was politically and personally harmless, and, if used skillfully, it might stimulate conversation on other matters. Moreover, responses might reveal attitudes toward society, politics, or other issues. Finally, and just as important, this kind of survey seemed to hold no potential for angering, troubling, or exploiting the respondents.

Some of my suppositions were corroborated by my colleague, Dr. Imanishi Kinji, during a field trip he made to Mongolia for ethnological research. He remembered my idea of the "taste test" and brought ten stills of movie stars with him. He obtained a set of responses from Mongolian men, and although he could not bring back the results because of the strict censorship after the war, what he told me later stimulated me very much. The

Originally published as "Bijinkan o chōsa suru," *Sōgō*, August 1957.

Mongolians he talked with were able to reply freely, as the photos did not violate any political and ideological control measures imposed by Japanese at the time. The Mongolians had tended to favor one girl, and, interestingly, most of them insisted she must be Chinese. They could not believe such a beautiful girl could be Japanese. Thus, even under political pressure, they demonstrated consistency in their esthetic taste and their high respect for the Chinese racial stock. Throughout the test, they had been quite open in expressing their opinions.

Rather than causing the subjects to withdraw or try to manufacture "proper" answers, the test had brought them out and stimulated them to talk. For that reason alone, I would have considered it successful. The test I used later, which I am going to discuss below, was designed to accomplish the same end. Called the Seven Beauties (S-B) test, its only tool was photographs of seven beautiful girls. It was intended to avoid positing any of the conditions that make people hesitate to reply honestly. The S-B test contained no element of inquiry into political ideology or behavior, and it did not threaten the security, position, or ego of the subjects.

I have seen the results of countless wasted surveys and have watched innumerable pedigreed scholars carry out fieldwork rendered useless by their lack of forethought and inappropriate methods. Surveys and field research are a fact of life now, thanks in part to the Americanization of academia, society, and public policy since 1945. Yet so often they not only yield nothing of value but are actually harmful in their effects on the subjects. Surveys are indispensable in providing the information by which creative public policy can be formulated and implemented, but I wonder how much that potential has been realized in the rural areas. Few teams or individuals start with the glaringly obvious first assumption: that the survey should eventually bring benefits to the village, or at least Japanese villages in general, and that they should by no means irritate, disturb, or cause any kind of damage. I have yet to hear of a case when a village directly benefited from a field survey. Yet I know many people who have acquired a degree, the prestige of a publication, or a promotion because they carried out some kind of rural fieldwork or survey. Fieldwork for its own sake is all too common.

The Japanese people, especially in the rural regions, are almost too cooperative in such studies, for they still respect academicians in general, and do not protest even when they are rankled. This attitude and the availability of grants send researchers scurrying into the countryside, ill-prepared and unsure of their most basic premises. In France, people are much more individualistic and they demand something in return. The number of surveys done in France is, consequently, much lower. But many farmers in Japan do not even ask the purpose of the project or its methods, and they do not demand payment.

In the survey that is described below, I risk failing to practice what I preach, for I can find little in its results that directly or indirectly benefited the people I talked with. Nor can I take credit for adding to the body of scholarly knowledge. But I feel confident that not only were the subjects not alienated, but they actually enjoyed the test procedures. In the sense that the human relations were good, and the people were relaxed and able to express their thoughts on many matters, I believe the survey was a success. I left them looking forward to the next visit of a scholar, rather than dreading it. But my first try with the S-B test was actually very incomplete. I would have liked to expand the test and design it in such a way as to measure change in attitudes toward politics and society, using essentially the same tools. As it turned out, we can only surmise the significance of my results for areas beyond masculine tastes in women's faces.

The Seven Beauties test was given in 1954. That summer, I visited several villages in the Kitagami mountains of Iwate prefecture in northeastern Japan, an area that used to be called the "Tibet of Japan." I brought with me the seven photographs. They were selected with the intention of drawing responses that would reveal how far men's taste in women has been modernized, which is almost equivalent to documenting the westernization of rural esthetic tastes. Out of seven photos, six (A to F) are pictures of movie stars and one (G) is a picture of a maiko, a young dancing girl of Kyoto, who represents a traditional type of Japanese beauty. I included one picture of a foreign movie star (A), and tried to arrange them in order between the poles of modern and Western (A) on down to traditional and Japanese (G). Although the selection of pictures is not entirely satisfactory,

A.  Audrey Hepburn               B.  Hara Setsuko

C.  Kogure Michiyo      D.  Tsushima Keiko      E.  Otowa Nobuko

F.  Yamada Isuzu          G.  Tomoko, a *maiko* from Kyoto

for reasons I will explain later, let me describe the results of the test first.

The method of the S-B test was very simple: the subject was simply asked to arrange the seven photos in order of his preference. Subjects were men only. They were asked to state their preference not in terms of any fixed standard of beauty, but simply according to which photos they liked better. In other words, their preference might mean lining up the girls in order of most to least sex appeal according to personal taste. I pledged that the results would remain anonymous.

After the test we gave point rankings for each photo: 7 points for the subject's first choice, 6 points for his second, and so on down to one point. We noted the name, age, educational background, and other details with the point list for each subject. Table 1 shows the test results from the villages in the Kitagami mountains and from several other groups, for purposes of comparison.

The series A to G was intended to provide an index of modernization of the subject's esthetic tastes. We graded the photos also: D was neutral (0); photos A, B, and C were plus 3, 2, and 1 and E, F, and G were minus 1, 2, 3, respectively. We multiplied the grade by the average number of points for each photo obtained in each local (or occupational) group, and then calculated a total for each group. That figure appears in the right-hand column of the table as the modernization of taste index (MTI) for each group. It should be noted that "modernization" does not connote any value judgment, and the index figure shows only a trend. The most remote communities (Sakamoto and Ōhira, in Akka Village) have minus 15, while the university graduate group shows plus 14.72. The difference in figures indicates the difference in degree of modernization (westernization) of the two groups.

The reader may draw any conclusions he wishes and judge the results himself. Let me make several comments for each group, however. To begin with the first location, Ekari village (top line in Table 1) is a community whose farmers achieved highly significant gains in the 1946–50 land reform through political negotiations between large landlords and poor tenant farmers. They were led by Nakano Kiyomi, the village mayor and a graduate of the University of Tokyo.[1] For many farmers,

Table 1  Esthetic Preferences as Indicated by Photo Priorities (classified by local group)

| Survey Group (no. subjects) | Type Grade | A +3 | B +2 | C +1 | D 0 | E −1 | F −2 | G −3 | Modernization of Taste Index |
|---|---|---|---|---|---|---|---|---|---|
| 1. Ekari (28) | Average | 2.36 | 4.57 | 4.29 | 4.89 | 5.39 | 3.11 | 3.39 | − 1.27 |
|  | Rank | 7 | 3 | 4 | 2 | 1 | 6 | 5 |  |
| 2. Ekari Intellectuals (6) | Average | 4.33 | 5.83 | 5.5 | 3.16 | 3.8 | 3.8 | 1.5 | +14.25 |
|  | Rank | 3 | 1 | 2 | 6 | 4 | 5 | 7 |  |
| 3. Akka (18) | Average | 1.94 | 4.22 | 4.22 | 5.39 | 5.44 | 3.44 | 3.33 | − 3.83 |
|  | Rank | 7 | 3 | 4 | 2 | 1 | 5 | 6 |  |
| 4. Sakamoto & Ōhira hamlets in Akka (4) | Average | 1.00 | 2.75 | 4.5 | 5.5 | 5.5 | 3.75 | 5.00 | −15.00 |
|  | Rank | 7 | 6 | 4 | 2 | 1 | 5 | 3 |  |
| 5. Ugei (31) | Average | 2.1 | 4.67 | 3.87 | 5.32 | 5.26 | 3.13 | 3.36 | − 2.09 |
|  | Rank | 7 | 3 | 4 | 1 | 2 | 6 | 5 |  |
| 6. Omoto (12) | Average | 1.92 | 5.00 | 5.67 | 5.75 | 5.08 | 3.25 | 2.17 | + 3.34 |
|  | Rank | 7 | 4 | 2 | 1 | 3 | 5 | 6 |  |
| 7. Total for 4 Villages (89) | Average | 2.24 | 4.58 | 4.31 | 5.26 | 5.31 | 3.20 | 3.20 | − 1.12 |
|  | Rank | 7 | 3 | 4 | 2 | 1 | 6 | 5 |  |
| 8. Freighter crew (7) | Average | 3.29 | 5.14 | 5.14 | 5.00 | 4.29 | 3.57 | 1.57 | + 9.15 |
|  | Rank | 6 | 2 | 1 | 3 | 4 | 5 | 7 |  |
| 9. College graduates (30) | Average | 5.03 | 4.87 | 4.17 | 5.1 | 4.87 | 2.5 | 1.47 | +14.72 |
|  | Rank | 2 | 3 | 5 | 1 | 4 | 6 | 7 |  |
| 10. Workers, Kyoto (49) | Average | 4.63 | 4.97 | 4.20 | 5.67 | 4.51 | 2.67 | 1.55 | +13.53 |
|  | Rank | 3 | 2 | 5 | 1 | 4 | 6 | 7 |  |

however, even though the land reform amounted to a vast social upheaval, basic lifestyles and consciousness did not begin to change until long after it was completed. Even now some people almost never bathe, or have a bath ten or so times a year.

In this village several leaders like Mr. Nakano had received higher education, and their tastes were quite different from the other villagers. They were placed in a separate category. The average of the entire village is a low minus figure (−1.27) in the taste index, but the average of the 22 villagers without the 6 leaders came out to be minus 6.89. This difference between leaders and other villagers confirms the existence of a gap felt between them, although village administration is generally smooth.

Akka village has one of the lowest population densities in Japan (10 persons per square kilometer; in Ekari, it is 26, while the average for all Japan is 218). Akka also probably has the lowest annual income (100,000 yen per household). The mayor at the time of my visit was not a native of the community. Since none of the villagers was equipped to carry out the role, a mayor had to be imported. The same was true of Ugei village. After I left, an Akka man was elected major, but he was illiterate. His name appeared in the newspapers as the only illiterate mayor in Japan. Akka's MTI (−3.83) is higher than that of Ekari's non-intellectual group (−6.89), however. That may appear dubious, but the test was carried out at the center of the village, where there is a bus stop and the village office, and the mayor and other non-natives were included in my data.

I listed the results obtained from two hamlets, Sakamoto and Ōhira, within Akka, although there were only four subjects. These communities are located furthest from the village center beyond the Suzu Pass (940 meters above sea level) on a road leading from Ekari village. I tested the four in Sakamoto and Ōhira to obtain a figure I thought would resemble that of Akka if all outsiders had been excluded. One of the four was a man aged 81. When he saw my photos, he could not believe the first (A) was a girl. "It is difficult to put them in order of my preference because there are six girls and one man!" he said. Without hesitation he picked G as his favorite. His MTI was minus 20. I assume that the preference of Japanese men in the early Meiji era would be about the same as his. When I saw this old man, who would never see a real geisha in his lifetime, pick out photo G, more than anything I felt the living strength of tradition.

Akka and Ugei villages were recently merged with Iwaizumi-cho. Like other communities so undeveloped that they could not even produce a mayor, these two became part of a town. It is likely that they have been exploited by the town, and that life there has grown harder than it was. Some hamlets in Ugei had neither electricity nor alcohol lamps. They used pine resin for lighting.

Omoto village is located on the Pacific coast and has a small harbor where boats can anchor. At that time large-scale land reclamation was under way for agriculture. Omoto is much more developed than Akka or Ugei. Out of all four villages only Omoto had a plus figure for its MTI. The inclusion of some outsiders working on the reclamation project in the test perhaps raised the MTI somewhat.

The total results for all four villages appear in line 7. Their main significance is merely that they indicate a tendency in the district. The sampling is entirely inadequate statistically, but the test itself was a secondary purpose in a trip originally intended as a study tour to observe life and attitudes in remote villages. I did not hold to a strict sampling method; I tested everyone I could, more or less randomly. No one but one old man in Ugei refused to take the test, and not one person backed off with an "I don't know." That much allowed me the satisfaction of knowing that the S-B test did at least part of what it was designed to do.

The freighter in line 8 was anchored in Omoto harbor. The results are from tests given to the crew members. Generally speaking, the crew had more Western tastes than local farmers. Incidentally, no subject in the groups on lines 8, 9, or 10 gave top rank to photo G.

College graduates (line 9) include scholars associated with my institution, the Research Institute for Humanistic Studies at Kyoto University; two professors at Tōhoku University; the vice-governor of Iwate prefecture; some of the staff at Iwate University; and some magazine editors. Thus, well-known scholars like Professors Nakamura Yoshiharu (socioeconomic history), Noda Matao (early modern European philosophy), Tsurumi Shunsuke (philosophy), and Dr. Matsuda Michio (pediatrics; Russian intellectual history) were among my respondents. Although as a group they put photo D at the top, it is not surprising that many chose A as their first preference.

I once tried to test several Quakers using the same photos. None of them put A at the top. People with well-defined beliefs, such as Quakers, have different esthetic tastes from other Westerners, but the results were interesting enough. Unfortunately I lost my memo and cannot include their data.

I obtained the data for line (10) from students who attended a humanities class I taught at a workmen's academy in 1957 run by the Kinrōsha Gakuen in Kyoto. The data for this group are three years later than the others. The subjects were mostly high school graduates, and two-thirds of them were labor union members. Most were in their twenties, but one was over 50, two in their thirties, and three in their teens. These figures represent the taste of organized workers who have some secondary education and a dash of highbrow preferences. It is interesting that the results here are similar to the preceding college-educated group. Except for photos A and B, the order of preference is the same in both groups.

Japanese society is characterized most dramatically by rapidity of change. Younger people today can no longer read prose written in the Meiji period, less than a century ago, and they are not interested in reading it. My survey provides a graphic chart of the change that is moving each generation precipitously forward, for each group represents one step ahead in the advance of our history. This comes out more explicitly when we classify the data by age group, as in Table 2.

Only the results for the four villages in Iwate prefecture are shown in Table 2. The insufficient sample size becomes blatantly clear in this table, but generally speaking modernized tastes seem to come out stronger as age declines. The somewhat unexpected results from people in their forties and those in their teens, however, can be explained by special circumstances. The leaders in Ekari village were mostly in their forties. They and many others of their age group whom I met on my trip had experienced

Table 2   Esthetic Preferences as Indicated by Photo Priorities (classified by age, 4 villages only)

| Age | Type | A | B | C | D | E | F | G | Moderniza-tion of Taste Index |
|---|---|---|---|---|---|---|---|---|---|
| Over 50 | Average | 1.85 | 3.82 | 4.92 | 4.38 | 4.92 | 4.00 | 4.08 | −7.05 |
| (13) | Rank | 7 | 6 | 2 | 3 | 1 | 5 | 4 | |
| 40–49(15) | Average | 2.53 | 5.67 | 4.2 | 4.93 | 5.33 | 3.07 | 2.93 | +2.87 |
| | Rank | 7 | 1 | 4 | 3 | 2 | 5 | 6 | |
| 30–39(18) | Average | 1.94 | 4.00 | 4.39 | 4.97 | 5.67 | 3.72 | 3.39 | −5.07 |
| | Rank | 7 | 4 | 3 | 2 | 1 | 5 | 6 | |
| 20–29(38) | Average | 2.32 | 4.79 | 3.97 | 6.03 | 5.34 | 2.76 | 2.79 | +1.28 |
| | Rank | 7 | 3 | 4 | 1 | 2 | 6 | 5 | |
| 17–19 (5) | Average | 2.8 | 3.8 | 3.4 | 6.0 | 4.8 | 3.0 | 4.2 | −4.00 |
| | Rank | 7 | 4 | 5 | 1 | 2 | 6 | 3 | |

some urban life. This did not seem to be true of the young people. I talked to only five teen-age boys during my travels, all of them from the most remote communities of Akka and Ugei. They have had scant opportunity ever to leave their villages, and their contacts with the outside world were much fewer than the generation that served in the military during the war. Hence, their responses were similar to those of their elders, because they were still so closely bound to the traditional village culture. (Village officials declared that they wanted rearmament and the reinstitution of military conscription as soon as possible; otherwise, they said, the youth of their villages would never even see Morioka, the prefectural capital.)

I am all too aware of the inadequacies of my first experiment with the S-B test, but I think it has potential. If it is administered within a comprehensive, controlled framework, with a much larger sampling, it ought to yield fundamental data for the study of the process of change in esthetic perceptions. Since this kind of test can produce relatively accurate and classifiable responses, the results may be a useful basis for the study of other aspects of society as well. I had planned to have an expert in Rorschach testing accompany me, but he was taken ill and could not go. I am quite certain that a comparison of Rorschach test results with those of the S-B test would show similar trends. In any case, the S-B test proved itself much more than a movie star popularity poll; it promises to be a good projective method to measure esthetic tastes.

There are advantages and disadvantages in using stills of movie actresses. Because their faces are familiar, the subject is likely to decide his order quickly and easily. At the same time, however, he may be influenced by the association of the image with a given film. Photo A, for example, may be perceived differently depending on whether one remembers Audrey Hepburn from her lively role in *Roman Holiday* or the somewhat somber figure she played in *War and Peace*. Such associations could disturb the response. A further impediment to free response is the social prestige accorded to successful film actresses. A subject may end up unconsciously choosing the most famous as his top preferences, regardless of attraction.

Originally I wanted to enlist the help of people in different social science and humanities disciplines in selecting representative faces to form a series of types. I thought it might be better to choose girls who are not well-known or popular. I was unable to get the necessary materials at that time, however, and used film stars instead. I feel a touch of shame at the elements of duplicity in my survey of tastes in northern Japan; the S-B test really served to open the door to the thoughts of farmers more than it produced any scientific data. But I believe this kind of test has potential value in scientific data collecting, and it certainly is useful in providing amusement. Having said all this, I may now be numbered among the hosts of useless fieldworkers.

# Note

1. An account of the land reform in execution is contained in Nakano's *Atarashii mura zukuri* [The Making of a New Village] (Tokyo: Shin Hyōronsha, 1954).

# 3

# Tradition Versus Modernization

TRADITION versus modernization has been the subject of intense discussion and deep concern for a long time, since the Meiji Restoration, in fact. That concern was expressed in many ways, but in the work of serious intellectuals, including Kitamura Tōkoku (1868–94), Ishikawa Takuboku (1886–1912), Natsume Sōseki (1867–1916), to name only a few, it was focused on the problem of tradition in the process of modernization and in its final goal.

Just to carry on life, an individual or a group of individuals must deal with what is newly emerging by using what has been accumulated and formed in their past in order to create their future. Confrontation and contradiction between the old and the new, and efforts to surmount them, are common in the experience of every people, not just Japanese. But in modern Japan the issue of tradition versus modernization has been especially prominent, for several good reasons.

In many instances underdeveloped lands were subjugated through invasion or colonization by advanced powers with alien cultures[1] and forced to accept ways of life different from their own. That never happened in Japan. Japan, too, was economically and in other ways very undeveloped at the beginning of the Meiji era, but it had a unique and relatively well-integrated, sophisticated culture that had penetrated deeply among the people. As the Meiji era moved on, Japanese deliberately set about absorbing elements from other cultures, while

Originally published as "Dentō to Kindaika," *Gendai Shisō*, vol. 11, November 1957.

maintaining their political and cultural independence, and by so doing they succeeded in modernizing their backward nation with astonishing speed. Their unusual experience, probably unprecedented in history, makes Japanese especially conscious of the ways tradition and modernization interact, conflict, or complement each other.

The very premise that Japan successfully modernized and overcame its backwardness has its critics. Indeed, a case can be made that the Meiji reforms were not thorough enough and that Japan remained a feudal state until August 1945. Indeed, such controls as the Peace Preservation Laws, aimed chiefly at restricting communist activities, symbolize the severe limits on freedom of thought and speech in prewar Japan, and there are other examples of undemocratic tendencies in political and economic institutions before the war. But it remains true that many Japanese worked hard and led calm, stable lives, either oblivious of such evil laws or resigned to them as unhappy necessity. The United States today is a modern state, despite the Taft-Hartley Act. That Japan was already a modern state before the war is widely accepted among historians.[2] The question concerning modernization is one of degree.

The elements of modernization may be described as (1) democracy in politics; (2) capitalism in economy; (3) shift from handicrafts and/or premodern manufacturing systems to factory production, accompanied by advances in science, technology, and mechanization; (4) mass education; (5) creation of a national military force, and (6) liberation of the popular consciousness from a communal frame and the growth of individualism. From the Meiji Restoration through World War II Japan failed in the first and the last (which are closely related), but it was successful in the others. The degree of modernization can be assessed differently depending on which element is given greater weight, but here I want to focus on the speed of development of productivity. No other country before it had industrialized as quickly as Japan did,[3] and a half-century later, only the U.S.S.R. had come anywhere near achieving comparable speed of development. In considering the modernization process as a whole, speed is one of the most important factors.

Compulsory mass education is another important area where

Japan has made outstanding progress very quickly. Illiteracy in Japan is now lower than in France. In that respect, Japan is probably one of the most advanced countries in the world. (Russia still had 73 percent illiteracy in 1917, China 80 percent in 1949, and India 83 percent even today.)

There were, granted, unfortunate effects. The rapid rise in productivity was tragic for the sweatshop workers in the early stage of industrialization, and popular education inculcated some degree of militaristic ideology in prewar Japan. But we must also remember that factory labor and compulsory education, in one way or another, forced change in the popular consciousness. The positive effects of those two factors in modernization were highly significant.

The changes and reforms made after 1868 were instituted from the top and were carried out at a breathtaking pace. To some Japanese, the fact that the reforms were initiated and implemented from above is something they are not proud of, but it should be accepted. Any underdeveloped country that seeks reforms within a short period must understand the reality that almost always it will have to be imposed from above, as in the cases of Russia, China, Turkey, and Egypt, for example. In all practicality, a nation's policy cannot be decided by the people when illiteracy is as high as 73 or 80 percent. Japanese tend to judge their own nation harshly, and give wide allowances for other countries. This is an unhealthy mental habit that robs them of objectivity.

The very speed of Japan's reforms, nonetheless, created severe difficulties for the developing nation. Japan accomplished some things in several decades that had taken the advanced European countries centuries to achieve. The distortions caused by such speed are reflected in every aspect of the thought and culture, perhaps particularly in the issue of tradition versus modernization. In the West, many contradictions arose as modernization was counterposed to tradition, but those countries had much more time and could resolve them gradually. To remain a sovereign, independent state, Japan had to resolve them very quickly. The sense of urgency may have heightened Japanese insights into the profound ramifications of what was happening, but it also prevented them from concentrating on one problem at a time. Change was so fast that the tasks at hand were abandoned before their completion. Kitamura Tōkoku and Ishikawa Takuboku, both passionately determined to illuminate the problems involved in tradition versus modernity, nonetheless failed to find workable solutions to the stubborn contradictions they saw.

After the Taishō era (1912–26) began, elaborate methods of dealing with social and other distortions were imported from the West. Whereas Meiji Japanese had been intense in their questioning, always struggling to see the possible outcome of solutions, the new generation tended to be more academic, emphasizing the proper framing of questions over the need for solutions. Increasingly they analyzed their society in terms of imported theory, often in disregard of its realities, and this unfortunate practice continues right into the present.

## Militarism and Nationalism

The conflicts that arose during the Meiji era between tradition and very rapid modernization have been carried over into the postwar era. Tradition alone cannot even be discussed without acknowledging the basic pattern of that conflict, and any realistic solution depends on establishing a valid historical perspective. The conflict remains basically the same, but its manifestations are different now. The postwar problem of tradition and modernization is complicated by new political conditions: Japan was placed under a seven-year occupation by American forces. The nation's pro forma independence was restored with the San Francisco peace treaty of 1951, but American troops remain. U.S. military bases are spread across the nation. In its international relations as well, Japan is in fact far from independent.[4]

Even though the fast pace of implementation created distortions, the Meiji reforms were achieved by independent people through their own efforts. On the other hand, the drastic changes after World War II were brought about under occupation by a foreign power. Many Occupation policies regarding the new Constitution, unionization of labor, punishment of militarist leaders, and so forth were beneficial measures supporting democratic modernization. They should have been made and implemented by Japanese, on their own initiative, but how could Japanese—exhausted by the war and long accustomed to keeping their thoughts to themselves or risk police harrassment—have taken initiative in the reforms? Some opposed all or part of the reforms, but their opinions were shut out by the Occupation forces. During the early postwar years, very few dared openly to express opposition. Even on reforms touching on the national language, no opposition views were expressed until Abraham Halpern took over the program and announced that issues involving the Japanese language should be handled under the direction of Japanese. Many problems that came up later derived from the confused circumstances of those years.

By no means did Japanese merely follow the enforced changes in dumb acquiescence, however. Postwar reforms did not generate heated reaction, that is true. But the reason was that the rate of approval was so high, not that Japanese felt powerless before authority. The Occupation policies could never have been carried out so smoothly if the majority of the people themselves had not been prepared and supportive. Yet among some, there was an almost neurotic reaction both to the defeat and to the Occupation. It had some incongruous expressions. The Communist party regarded the Occupation as a liberating force. The Socialist party tried to maintain lese majesty. The conservative Liberal party opposed the land reform, despite the fact that it prevented a major shift of the rural population to the Left. These are extreme examples, but everyone developed some sort of misunderstanding of the situation. I myself never thought that the great turnabout in Occupation policy itself would take place so early and so easily. We knew little of the Russo-American confrontation.

The Occupation, really a transition period, created abnormal circumstances, but if the principles of the reforms had been consistent throughout, any abnormalities eventually could have been absorbed into the normal conditions of the nation. But international tensions, namely the Korean War, forced change in the principles themselves. The axis of the shift is the interests of the United States; that is a constant. It is natural that American policy should ultimately be geared toward its own interests, but the effect of changes in international relations transformed Japan from a nation aspiring to be "the Switzerland of the Far East" to a rearmed state. The shift allowed a man once imprisoned as a Class A war criminal to become prime minister. There was a great change in values, and everyone has been forced to adjust to another new set of circumstances.

Japanese who once supported Occupation policy have had to make a choice: to be pro-American and replace their pacifism with approval of rearmament, or to become more or less anti-American or antigovernment. Thus, Japanese generally fall into one of four categories: (1) people who shifted attitudes with the change in U.S. policy and remained pro-American; (2) people who intended to stay firm in their support of the original U.S. policy and then rejected the turnabout; (3) people who seek to escape politics (and consider themselves politically "neutral," but by their apathy end up supporting the pro-American government of Japan); or (4), those who are antireform, or reactionary. This last group does not seem to have recouped their power over the press, but in society it is gradually regaining influence. The change in the political situation has induced the revival of nationalism in Japan.[5] The problem of tradition is now a daily theme in the press, and all of the above groups of people have revealed their attitudes toward it.

Those in group 4 are by and large right wing, hence they are usually extreme patriots, but in postwar Japan it is difficult to sustain that level of nationalistic feeling. One reason is that their funds come from capitalists, who do not generally appreciate anti-American thinking. Thus, postwar right-wingers can be anti-Soviet but not anti-American. Yet if one takes a nationalistic stand one has to be more or less anti-American, and that is why it is so hard for the right wing to win wide support. Emotionally, they are very much oriented toward the preservation of tradition, but without a solid base of nationalism, their traditionalism is theoretically bankrupt and lacks persuasiveness.

The pro-Americans in group 1 are more or less nationalistic, but like group 4 they are hindered from moving too far. Some are totally uninterested in the matter of tradition, especially as America has so little old tradition to be maintained and does not belabor Japan's. But many of the power elitists in group 1 use tradition as a popular rallying point and also as a camouflage for reactionary policies. The United States supports their stand on preserving tradition, in the interest of directing the attention of the Japanese people toward cultural rather than political affairs. Ultimately this group is cosmopolitan: they tend to admire what all foreigners, not just Americans, admire. Their attitude is a kind of topsy-turvy traditionalism resulting from idolatry of foreign things, ideas, and opinions. Like foreigners they praise Kabuki and ignore calligraphy or *nanga* paintings, which are among the arts most difficult for Westerners to appreciate.

Generally speaking, Japan's intellectuals consider themselves liberals, but they are not necessarily determined to fight for the preservation of freedom. Rather, they seek freedom from any kind of "ism." All ideologies are normative by nature, which they find uncomfortably restrictive. They have an especially strong aversion to nationalism because of its associations with the war and the unhappy prewar years. Because of their high level of education, most Japanese share the attitude of intellectuals toward nationalism.[6]

Group 3, the political apathy group, in fact, reacted against the impatient modernists who wanted to clear away the burdens of tradition. However, they are not traditionalist. They particularly oppose any tradition that is connected with ethnocentric behavior. They are fundamentally cosmopolitan, a characteristic they share with group 1. At present at least, their thinking represents a dominant attitude in Japan.

The problem of tradition is most complicated in the thinking of group 2. They have a strong antipathy toward nationalism, which they see as a form of fascism, but they are intense in their desire to achieve full independence for the nation. Their position has been strengthened by the rise of nationalism in other Asian and African countries (although they see it too optimistically), and consequently they veer toward nationalism themselves. This tendency became particularly pronounced after the Korean War. Because nationalism is always based upon a nation's self-confidence, moreover, the value of Japanese tradition is important to this group.

Group 2 consists of Marxists and bourgeois liberals. They agree on the question of peace and the need to uphold the new

Constitution, but they are at odds on other issues, one of the most divisive being tradition. Some bourgeois liberals were labeled modernists by postwar leftists and criticized, but some gradually began to consider tradition more carefully, somewhat as follows. a) First of all, they realized they had underestimated the scope and seriousness of the "reverse course," the turnabout in Occupation policy; b) from there, they saw that the path toward modernization was not straight, although they remained optimistic about progress; c) as long as they could be realistic, they saw that nationalism was the crux; d) at the same time they understood the point Einstein once made: "How relatively small, as compared with the powerful influence of tradition, is the influence of our conscious thought upon our conduct and conviction";[7] and e) they have come to attach importance to the tradition (though not necessarily all of it) of the Japanese nation, and to voice their patriotic feelings.[8]

On the other hand, leftists attach importance to tradition for a political purpose. As in the U.S.S.R. and China, they believe full national independence requires emphasis on tradition. There are different opinions on this among leftists, but it is possible that such a position was proposed by the Communist party and leftist intellectuals followed suit. Their opinions sometimes do not coincide with those of bourgeois liberals.

Thus, the problem of tradition has been discussed most seriously among people in group 2. I would like to focus my discussion on this group's views in dealing with the whole issue of tradition and modernization after World War II. I am personally familiar with the process of their discussion, but more, I believe this is a good point of departure for a full discussion on modernization and tradition. Other groups have debated tradition, but only in a fragmentary way, with no intention of generalizing it into theory. In group 2, it seems that the problem has been taken up seriously in terms of nationalism and in relation to the fate of the Japanese. This discussion sometimes lacks a completely accurate perspective, but it offers a channel for theoretical dispute and the possibility of clearing up errors along the way.[9]

## Futility of Borrowing Policy

"Let us show that Japanese, too, have produced great works; let us meet the crisis of cultural imperialism by awakening our national consciousness and regaining our national pride" (*Nihon bungaku nyūsu*, bulletin of the Nihon Bungaku Kyōkai [Society for Japanese Literature], No. 5). This proposal, written by Izu Toshihiko, expresses a basic attitude toward tradition among postwar leftists, especially members of the Nihon Bungaku Kyōkai. It represents a cultural policy that was probably determined in line with the Communist party's concept of a democratic united front for national liberation. These people encouraged building a strong national consciousness and national pride, and they warned that at times it would be necessary to use culture for political ends. It does not matter which party makes policy, if the policy is good. However, as far as policy concerns culture, it should not be the exclusive preserve of a limited number of people; it must be understood and accepted even by people in intellectual circles, where distrust of leftists is particularly strong.[10] It is useless, actually dangerous, to discuss culture only in terms of a given political goal. I do not expect all essays by partisan critics to be academically solid, and they are free to write propagandist tracts. But to mechanically apply a given policy to each cultural problem is no solution. The solution is to create new approaches that cut into and reconcile the contradiction between the normative conditions and the objective conditions. An effort simply to find ways to keep tradition A or tradition B going, without first solving the basic conflict, would be shallow and ineffectual. The political goal also would not be achieved. Generally, the leftist theory of preservation of tradition has this weak point. Let us look at it more closely.

## Illogical Dogmatism

My article "Daini geijutsu" [The Secondary Art of Modern Haiku] (essay eleven in this volume), in which I stated that modern haiku should not be called a genuine art, has been widely criticized. Except for a few, including Odagiri Hideo, leftists in general are outraged by my modernist approach.

One leftist takes issue with my negative stand on modern haiku on grounds that (a) this short form of poetry is found nowhere else in the world, and therefore should be encouraged, not disparaged; (b) it has a long tradition; and (c) it is widely loved by almost everyone except a few modernists. He questions my attitude; is it not antipopulist to criticize haiku and recommend giving it up? I can only reply that our emperor system, too, is unique, has a long tradition, and is widely loved, and the Left is out to destroy it. Yet I do not attack that effort.

Akagi Kensuke, poet and leftist, has written that my assessment of haiku as a secondary art is invalid because even now, several years after my article came out, the genre is as alive as ever. This seems a patently spurious argument. It is thirty years since Marxism reached Japan, and revolution has still not yet taken place. But I do not think Marxism is therefore invalid.

The problems of culture can never be defined by formal logic alone. But some Marxists do not even follow formal logic as it is generally conceived. They are dogmatic to the point of impracticality. Dogmatism does not provide solutions, except in the minds of those who think Marxism is infallible, but it appeals to the indulgent wish many Japanese have to preserve anything that is old. The leftists may freely criticize anyone who is out to destroy tradition, but at least they should offer arguments that are logically formulated. My point is that any defense of traditional art, haiku or whatever, is likely to be irrational, no matter who engages in it.

## Conservatism of the Japanese Left

Marxists generally are considered to be progressive, but the preservation-of-tradition policy brought conservatism into Japanese Marxism. Recall the discussion on maintaining the original Kabuki scripts intact by Kondō Tadayoshi (1901–76), specialist in Tokugawa-period literature and former president of the Nihon Bungaku Kyōkai, and Ino Kenji (1913–), scholar of modern Japanese literature and critic. Their discussion introduced rather casually constructed policies on culture, without considering how the preservation of Kabuki could be reconciled with other party tenets. I will not repeat the entire argument

I developed against their position, but will only mention my basic criticism.[11]

Apart from those in the art-for-art's-sake school, anyone who is intent upon changing society must discuss art and literature by taking into consideration the influence of a given work on popular thought and behavior. But Kondō and others seem oblivious to this crucial point. They simply remain "firmly determined to prevent Kabuki from being left in the care of the enemies of history and to take it back into our hands." By this they probably mean that if leftist spokesmen do nothing but find fault with Kabuki on grounds of its feudalistic values (as Murayama Tomoyoshi, playwright, is doing) instead of admiring and trying to protect it, then Kabuki will become a tool of reactionaries, many of whom are staunch fans. (Recently, the U.S. ambassador to Tokyo, Robert Murphy, entertained some well-known Kabuki actors, which may seem significant to some observers.) In any case, what do they mean by "taking it back?" They cannot screen Kabuki scripts or revise them. Those functions come under the control of Shōchiku or Tōhō, capitalist enterprises that could not conceivably have greater sympathy for Kondō and other leftists than for Japan's power elite and the United States. Apparently, then, "taking it back" merely means encouraging progressives to admire Kabuki without feeling guilty and to build confidence in themselves by taking pride in the cultural achievements of the Japanese people.

Kabuki is a product of feudal ideology. It is one thing to believe that art has little impact on the way society is run, but it is quite another to criticize the degrading influence of westerns or cartoons while bypassing the possible effects of the feudalistic threads in Kabuki. The result is a fatuous contradiction. Today I support the effort that Kondō and others are making to protect the new Constitution, not only because I am against rearmament but also because I want to protect the modern patterns of human relations that are guaranteed by the Constitution and prevent the revival of feudalistic thinking. But people like Kondō, while they are serious in rejecting feudalism in anything contemporary, easily accept the brutality of the murders in the drama *Chijimiya Shinsuke*, which they interpret as "a deep tragedy of humanity," and allow the murder in *Terakoya*—perpetrated to keep a domain house intact—to go uncriticized on grounds that it is "a silent resistance against the enemy of humanity." Their attitude toward Kabuki betrays an a priori determination to praise the genre, and they only add a few new interpretations in order to justify that effort. The same approach can be applied to any "degrading" western film as well, which makes it self-defeating.

There is an element of cultural conservatism among so-called political progressives who criticize society of the modern or contemporary periods and praise the middle or ancient periods. This is what Kondō does in "Kabuki o mite" [Impressions of Kabuki]. He praises Kabuki, while condemning modern drama as un-Japanese. He deprecates all Western-based music, art, literature, etc., as "miserable." His position is based upon Ishikawa Takuboku's attack on the tendency to worship anything foreign. But Ishikawa himself struggled with the conflict between his own desire for westernization and his nationalism, and this conflict finally led him to socialism.[12] Subjective idealism that accepts only what is convenient will not contribute to well-balanced nationalism. Cultural criticism that ignores the actual modernity of Japan becomes empty moralism that lacks all power of persuasion. It is an irony of history that the Marxist theory of preservation of tradition resembles the reactionary "conquest of modernity"[13] theory of wartime Japan.

In his article Kondō tried to denigrate Tsubouchi Shōyō (1859–1935), Mori Ōgai (1862–1922), and Osanai Kaoru (1881–1928), intellectual pioneers who introduced to Japan the modern novel, Western literature, and theater, respectively. Tōma Seita (1913–), Marxist historian, criticized even Futabatei Shimei (1864–1909) for his intellectualism.[14] No one lacks some defect or weakness, and we are free to criticize, but consistency and logic are important. If the Left would defend modern writers with the same enthusiasm as they defend Kabuki, all writers would be on more solid ground in their work. But when leftist critics shun the modern writers, while heaping praise on old stage drama, one can only conclude that these leftist critics ultimately are against modernity itself.

## Perils of Emulating Socialist Models

Lenin's policy on art was used as the base for the argument supporting Kabuki. Pro-tradition leftists played up the fact that Lenin permitted the stage presentation of bourgeois plots like *Carmen*, *La Traviata*, and other operas in 1919 just after the revolution. It is fine to acknowledge to Lenin's policy, but it is a mistake to use it to justify the leftist policy of preserving Kabuki at a time when Japanese democracy is in danger. The context is totally different: Lenin's party was in the position of authority in the U.S.S.R., while leftists in Japan are part of the powerless minority.

The leftist theory of preserving traditional culture is derived from Russian and Chinese models. It rapidly gained ground after Minami Hiroshi, social psychologist, visited those countries in 1952 and reported that in both the traditional arts, including the Russian ballet and Chinese Peking Opera, were being widely performed with the support of the government.[15] However, as the diagram below shows, the theory is very inconsistent unless leftists in Japan have given up their intention

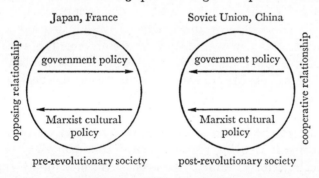

of revolution. The political systems of Russia and China are different from those of Japan or France. In socialist nations both government and cultural policies have the same orientation and they complement each other, whereas in capitalist nations, leftist cultural policies naturally clash with the national policy. If a leftist claims the necessity of protecting traditional art in a nation whose revolution is still to come, arguing that another, post-revolutionary nation is doing so, that means he has given up the goal of revolution. Or, he is assuming that Japan completed its revolution in 1868 and that now reformism is enough. Such attitudes are perfectly acceptable, but as long as the leftist aspires to revolution, he should not support a cultural policy in favor of preserving tradition.

No revolutionaries in Russia or China even considered maintaining or protecting classical ballet or drama before the revolution. Lu Hsun said that young Chinese should read the Chinese classics as little as possible, or not at all.[16] Ts'ai Yuan-p'ei reportedly once said, "Although the traditions of old China are important, it is not necessary to worry about them now. Even if old materials and forms are broken up and scattered, we can put them together again after the revolution. Now we should devote ourselves to the revolution."[17] Mao Tse-tung did not really care about keeping alive the traditional artistic performances of Mei Lan-fang or Ch'eng Yen-ch'iu during the process of the revolution, but he did consider adopting the Roman alphabet in place of Chinese characters. Now that the revolution has been accomplished, Chinese are turning back to tradition because they have confidence that their social reforms will proceed rapidly. They support the Peking Opera, which the Chinese public loves, as a symbol of joy in the achievement of the revolution. At the same time, modern plays are widely performed and have become popular to the extent that even the Peking Opera is being influenced by their techniques.

Moreover, the Peking Opera now is performed differently from before the revolution. Scenarios are strictly screened and their content is being revised. The drama *Shihyühuan* [Finding a Bracelet], for example, has been performed many times in Japan by a troupe led by Mei Lan-fang. In the drama a girl meets a promising young man, and they are attracted to each other. But the young man is forced to leave, dropping a bracelet behind. The girl finds it and is filled with joy. A neighborhood woman sees her pick it up and teases her. Before the revolution, the local woman was portrayed as a vicious conniver who took money from the girl, falsely promising that she would bring the two together again. Because such conduct is considered immoral, that part was revised. Another example is *Sanch'ak'ou*

[Three-forked Road], also warmly received in Japan. In this drama, the escort of a general gets into a swordfight with an innkeeper in the darkness, without knowing that his opponent is an ally. I wondered why such a stupid thing could happen, so I inquired, and heard that in the prerevolution plot, the innkeeper was an evil enemy who tried covertly to kill the escort's master, hence the ensuing fight. The plot was revised to make the fight a case of mistaken identity, because the original circumstances were considered educationally inappropriate.

Whether the revisions are commendable or not, they are possible only because the Peking Opera is entirely under the control of the state authorities, and they do not care about profit—only whether the Opera is useful or not. Do the Japanese leftists who advocate vigorous support for classical Kabuki know how the arts are controlled in China? Or do they ignore that aspect? If they went to China, their hosts would not mention the revisions if they could avoid it. (Perhaps Chinese do not want to be criticized for oppression of the arts by the freedom-conscious Japanese.) Kondō wrote that he has become more certain of his own theory after seeing numerous performances of the Peking Opera in China, but that puzzles me. It would be helpful if he would elaborate on this point; otherwise he seems to be undercutting his own basic stand.

In the U.S.S.R. and in China presidents and deans of universities are all appointed by the state authorities, and school texts are all standardized by the government. There is no such thing as a strike. Some people, nevertheless, think such a system has great merit. An effort to emulate the methods and principle of retaining tradition in socialist countries, without considering the differences in the respective institutions, would be just as shallow as voicing an irresponsible opinion. It is a problem that arises in areas other than the arts as well.

The cultural standards of Russia and China before their revolutions were generally much lower than that of contemporary Japan. They had fine artists and writers, like Gorki and Lu Hsun, but high standards of culture did not penetrate to the common people. Finally, even apart from the differences in national institutions, it is not practical to imitate cultural policies in the U.S.S.R. or China because of the different cultural backgrounds.

## Sterility of the National Literature Debate

Takeuchi Yoshimi and Kawamori Yoshizō have raised the question of the necessity of a body of national literature[18] that, by concerning itself with national problems, would support the reform movement in Japan and also have wide appeal among all classes of people. In Japan, as they point out, modern literature has tended to be either "pure" literature aimed chiefly at writers and intellectuals who enjoy literary art for its own sake, or lowbrow, popular literature with strong appeal to the general public. The idea of a new national literature that might bridge the gap strikes a responsive note among journalists, mainly because the concept is solid and relevant and has created much interest. Despite general sympathy, however, it has not yet borne any real fruit. There may be several reasons. When Takeuchi and others came out with their proposals I expressed my support for the idea and added several points to be considered (*Mainichi shinbun*, 28 October 1952). Let me summarize what I said there regarding the lack of productive results from the national literature debate so far.

Generally, the resolution of a question very often is contained in the question itself. If the question is scientific, the answer obtained will be scientific. If it is moralistic, the answer will be moralistic. Although all great questions are framed on a moral basis, the definition of the substance of the question itself must always be objective. Otherwise we cannot arrive at any resolution. The problem of a "national literature" clearly is based upon a patriotic concern, but the term "nation" was ambiguous from the outset. There is no way to measure exactly what part of this entity we call Japan is the "nation," and few people have ever even tried. Thus when Takeuchi says, "The people want to be liberated as a nation and they want to change themselves to achieve that end," he neglected to consider all those people who had no special sense of crisis. He did not take the size of the readership seriously enough and failed to consider the impact of such popular authors as Nakazato Kaizan[19] or Yoshikawa Eiji[20] in relation to the issue of popular appeal.

Moreover, when the debate was taken up by leftists, they totally rejected the proposal so important to Takeuchi Yoshimi that literature be autonomous, and they made the "national literature" virtually synonymous with the "democratic literature" of the Left. One can understand the raison d'être of leftist avant-garde literature, but the point of departure for the national literature seems to be exactly the same, which precludes it becoming a literature for all Japanese at present. Noma Hiroshi, leftist novelist, comments that "I think of this as part of the campaign to reorient Japanese thought . . . it might help to change the basic patterns of understanding and feeling among Japanese."[21] He should have been talking about revolutionary literature, not Takeuchi's national literature. The confusion derives from the lack of definition of "nation." As soon as Tōma Seita declared in *Kokumin bungakuron* [Discussions of the National Literature] (Minka Geijutsu Bukai, ed.) that "a national literature can be created not out of the thinking of intellectuals (like Futabatei Shimei), but only out of the thinking of the people of the nation—it must emerge from the idea of unity between worker and farmer under the leadership of the proletariat," some on the Left took up the thread. When they then went further to say that the methodology of national literature should be socialist realism,[22] the original idea completely disappeared from the national literature debate.

The subject of tradition often enters into discussion of this issue, but no new ideas have been expressed. The Nihon Bungaku Kyōkai took up the topic of "a national literature" in its general meeting in 1954, but the speakers confined themselves to studies of ancient and medieval literature, like the *Azumauta* of the *Man'yōshū*, Ihara Saikaku (1642–93), Shimazaki Tōson (1872–1943), etc., using conventional methods. Serious efforts to create a national literature should analyze and assess modern writers—Tokutomi Roka,[23] Natsume Sōseki,[24] Nakazato Kaizan, Kikuchi Kan,[25] Yoshikawa Eiji—whose popular appeal has not waned since the Meiji era in spite of differences in artistic values and ideologies. The elements common to their works should be properly recognized. But no one has made that effort.

Kurahara Korehito and other leading figures in the Communist party responsible for cultural policy compromised, and they accepted almost all Japanese modern writers as contributors to the national literature, but the political effect of that stance has been nil.[26] To accept even the works of writers who do not have wide popular appeal makes one suspect that their compromise was made not for literary but for political reasons, or that they have abandoned Marxism. For whatever reason, it is hard to trust them. What puzzles me most is why Kurahara, who approves of even pure bourgeois writers, is so intolerant of popular writers. Nakazato Kaizan, for example, was once an eager student of socialism, and so even in the eyes of leftists he must be at least as acceptable as Tanizaki Jun'ichirō in ideological terms. Furthermore, one would think that his refusal to join the Bungaku Hōkokukai (Literary Patriots Association) in the war years would elevate Nakazato above most bourgeois writers. Still, Kurahara does not approve of him. Perhaps Kurahara is still slave to the old division between highbrow "Iwanami culture" and lowbrow "Kōdansha culture," but that split is no longer important.

I do not recommend that popular writers such as Nakazato Kaizan or Yoshikawa Eiji be made models for the national literature, but if this new genre is to avoid becoming an obscure avant-garde literature and is to create instead something with strong appeal to the general public, the works that have attracted the most readers should be carefully studied first, regardless of their ideologies. If Tokuda Shūsei and Higuchi Ichiyō can be regarded as national literature writers, then Nakazato and Yoshikawa must also be included. If works by Nakazato or Yoshikawa are second-rate, we must not therefore reject them but recognize that ours is a society whose traditional national literature contains second-rate works, and then start trying to make improvements. Had the debate involved such critical testing of works by different authors, it would have produced new ideas on how a writer can grasp the basic personality of the Japanese. The results could have been helpful for leftist writers and writers in general. But from the outset there was no chance to move in such directions because of the prejudice against mass appeal as vulgar. Therefore, there has been no reflection on other possibilities, such as films, which have a much more potent popular appeal than literature.

In brief, the failure to be scientific in observing reality has kept the discussion of a national literature at the level of a moralistic-political chorus that is far removed from the original idea.

While the argument attracted many critics, a large number of bestsellers that denied or ignored fundamental national problems had great success, demonstrating the vanity unrealistically in trying to channel popular literature into moralistic lines.

## Tradition and Beyond

I have said a great deal about the opinions of others on the broad issue of tradition and modernization, but let me briefly summarize the gist of my comments so far. A study of the term "tradition" is not in itself very useful in determining the place of tradition in modernizing or modern society, but to clarify exactly what the word means is crucial, for it is a basic premise. I tried to stimulate thinking on this a few years ago by taking up the term itself,[27] but I failed. My thesis was ignored, and no one took the opportunity to develop a better premise by revising or denying my view.

The Japanese term *dentō* [tradition] does not originally belong to our language. It was devised as a way to translate the English or French term "tradition." Literally it means something transmitted through generations within a society that restricts the behavior of its members. Logically, then, it should cover everything, for all is transmitted somehow, or it dies out. However, while "custom" is something transmitted unconsciously, the term "tradition" implies a value judgment made on the transmitted element, according to Seligman's *Encyclopedia of Social Science*. Following that reasoning, tradition has a meaning intermediate between unconscious custom and ideas. While *dentō* puts more weight on the side of custom, the term in Western languages leans toward ideas; it is, in short, a vaguer term in Japanese.

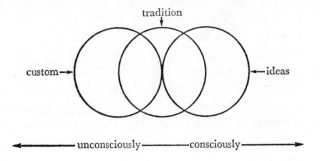

Look at some examples. "Because I was elected to the city assembly, I will try to uphold your expectations by keeping our good *traditions*, seeking the security of citizens, . . ." (speech of a city assemblyman in Kyoto, 1951). "We farmers wish to transfer our land that has been passed down for 350 years from our ancestors to our children as our *tradition*" (speech by Aoki Ichigorō during the cabinet committee hearing on the Sunagawa Incident in the House of Councilors in 1955).

Both examples are typical of the way *dentō* is used. The content of the transmitted thing is not important in the context, and more emphasis is placed on attachment to something that has been maintained a long time. It is more than mere sentimentalism, but it is still basically a feeling. It should not be employed in a logical defense of the old simply because it is old, for that would create barriers to improvement and reform. Einstein once said that it would be "foolish" to despise tradition, but with our growing self-consciousness and increasing intelligence we must begin to control tradition and assume a critical attitude toward it, if human relations are ever to change for the better. In the process of modernization since the Meiji era began, the control of tradition has been relatively successful. Today, any discussion of tradition inevitably involves a degree of negative criticism. If people are indiscriminately positive toward anything old, they will end up supporting a revival of feudalistic sentiments and old morals. To be eclectic toward tradition is as important as screening what is new. We must very seriously consider what to retain and what to throw away from Japanese literature, for example. And I think the Socialist, Communist, or any other reformist party is obliged to publicize its selections.[28]

Despite the fact that the term *dentō* is used so much, contemporary Japanese are not "tradition-directed" but "other-directed." Their ways of thinking and acting are no longer restricted by tradition. People are interested in tradition mainly because they are embarrassed if they do not know something about the traditional arts and customs when asked. This is nothing but "conformity behavior." In this case, foreigners are included among the people to whom one has to conform. Once a famous foreigner admires Kabuki, Japanese think they should admire it too. It would not be effective to discuss "tradition" without recognizing this tendency in postwar Japan.

Nothing can start from zero; all human actions need the support of the accumulated past. The postwar history of mountaineering in the Himalayas is a good example of how strong the influence of tradition is. Mountaineers from nations with a long alpinist tradition—England, France, Germany, and Japan—succeeded in climbing Himalayan peaks. But the United States and the Soviet Union, two superpowers, both lag behind, possibly because the tradition of mountaineering is relatively new there.[29] Still, a "good" tradition must be used, built upon. To have a good tradition means to create something on the basis of it. Because discussions on tradition in postwar Japan place greater emphasis on the maintenance of old traditions unrelated to contemporary life, Japanese lack a strong sense of using tradition, incorporating it into the building blocks of present and future.

Once it was considered an important endeavor to prove that certain of the traditional arts originated among the people. It was a significant trend, but it is just as important to analyze why certain arts with popular origins were taken over, really, by the ruling class and lost their "popular" quality. Nō, Kabuki, sumo wrestling, and many of the traditional performing arts were revived and redeveloped under the protection of the powerful bureaucrats of the Meiji government. In 1882, for example, the opening ceremony for a new Kabuki theater, the Shintomiza, was attended by Sanjō Sanetomi and other government leaders, and army and navy bands played. These arts remain in the same state today, and they are what modernized, contemporary Japanese watch. In effect, then, one cannot discuss tradition if one ignores what happened to it during Meiji and after. But this point has been so thoroughly overlooked that today tradition seems to generate either moralistic or idealistic discussions and no more.

If one examines tradition from a practical vantage point today rather than simply in appreciation of the past, if one regards it as being basically uninterrupted between Meiji and the present, inevitably the discussion will deal with Meiji culture. But culture must not be considered only in terms of economic history. Such terms as "semi-modern" or "semi-feudalistic" cannot explain the creation of, say, the beautiful paintings by Yasui Sōtarō and Umehara Ryūzaburō (which have a charm that cannot be found in American, Russian, or English creations). In fact, no social reform can get rid of everything old at once. Even in the Soviet Union something uncommunist, something feudalistic remains. Society in Meiji Japan also was half modern and half feudal, but that was historically inevitable. Japan's modernization contained and created numerous serious problems, but on the whole it advanced relatively smoothly. That Japanese were successful in maintaining their cultural and political independence is certainly among the most important results. And if national independence, the basic goal of nationalism, is a prime measure of modernization, the idea of retaining tradition discussed in isolation from nationalism becomes a disembodied ethnic cosmopolitanism.

Nationalism cannot be summed up in a few sentences, but in the case of Japan an important point is that nationalism once was linked with militarism and aggression. It became repugnant[30] to the Japanese people, and today they regard it gingerly, if they do not reject it outright. Now it is time to discard that bias and try to assess nationalism more objectively.

According to Abe Kōzō,[31] nationalism in Japan was not firmly linked with social reform, as it is in the rest of Asia and in Africa today. Instead, it arose from "the desire of the lower-ranking samurai in the ruling class to maintain their privileges." It was "born completely independent of popular sentiments," he says. This dogmatic opinion still appears as a representative view in the major newspapers, but it is not accurate. In the first place, nationalism elsewhere in Asia and Africa, except in China, is not necessarily linked with social reform, although Japanese are ready to support nations that are struggling to build their countries through nationalism. But they should not idealize the movement and ignore the realities in those countries. From my own encounters at P.E.N. Club meetings and talks with explorers, scholars, and writers who have visited these places, I do not receive the impression that nationalism today in modernizing countries is more responsible or less narrowly focused than it was in Japan during the Meiji era. On the contrary, it seems less responsible and less directed at broad national welfare. If Japan is to protect both its political and cultural independence, we cannot reject its nationalism in penance for what happened in the past, no matter how evil that past was.

The Japanese people should be more aware of their nation— they must shoulder the burden of responsibility for the history of their nation in past, present, and future. If they did, they would have more confidence in it, and that confidence would lead them to take positive, generous interest in other nations. They must start by reorienting their attitude toward Japan's nationalism and modernization. Neither falls into what is called the "classical" pattern, but that is nothing to be ashamed of. What country, except England and France, perhaps, ever followed "classical" patterns of nationalism or modernization? And if those countries did, it was because they themselves defined the terms. The very fact that Japan is not classical is part of Japanese tradition, and we have no choice but to bear our tradition and move on. But in so doing, it is absolutely necessary to reevaluate the history of modern Japan. Japanese today tend to forget the enormous strain and effort that went into modernization in the Meiji era. They think of it as something that just "happened," almost mechanically. But their understanding of that process, and the important role of nationalism, will never be complete or accurate until they appreciate the tremendous, back-breaking work that went into the achievement of modernization.

Reforms are not always successful. In Afghanistan, King Amanullah Khan (r. 1919–29) attempted radical modernization from above, but reactionary opposition forced him to abdicate and flee. Today, that nation is one of the least modernized and antimodern countries in the Islamic world.

Our grandfathers of Meiji Japan succeeded in radical modernization, and they did so without losing national independence, even though the costs were high. It is meaningless to talk about Japanese tradition without recognizing the painful efforts of that first "modern" generation. How easy it is to lament that "our nation was pushed onto the capitalist road from above" and deprecate the originality and efforts of industrial capitalists, such as Kaneko Naokichi, Mutō Sanji, and Fujiwara Ginjirō, just because they were capitalists; but that very negativism blocks a creative grasp of our nation's tradition.

I recently saw a movie on the construction of the hydroelectric power plant in the Kurobe Valley. It will produce a quarter of a million kilowatts of electricity, and it requires the construction of a long tunnel through the Japanese Alps and a huge dam in the valley. It is the second largest plant of this kind in the world. To me, a people who can handle such a project deserve full confidence and respect. I am also impressed whenever I see people carrying construction materials on their backs in the time-honored way, working with others who are boring tunnels with the latest machines, all wearing the traditional worker's *happi* coat with the centuries-old white cloth wound around their heads. Every creative project proceeds with the new and the old worked in together. Such scenes symbolize the way tradition and modernization should be related. Both the *happi* coat and the white head cloth are traditions. They may be displayed in folk art museums in the West, but when they are used in the context of new, creative activity in Japan, they come alive with a beauty that is enhanced with their age.

I do not think much effort should be spent maintaining traditions that have been transmitted without any relation to modernization. The beauties of old Japan that early foreign residents admired will gradually disappear. What we must pass on, however, are the rationalism of Arai Hakuseki,[32] the meticulous scholarship of Motoori Norinaga,[33] and the wisdom and courage of our grandfathers who achieved the Meiji Revolution.

# Notes

1. Germans and Indians, for example, generally regard culture as something internal and civilization as external, placing the former above the latter. I approach culture as inclusive of civilization; I see it as a pattern of human behavior in a given society. A specific value system determined by what has accumulated in the past—both tangible and intangible elements—governs the behavioral mode.
2. The title of E. H. Norman's classic work, for example, is *Japan's Emergence as a Modern State* (New York: Institute of Pacific Relations International Secretariat, 1940). Norman does, however, point out the imperfect nature of Japan's modernity.
3. See Ōuchi Hyōe, Arisawa Hiromi, Wakimura Yoshitarō, and Minobe Ryōkichi, *Nihon keizai zusetsu* [Graphic Outline of the Japanese Economy] (Tokyo: Iwanami Shoten, 1955), p. 2.

4.   To those who bristle at this statement, let me just point out how hard it is to assert Japan's independence in the face of the government's lack of autonomy on the question of easing restrictions on its China trade, for example. Or look at what happened during an emergency on the Japanese *Sōya* expedition in Antarctica in February 1957. Many lives were involved, but the Japanese Maritime Safety Agency had to get American approval before it contacted the Russian icebreaker *Ob*, which happened to be closest to the ice-trapped *Sōya*, for help.
5.   My ideas on why the emergence of nationalism was somewhat belabored in postwar Japan are contained in an article in the November 1952 issue of the *Fujin kōron*, entitled "Nashonarizumu to bunka" [Nationalism and Culture].
6.   This attitude includes what Fujita Shōzō calls "the inclination toward a peaceful, private life" in the epilogue of his article "Tennōsei to fashizumu" [The Emperor System and Fascism] (1957) contained in the fifth volume of the *Gendai shisō* [Modern Thought] series published by Iwanami Shoten.
7.   Albert Einstein, *Out of My Later Years* (New York: The Philosophical Library, 1950), p. 133.
8.   The entire process from (a) through (e) is an assumption based upon my own experience. Tsurumi Shunsuke once told me that I was gradually shifting toward nationalism and that since it was a sort of "conversion" I had better make an announcement to that effect. So I took this opportunity to sum up the process.
9.   I am, in fact, a participant in the debate and have written a lot about the subject since the war. Therefore I am not the right person to write an impartial review. I think it more honest to present a critical introduction, rather than a summary, expressing my own opinions. A full view is best achieved by reading the statements of my critics in their own articles, in conjunction with my inevitably partial opinions.
10.   Usui Yoshimi, in his article "Kokumin bungakuron" [Discussion on the National Literature] in the July 1952 issue of *Gunzō*, says: "The independence of a nation is one of the most crucial issues today for everyone involved in the matter of cultural creation. Nonetheless, there can be no trusting a literary standard which is so affected by political demands that every time a political program is needed by a leftist party, the new policy is immediately applied to literature, and our criterion of judging literature changes completely."
11.   For details on this argument, see the following: "Kabuki o mite" [Impressions of Kabuki], correspondence of Ino Kenji and Kondō Tadayoshi, appearing in the November 1951 issue of *Bungaku*, whose theme is "Approaches to Our Literary Legacies"; my article, "Konnichi ni okeru Kabuki" [Kabuki Today], in *Bungaku*, March 1952; "Futatabi Kabuki ni tsuite" [On Kabuki—Part II] by Ino and Kondō in *Bungaku*, May 1952; my article "Futatabi konnichi ni okeru Kabuki" [Kabuki Today—Part II], in *Bungaku*, August 1952.
   Although there is a considerably wide difference in views between Kondō and Ino, my discussion will center on Kondō's opinion, rather than the specific points of difference. In writing this section, I also referred to Hirosue Tamotsu, "Kabuki-ron no kadai" [Themes in Discussions on Kabuki] in *Nihon bungaku no dentō to sōzō* [Tradition and Creativity in Japanese Literature], Nihon Bungaku Kyōkai, 1953.
12.   Takuboku, the poet who renovated tanka, was a critic and a revolutionary romantic. Generally, leftist discussion on Takuboku ignores the modernity in Takuboku's thinking, resulting in a corruption of his socialist ideas themselves.
13.   The review *Bungakukai* organized a symposium of writers and philosophers to discuss the problem of "the conquest of modernity" and published the results in 1942. Most of the participants violently attacked science and modernity and demanded a return to national tradition.
14.   Rekishigaku Kenkyūkai (Japan Association for the Study of History), *Minzoku no bunka ni tsuite* [On National Culture] (Tokyo: Iwanami Shoten, 1953), pp. 170–73.
15.   In his *Nihonjin no shinri* [Psychology of the Japanese] (Iwanami Shoten, 1953), Minami attacks the traditional and feudalistic mentality of Japanese. Yet he applauds the traditional performing arts, which are supported by the same mentality.

Minami may have resolved this contradiction for himself, but he does not indicate how. I hope he will explain more carefully when he discusses nationalism.

16. Rojin (Lu Hsun), " 'Fun' no nochi ni shirusu" [A Note after the *Tomb*] (Iwanami Shoten edition, *Rojin senshū* [Collected Works of Lu Hsun], vol. 5).

17. Tō Shōson (T'ao Ching-sun), *Nihon e no isho* [My Last Testimony to Japan] (Sōgensha, 1952). I have quoted these two statements frequently, hoping their profound implications would penetrate, but little attention has been given to them. No leftist opinion has been offered regarding their political and historical significance. The fact that these people are unable to respond openly to such views creates a weakness in theory in leftist discussion on tradition.

18. See Minka Geijutsu Bukai, ed., *Kokumin bungakuron* [Discussions on the National Literature] (Kōbunsha, 1953) for some important statements on this issue. See also Takeuchi Yoshimi, *Kokumin bungakuron* [Discussion on a National Literature] (University of Tokyo Press, 1954); Usui Yoshimi has begun "Kokumin bungaku ronsō" [Debate on the National Literature], a serialized essay in *Bungakukai*, starting in the October 1957 issue.

19. Forerunner of contemporary writers of popular literature; his *Daibosatsu-tōge* (1913–44) is Japan's longest novel, and probably the world's.

20. Leading author of popular literature; his *Miyamoto Musashi* was the top bestseller during the Pacific War.

21. "Kokumin bungaku ni tsuite" [On the National Literature] (*Jinmin bungaku*, September 1952).

22. The concept of "socialist realism" is not necessarily defined clearly even in the Soviet Union. My interpretation is "a realism that conforms to Communist party policy and emphasizes the educational effect of a given work." In noncommunist countries, socialist realism could not possibly have a very wide audience unless a large segment, one-fourth or more, of the population support their Community party, as in France. In Japan today there is no chance that socialist realism could provide the methodology for a national literature meant for everyone.

23. Romantic writer (1868–1927); author of *Hototogisu*, the most popular novel in the Meiji era.

24. Outstanding author of modern Japanese literature (1867–1916); novels: *I Am a Cat, And Then, Kokoro*, etc.

25. Novelist and founder of the review *Bungei shunjū* (1888–1948).

26. "Geijutsu ni okeru kaikyūsei to minzokusei" [Class Identity and Nationality in the Arts] (*Shin Nihon bungaku*, June 1952).

27. "Dentō" [Tradition] in *Bungaku kōza*, Chikuma Shobo edition, September 1951.

28. Modernization does not necessarily discourage tradition; in fact, sometimes it activates it. In Japan and India, for example, the introduction of the railway encouraged more people to make religious pilgrimages, and in Nepal the largest volume of imported goods after opening trade with foreign countries was candles for religious use. At the same time, modernization deprives tradition of its mysterious qualities. As a comparison of pilgrims in Japan and India shows, the more advanced a nation is, the less religious its pilgrims become.

29. In 1958 Americans at last succeeded in conquering a peak of more than 8,000 meters (26,240 feet) when two U.S. climbers ascended Hidden Peak (26,470 feet).

30. Maruyama Masao used the expression, "lost its virginity" regarding nationalism in Japan, emphasizing the moral aspect. The loss of virginity may not be an asset, but the subsequent maturation is what counts. It is outmoded idealism to think that once virginity is gone, everything is over.

31. Abe Kōzō, "Nihon no nashonarizumu" [Japanese Nationalism] (*Asahi shinbun*, August 14, 1957).

32. Statesman and encyclopedist scholar (1657–1725); first scientific historian of Japan; he wrote an outstanding autobiography half a century before Rousseau.

33. Philologue and positivist scholar of Japanese classics (1730–1801).

# 4

# The Classics in Contemporary Japan

WITHIN the broad theme of *humanisme* it may be out of place to venture a discussion on the humanities of a single nation, in this case, the classics in Japan. *Humanisme*, or neo-*humanisme*, is, by definition, universalistic, or at least oriented toward universalism. But it is increasingly evident today that *humanisme* is in trouble. Responses from across the world to questionnaires prepared by Unesco without exception indicate misgivings that *humanisme* has any future at all. Obscure debates on the merits and necessity for humanistic education (the humanities and classics) can no longer contribute anything to the state of *humanisme*. A useful approach must be objective and must acknowledge the realities we live with. That being so, perhaps it is of some value to assess *humanisme* in individual countries. The case of Japan may be especially interesting, as no people have opened their doors more widely and willingly than Japanese to the humanities of other countries.

When the Chinese classics began arriving in Japan in the ancient period, their impact was immediate and forceful. Inspired by China's literary achievements, our ancestors set about to produce their own in the *Man'yōshū*, *The Tale of Genji*, and the other masterpieces of early Japanese literature. Japanese continued to study and borrow from the Chinese classics and to apply what they learned. Confucianism became the standard for ethical life among the intelligentsia, and it remained so until

Originally presented as a paper, entitled "Gendai Nihon ni okeru koten no arikata," at a symposium held during the General Assembly of the International Council for Philosophy and Humanistic Studies (ICPHS), September 1959.

the late nineteenth century. Under the Tokugawa bakufu (1603–1868), Confucianism also provided the code of ethics for the nation at large, enabling a centralized authority to preserve the established feudal order and maintain peace through a policy of national seclusion for two and one-half centuries—an extraordinary length of time for any country. At the same time, knowledge of the Chinese classics spread. *Kuwen Chenpao*, a collection of poems from the Ch'ing dynasty (351–94) to the Sung (960–1279), and *T'ang Shih Hsuan* [Selected Poetry of the T'ang dynasty] gained as wide a readership as the Japanese literary masterpieces. If harmony and stability are the most important elements in the nurturing of a culture, then Japan under the Tokugawas may well have provided a near-perfect cultural nexus. But few people today consider that period the "golden age" of Japanese culture. Its stability verged too closely on stagnation.

The status quo was demolished in 1868 when the Meiji Restoration ended Tokugawa rule. The question of whether the Restoration was a bourgeois revolution or not can still ignite controversy, but no one denies that it was a cultural revolution of a radical kind. The leaders of the Meiji state were determined to wipe out all remnants of the feudal age and to bring Western civilization to Japan. The attempt to obliterate a tradition—which, incidentally, Arnold Toynbee commended—may seem an incomprehensible act of folly, but Japan sensed the mortal danger of colonization by the very Western powers whose civilization offered the means of defense. There seemed no choice but to modernize after the model of the West. This cultural revolution was harsh and violent. Some first-rate Japanese-style painters, for example, had to support themselves by going to work for arsenals, drawing diagrams of cannon instead of birds and plum blossoms. Traditional songs and ballads were no longer sung in the new schools. The reason for that lay in their provenance. The Tokugawa ideal of beauty was personified in the highest-ranking courtesans of the Yoshiwara, the extravagant, formal gay quarters of Edo (Tokyo) where pleasure was crystallized into an art. The songs and ballads of the period grew out of the esthetic sense cultivated in the Yoshiwara, and, weighted with such an indelible heritage, they had to go. No Westerner, perhaps to his good fortune, has ever experienced such a revolution, but for that reason it may be difficult to fully appreciate the impact of cultural discontinuity on the Japanese people in the aftermath of the Meiji Restoration. But without sympathy for the experience of shattering discontinuity, it is impossible to understand the modern culture of any of the late-developing nations.

Of course it is impossible to overhaul a national mentality in a single sweep. Japan, like any other late-modernizing nation, experienced periods of strong reaction, but most Japanese have supported modernization policies. They themselves are the beneficiaries of those policies which, despite a threefold population increase since the Meiji Restoration, have raised the standard of living. The people are aware that their country's modernization and industrialization are directly responsible for improvements in their own living conditions. The wars that have involved Japan since the late nineteenth century have all been accompanied or followed by major spurts of development. That in itself can be no source of satisfaction, but more noteworthy is the fact that those highly educated in the Japanese and Chinese classics tended to support aggressive wars, while some Christians and socialists, people who studied Western culture, opposed war every time. Surely a grounding in the classics heightens one's esthetic sensitivities, but it is extremely doubtful that education in the classics today can produce people who do not fear ideological or moral martyrdom. Clearly we cannot ask too much of this great reservoir of man's wisdom.

In Europe, modern science fought an uphill battle against traditional thought, notably Roman Catholicism. No such conflict occurred in Japan. First of all, on the basis of a compromise reached between them, both modern science and traditional Western thought were taught in Japan. Second, science and technology were considered essential to the country's modernization. Third, the substance of Japan's traditional thought could not hold its own against new ideas. Japan had—and still has—political and social reactionaries. But few have ever opposed anything that had to do with science. In that respect Japan is very different from Europe or India, where even today innovation in the realm of science often meets resistance. With such a long tradition behind their unanimous respect for science, it is not surprising that Japanese are perhaps more wholeheartedly enthusiastic than other peoples about "progress" as well. In the field of education, Japanese experience no basic conflict between science and the classics, simply because the superiority of science is taken for granted in their society. Any problems that do arise only concern the allocation of teaching time.

Not all Western literature is "progressive," at least not in every respect, and there are numerous writers who would counter the most basic assumptions of modernization. But Japanese of the Meiji era believed that Western literature provided an ally in their efforts to modernize society. Modernization, in fact, became synonymous with westernization. By 1871, only a few years after the Restoration, Mill, Rousseau, Shakespeare, Defoe, and Dumas (père) had been translated into Japanese and were widely read. The Japanese passion for Western literature has grown steadily stronger since then, except during the World War II years when the military dictatorship forcibly suppressed it and attempted to use the Japanese classics to propagandize antiforeign sentiment. But suppression only tantalized: the postwar boom in Western literature was unparalleled. It may be important to remember that the influence of Western works on Japanese thinking has been that much more powerful because so many people can read. In a nation where all but 3 percent of the population is literate, and where the habit of reading is stronger than in any other, the written word, from whatever source, is bound to have greater effect.

A huge reading public makes it possible to publish cheaply. A complete translation of *War and Peace* can be had for only $2.50, and a translation of Maupassant's *A Life of a Woman* for 50 cents. Low prices, in turn, give anyone access to books. Works by the great Western novelists, Stendhal, Maupassant, Tolstoy, Dostoevski, and numerous others are now "classics" in the minds of Japanese, many of whom feel a stronger affinity for these works than for the classical literature of their own country. Few contemporary Japanese novelists enjoy a wider readership than the prominent Western authors. Literary critic Nakano Yoshio[1] interviewed twenty well-known Japanese authors and reported that almost all acknowledged that Western writers had stimulated their early interest in literature. Also, most critics of modern Japanese literature studied European or American literature in university. Without years of cultural or social westernization behind them, it would be difficult to explain the phenomenal success of Western writing among Japanese. Certainly this is one area where the government had no direct influence, nor was Western literature taught as part of the required school curriculum.

On the other hand, the traditional classics, the great literary works of ancient China and Japan, have been steadily losing their appeal. Poorly prepared or simply dull teachers make the classics even less interesting. When I was a middle-school student, the Japanese and Chinese classics were required subjects, and the hours spent in those classes were unbearably boring. Today, I am very aware of the subtle qualities and profound values in the classical literature of Oriental peoples, but I was a child then, and children are affected by their teacher's personality at least as strongly as by the content of a textbook. Insipid instructors (recalling of American mathematician Norbert Wiener's cynical image of blind kittens sewn up in a basket to protect them from the harsh world) do not inspire a child's trust. We liked our English and natural science teachers; they were vigorous and progressive. But the Japanese and Chinese classics teachers always seemed to be lost in awe of the ancient sages. Worse, the Japanese classics teacher was unable to write decent prose in modern Japanese, and this only deepened our contempt. Things do not seem much different today.

A one-thousand year tradition does not just dry up, however. It keeps following in the innermost regions of our consciousness, waiting for the time when it can surface. Several years ago, Yoshikawa Kōjirō, professor of Chinese literature at Kyoto University and a man with a very modern outlook, and Miyoshi Tatsuji, an extremely cultured man and first-rate poet, together published an annotated selection of T'ang dynasty poems. Much of the book's value lies in their excellent translations and annotations and very well-written guides to the appreciation of ancient poetry. The work sold 250,000 copies.

At only 30 cents a copy, this book contributed much more to an understanding of Chinese literature than did the efforts of teachers and local boards of education to have the Chinese classics incorporated as a compulsory subject in the high school curriculum. (I should add that the focus of interest in the Chinese classics generally has shifted from their ethical to their esthetic value.) In short, if we wish ancient literary works to be accorded a higher place in formal education and in our cultural life, we must first train well-qualified teachers equipped with the technical knowledge needed to teach the classics and a keen sensitivity to modern values. But in Japan, and probably elsewhere, too, college graduates who teach high school literature must be content with a far more modest income than what their peers employed in private corporations earn. It is not easy to recruit talented students to become school teachers.

One very important service the classics perform is to transmit the traditional culture and values of a nation to succeeding generations, but the tradition is carried on as much by the masses as by the elite. Along with the classics and highly sophisticated literature, popular literature, which reaches so many more people, is an important repository of tradition. The values implicit in Japanese reverence for ancestors, love among family members, and the "life-is-transient-nothingness" attitude are permanently rooted in the soul of the people, but not on account of any formal or classical education. These values are conveyed in other ways, an important one being popular literature. The volume *Japanese Popular Culture*[2] goes into this subject in some depth, examining the relationship between traditional tastes and ways of thinking, and modern mass culture.

Social change in Japan has probably moved more rapidly than in any other nation in modern history. This change shows up dramatically in the language. French people have no trouble reading Molière (1622–73), but most Japanese find it difficult to read a literary work written in their own language only eighty years ago. The style of mid-nineteenth century writing can be called "old" now. Its strict literary conventions and set forms, as well as the very large number of Chinese characters in use then, are daunting to today's young people, whose written idiom is colloquial, and who can call up only a limited number of characters without recourse to a dictionary. Yet few seem very concerned about the passing of the ideograph—the vehicle of the written word in Japan for a millennium and a half. On the contrary, its persistence confounds the typewriter and other modern tools of instant information, to the frustration of those with vested interests in efficiency. Understandably they recommend limiting the number of Chinese characters even more, simplifying them further, or even abolishing them altogether. Some large corporations have dispensed with characters and use typewriters that contain only the phonetic syllabary of forty-seven symbols. Protests from the minority who value Japan's ideographs are no match for the powerful lure of profits and time-saving. Capitalism seems bent on robbing tradition of all its defenses and taking away the memory of our language with it.

Considering the indifference that prevails in the cultural milieu, to revive appreciation of classical literature may be a stiff challenge. But it is worth the effort, and there are several ways to do it. Let me offer my thoughts on what we need to do to reset a base for the classics in our total education. The first requirement, of course, should be language. Genuine appreciation of the classics of any country is possible only if one knows the language in which they were written. Today, however, even Europeans find it difficult to master Latin, and it is that much more difficult for Japanese who wish to learn it. To master classical Greek or Chinese is even more arduous. Keeping that in mind, let me make some suggestions.

First, it is absolutely necessary to train highly competent teacher-scholars. It becomes the mission, if you will, of such people to spread their love and knowledge of the classics among the population, using their sense of the contemporary mind to find ways to appeal to modern readers.

Second, while the layman cannot be expected to learn Greek, Latin, or Sanskrit, the great works in these languages can be made available to him through good translations. Even if a person reads only a few of the great Western or other classics, they will provide some foundation for further reading in the modern literature of the culture, works that are successors of the classical giants. A program of modern literature must be planned with such considerations. If the schools provided guidance in reading the modern literature of other countries and recommended certain foreign masterpieces for extracurricular reading, students could become familiar with these works and their traditions. It would be wise to draw up a standardized but broad reading list. I made such an attempt myself in "Fifty Selected Modern Novels," which is the appendix to my *Bungaku nyūmon* [An Introduction to Literature].[3]

The Chinese classics make different demands on us. Japanese itself is deeply indebted to the Chinese classics. Indeed, an understanding of our own classical literature is impossible without knowledge of China's. It is important to read the great Latin historical classics, but Japanese have more to gain from Ssu-ma Ch'ien's *Shi Chi* [Historical Memoirs] and Pan Ku's *Han Shu* [Historical Records of the Former Han] than from Thucydides, Livy, or Tacitus. Japanese ought to have a head start, for the Chinese classics permeate the culture we grow up in, but the fact is that classical Chinese is more difficult for us than Latin is for Europeans. I do not think it necessary to read them in the original, or to demand that Chinese be taught as a compulsory subject. It is enough to provide good Japanese translations and carefully annotated texts accessible to anyone.

Finally, Japanese classics should be part of compulsory education. Since it is too much to ask that ancient literature be absorbed intact, as the purists would have it, good annotated and abridged texts are a valuable tool for the gifted teacher who can instill the germ of intellectual curiosity. It is not always easy to arouse interest in that large body of our classical literature which dwells on resignation, inner reflection, and the transience of this world. Arising during the centuries of isolation, this style achieved peaks of emotional delicacy, but it lacks universality, and it did not encourage a coherent structure of thought and philosophy. It is not necessary to ask boys and girls alive with dreams and eagerness to strap their thoughts to the negative, meditative mood that suffuses these works. We can simply refocus our selection. For young people in school, it may be enough to read the literature of the post-Meiji Restoration years. Traditional Japanese values are very much alive in literature well into the modern period. The works of Natsume Sōseki, Shiga Naoya, Tanizaki Jun'ichirō, Kawabata Yasunari, and others all attain much of their esthetic and philosophical depth from their very dependence on those values in the fabric of their prose.

Still, no matter how strong Japan's classical traditions and values, there is no denying that our contemporary culture is

hybrid. It is probably inevitable that the cultures of the modernizing nations of Asia and Africa, also, have become more or
less hybrid. While modernization on the pattern of a model
carries the risk of superficial imitation, I do not believe that
the heterogeneity produced by mixing indigenous and external
cultures is either unproductive or superficial—nor contemptible
—in itself. In Japan's case, we probably went too far in
Americanizing our society after World War II. But in the whole
picture, is there any nation today whose culture is as pure and
integrated as in its medieval period? The conditions that make
such a culture possible no longer exist. There is no useful end
served by vaunting the "glorious" ancient civilizations of the
East and dismissing their modern transformation with contempt.
Such an attitude is offensive and it effectively bars any communication, much less understanding. We are not museum-keepers.
We live in the present, not the past, and we, too, are struggling
to keep up with the contemporary world and move on in a very
difficult age.

Cultural diversity is a fact of human life. We do not need to
mentally sift the elements to try and "purify" a culture for our
own satisfaction, or exclude from consideration all cultures
besides our own. Neither is it necessary for cultures to withdraw
into themselves. Mixing is not always evil. The personality with
contradictory elements can offer much creativity and stimulation, as long as the "mixture" does not result in harmful or
disturbing behavior.

To achieve understanding among nations, perhaps we must
pass through a stage of superficial knowledge and ridiculous
imitation. How Japanese chuckle (or groan) when they see the
common *geta* (wooden clogs) and *tabi* (socks) used to ornament
the walls of tastefully decorated living rooms of upper-class
Americans who think they are being chic. On the other hand,
Japanese intellectuals also considered *ukiyoe* common, even
vulgar—until Europeans came along and pointed out the artistic
merits in this art form. That is only one example of how foreigners were able to awaken Japanese to treasures in their own
culture. It was a French poet, Charles Baudelaire, who recognized the value of Edgar Allan Poe. Some young Japanese interpret Stendhal's *The Red and the Black* as a story of adultery and

fail to see its value as a social critique. Nonetheless, it is better to misunderstand somewhat than not to read the book at all. Often, moreover, one fully understands only later where the true value of a work lies.

Unesco has begun a noteworthy project of translating the literary masterpieces of the world into different languages. This effort will only accelerate the trend toward the formation of hybrid cultures, but rather than shrinking from the prospect, I think Unesco should go one step further. If the organization can enlist the assistance of a literary team of scholars from all over the world, it would be possible to publish a "Selected One Hundred Works of World Literature" or some similar title. With good translations, these works could become available to people in every nation.

To understand others is, in a sense, to abandon a portion of the self. Holding fast to a tightly bound self, one can never really understand or work closely with others. I believe that to assimilate the classics of other nations is a part of our job of learning more about those nations. The elements of tradition that will fade away as the world inches further toward uniformity are, in a sense, being selected out, and we should not mourn their passing. In any case, tradition does not give up easily. At first glance, Japanese seem to be westernized and very cosmopolitan, but they remain inherently Japanese. Sometimes they seem hopelessly Japanese.

# Notes

1. Nakano Yoshio, ed., *Gendai no sakka* [Contemporary Writers] (Tokyo: Iwanami Shoten, 1955).
2. Katō Hidetoshi, ed., *Japanese Popular Culture* (Tokyo: Tuttle, 1959).
3. Kuwabara Takeo, *Bungaku nyūmon* [An Introduction to Literature] (Tokyo: Iwanami Shoten, 1950).

# 5

## Another Look at Japanese Culture

IN their approach to a nation's culture, Japanese most commonly begin by examining it historically. Another way is to start from a description of the nation today and its people, and then draw conclusions. When using this approach, however, one must beware of the danger lurking in the creeping platitudes of the image-setters.

If we were to go by the official guides, standard travel books, or even textbooks, this country is charmingly beautiful. In fact, however, Japan's vistas are not even picturesque. Japanese seem to be doing their best to defile what really should be lovely scenery. Almost no "scenic spot" remains where you do not have to dig to find something pleasant, or even pleasing to imagine as it once must have been. Yet people call the place "beautiful." After all, the guidebooks claim it is. Nowhere is it mentioned that the place is polluted with neon signs, billboards, and rubbish. What is not noted in print seems not to exist. This ostrich mentality extends to Japanese scholars, also. They could do very well without it.

A culture must be examined as it is in the present, which requires some understanding of the historical conditions that determined it. To Naitō Konan (1866–1934), an eminent historian, one should not have to go beyond the Ōnin War (1467–77) to learn all one needs to know about Japanese culture. Until that war, playing football and composing poetry were the

Originally delivered as a speech, entitled "Nihon bunka no kangaekata," in Okayama, fall 1961. Revised and published in *Sekai*, September 1962.

major cultural activities, but these were enjoyed only by the upper classes in Kyoto and Nara, Japan's ancient capitals. The war cut off many highly educated members of the elite from their livelihood, and they had to fan out through the country, where they taught their accomplishments to make a living. It was these people, said Naitō, who pioneered a wave of court culture into the rural areas. He may be right—that one need go no further to find out what this culture is about.

Those who attach importance to history tend to search for origins. As a result, they usually end up placing foreign labels on everything. The tea ceremony can be traced to Lu Yu (c. 720–804) and others in China. Japanese ideographs are actually Chinese characters. The phonetic syllabary, moreover, is completely derived from the ideographs. Japan has Christian churches, but they derive from a Middle Eastern Jew called Jesus. The usefulness of such puttering among origins is probably limited to "Information Please" and other television quiz programs; otherwise, it only leads to such radical dismembering that the culture under scrutiny is left with no identity. The marvelous culture of the French, for example, would be reduced to a collage of Christian, Greek, and Roman elements. Obviously we need no apology for the external sources of our culture.

Among the imports Japan brought in are many that were much improved once they arrived. Cameras made in Japan enjoy a reputation as the best in the world, but a Frenchman named Louis Jacques Mandé Daguerre (1789–1851) invented the camera. Which deserves emphasis in assessing Japan's cameras—their history or their current state? Japan's photographers also stand up well in a comparison with their French counterparts. The point is that the merit of something now does not rest on where it comes from. Baseball is very popular in Japan, and it will remain so, even though Japanese players are still not as strong as American. The fact that Japanese like it is more important than where the game started.

It is not wise to go overboard in studying history in order to know the present, for it is endless, and it may work at cross-purposes with your goal. To understand the Shōwa era, you must study the Taishō era; to understand the Taishō era, you then have to study the Meiji era. On you go until eventually the old begins to seem far superior to the new. Then you find yourself declaring that unlike England, where capitalism reached its classical, orthodox form, Japan is backward. That is a value judgment, but is it necessary? Perhaps you are technically correct, but non-classical or "unorthodox" development should be just as acceptable. Neither the United States nor the Soviet Union can make any claim to orthodoxy in economic development compared with England and France. Japan has legislated peace into its Constitution and has no colonies or overseas territories; is it not, then, more advanced than England and France? In sum, there is no definitive benefit in judging the present against what you can cull from the past, or in measuring Japan against an inevitably degrading Western yardstick. The appreciation of contemporary Japanese culture must derive from some other approach.

The one basic point that can be made with certainty—apart from whether it is "good" or "bad"—is the fact that Japanese society has undergone change more rapid than has ever been experienced in any other country. An understanding of what that change means is crucial to understanding Japanese culture today. The rate and effects of change in Japan are starkly clear when one visits France, England, or the United States. Think for a moment. Few Westerners, in any country, cannot read something written in their language in 1901, but I wonder how many Japanese high school students can read *Ichinen yūhan* (One and One-Half Years, 1901) by Nakae Chōmin (1847–1901). College students may pretend that they read Chōmin, but I doubt that they really understand what they are reading. Even if they knew all the characters he uses, they probably would still be unable to read with clear understanding. This is not true in France. High school students can grasp most of Pascal or Gide without abridgement, whether they hear the prose or read it. The reason for the difference is simply the faster pace of social change in Japan. This basic fact must be absorbed before one attempts to formulate any judgment about Japanese culture.

Why did such rapid change occur in the first place? In the Tokugawa period Japan rested—I will not say "slept"—for two hundred and fifty years. During that extended interlude, the country quietly prepared itself until necessity suddenly forced the people to mobilize their ingenuity and achievements in order to adopt the modern civilization of the West. Our grandparents worked hard, sometimes desperately, and they worked very quickly, for they knew that their survival hinged on success. It was a unique cultural revolution brought on by the Japanese people as a whole. Perhaps there was no choice, but whatever the reason, they made the revolution and dauntlessly carried it through to the finish.

How can we say whether it was "good" or "bad"? In the same way, we cannot judge the radical change in dress from kimono to Western styles as anything but practical. All we can say is that it was fast; few countries have experienced such a complete turnabout even in dress in the short century since 1868. I recall a photograph taken of Jawaharlal Nehru at an interview with Nikita Khrushchev, in which Nehru is wearing a cap, true to Indian tradition. Whenever Nehru attends formal meetings he always wears close-fitting trousers and this hat. A photograph showing him otherwise would damage his image in India. India has had no cultural revolution; women wear saris even on road construction jobs. Such loyalty to tradition may be commendable, but it stands in the way of modernization and industrialization for India. My point is that by emphasizing the present in examining a culture, I suggest that facts right before us should be dealt with before one launches into lofty historical comparisons.

Japanese culture cannot be understood against a Western model, for no Western nation has had such a revolution. How pointless and denigrating it would be to hold up the image of the United States in assessing the Soviet Union, for the United States had no socialist revolution. In the early years of the Meiji era, the late nineteenth century, when Japan's cultural revolution was at its most intense, no one found it strange that talented artists were doing menial work, because everyone was swept up in it. Certainly Cézanne never sat at the reception desk at some textile factory to earn his livelihood because his pictures sold poorly. The cultural revolution in Japan was that grim.

Other things happened that would have been inconceivable in the West, like the sudden damper the schools put on the songs, even local folk songs, that our grandparents had known and loved since childhood. After the Meiji Restoration a large part of our heritage in songs and ballads, including *tokiwazu, shinnai, utazawa,* was abruptly set adrift from the education of the people. This was a revolutionary event. Search another culture, if you like, for the object lessons it can give your own, but never hold up a culture undisturbed by revolution against another which had to endure revolution for decades, and then try to claim superiority for it.

Our Meiji grandparents were in a rush. They overlooked a lot and did not implant some things deep enough in their urgent westernizing. Democracy is a battered target of those who want an example of an import whose growth was stunted. They may be right, that democracy remains only partially matured even today, but we must remember that Japan started from scratch on the road to democracy, and only a hundred years have passed. The democracies of the West had a long period of preparation before their present systems blossomed. In the process, moreover, how much blood was shed, how many monarchs were executed and people uprooted? Japan's democracy may be far from mature, but what has been achieved, and in a much shorter time, is actually remarkable. And it has been done with relatively little violence.

An element of insouciance in their temperament sometimes serves the Japanese well. When they go abroad they make a point of seeing what is pleasing or beautiful, and bypass or block out what is not. This tendency to home in on what they wish for may be an important cause of Japan's advance as a nation. But it is necessary to see both good and bad, beautiful and ugly, dispassionately. Japanese visiting France, for example, might note that the primary school buildings in their own country are far superior to those in France. Japan has many other worthy achievements, but some Japanese would rather stress the weak points in their culture. They are right when they point out its inconsistencies and its flighty restlessness. Their claim cannot be countered by any argument about the deep and quiet currents of simplicity and tranquility that run in the heart of the culture. To see quietness, unpretentiousness, as the essence of the culture is nonsense. Contemporary Japanese culture is characterized less by quiet simplicity than any I can think of. Give some of the Western countries credit for learning to love quietness, but Japan is restless; today it is all motion and noise. Let us go back to Nakae Chōmin as we think about why Japan has become so twitchy. Chōmin once acted as a "chief of staff" in the Freedom and Popular Rights Movement in the late nineteenth century, and he was also a creative thinker, rich in talent. Unfortunately, few young Japanese or even intellectuals have ever read much of what Chōmin, or any number of other great Japanese thinkers, wrote, because—and this is also a byproduct of Japan's cultural revolution—they think they must read Hermann Hesse and other European writers first. They tend to think that their ancestors produced nothing worth reading, and so Chōmin is of secondary importance. He wrote *Ichinen yūhan* after his doctor announced that he would die of cancer of the larynx in "one and one-half years." I would like to quote a passage from the book, written in context of a discussion on the lack of philosophy in Japan:

> Compared with other peoples, the Japanese can reason things out very clearly. They are adept at changing in response to the needs of the times, rather than stubbornly clinging on. That is why Japanese history has never seen the tragic and pointless wars of religion that so fill the history of the West. Japan successfully revived itself in the Meiji era [i.e., the Meiji Restoration] with swords that hardly touched blood. Three hundred feudal lords willingly handed over their land and power to the emperor. This was possible because of their lack of stubbornness. The same quality explains how Japanese could suddenly shift from traditional to Western in manners and customs without any lingering attachment for the past. It is also lack of obstinacy that gives rise to a very bad disease called "frivolity" and another bad disease called "flabby purpose and indecision." The same disposition also explains why Japan has no original philosophy nor any political principles, and why no political struggle ever lasts very long. Japanese are cunning and crafty, not cut out to accomplish any great work. The people are practical and cannot possibly be expected to go beyond the confines of common sense.

That is why I urge a swift and fundamental reform in education and a drive to create living people rather than dead scholars.

This very interesting point may serve as a basic theme in an examination of Japanese culture. In Chōmin's view, Japanese are quick-witted and can find reason in things easily. Once they judge that something is more important now, they can immediately switch gears and act upon it. That lack of persistence—stubbornness—removes the need for such absurd activities as a religious war. Thus Chōmin identified positive points in the Japanese temperament. There have been struggles related to religion such as the uprisings of the Buddhist Ikkō sect at the end of the Muromachi period (1392–1573), and the Christian rebellion at Shimabara from 1637 to 1638, but they were on a small scale and can hardly be called "wars" compared with those in Western history. On the contrary, Japanese absorb the new rather than struggle to keep the old. They changed their lifestyle completely after the Meiji Restoration, and today imported sports and goods are an integral part of Japanese life.

Chōmin is not completely positive about this temperament. A proverb goes, "A sage does not adhere to things," but Japanese tend to relinquish their hold too easily. They too easily become frivolous, said Chōmin, taking in everything. Almost every conceivable sport is played in Japan. Baseball and tennis are a passion with many, and swimming, too. But few know the traditional strokes once taught by the Shinden and Suifu schools, both of which were developed during the Tokugawa period, but they do the crawl, butterfly stroke, and other strokes learned from the West very well. Europeans, on the other hand, have imported judo, but they do not play baseball or sumo. In food as well, Japanese have managed to reproduce much of the world's cuisine. Tokyo's innumerable restaurants offer all manner of cooking from countless countries, but in London or Moscow it is quite a special establishment that offers Chinese noodles or Japanese curry or Mongolian grilled mutton. Japanese are eager to try everything. Their very enthusiasm is childlike in a way, but at the same time it reveals an aggressive spirit and a healthy vigor.

There are merits and demerits in almost any aspect of culture

or personality, and Chōmin sees both sides of the Japanese temperament. But when he urged "a swift and fundamental reform
in education and a drive to create living people rather than dead
scholars," he obviously stood for the cultural revolution. There
he was telling his countrymen to overcome their demerits and to
push on in the spirit of progress, not clinging to the past, but
refining their capacity to discern reason.

Japan's rapid advance after the Meiji Restoration owes much
to the kind of temperament Chōmin identified, but where does
that temperament come from? In my view, perhaps the single
most important factor is the absence of "God." Over all Japan's
myriad gods and deities, there is no single Allah or Jehovah, no
monopolistic god that devours all the others. One all-powerful
god would not permit constant shifting from one thing to another.
For Japanese, one all-knowing god would be constricting.
When one does something uncommendable, he may hide it from
his wife, children, and other people, but if that god were above
him, he would be uneasy. The Japanese would begin to repress
his eagerness as he heard his god reprimand him for wearing
a suit instead of Japanese clothing. "Do you think it is right to
discard tradition?" comes the voice. That god would scold when
he caught someone beating a drum as a Nichiren Buddhist one
day and singing hymns at church the next. In France and
England, where city halls are constructed on medieval models,
such buildings are beautiful but not practical. They are heavy
and badly lit. But if Europeans were to try to build a well-
lighted building with glass walls, like the Tokyo Metropolitan
Government offices, they would probably hear the voice of God
reminding them "Are you not ashamed of yourselves for trying
to betray your tradition?" In Japan, no such voice is ever heard.
As it is, none of Japan's thousands of gods has too much power.
An old maxim goes, "If one god throws you out, another god
will pick you up."

Japanese worked hard to raise production after the Meiji
Restoration, and the pace at which they succeeded in industrial
growth is the most rapid in history. I believe that the absence of
an almighty God was instrumental in that success. This assumption needs more study and development, but I am convinced it
is basically valid. There are those who believe Japan's failure to

adopt Christianity is somehow shameful. Certainly the religion has many very strong points, but Japan is not to be condemned for its refusal to become a Christian nation. If Christianity is a prerequisite for improvement, then most of Asia and Africa is doomed. Japanese must continue to live with their huge family of deities, and I am quite sure they will do so productively. The absence of God is linked with "frivolity," but, for better or worse, that very frivolity or dilettantism is an important prop for survival in an age when scientific progress knows no bounds.

Japan was only recently a backward nation. But by means of a protracted cultural revolution beginning just after the Meiji Restoration and the efforts of its people, its progress has been startling. What logic is there, then, in exhuming the glories of the age of Hōryūji temple or the haiku of Matsuo Bashō in order to learn about the culture? How much more instructive to study recent phenomena, such as the school excursion.

The critics of school excursions claim that these mass, several-day sightseeing tours in fleets of student-filled vehicles hinders the healthy development of the individual. But describe to Americans or Russians how trains and boats are chartered for these educational trips, and they are bound to be impressed. The excursions may not enhance the child's individuality, but the children love them. All Japanese, rich or poor, go in large groups to visit the famous sites in their country sometime during the primary and junior high school years. It is quite an achievement. An international survey to find out what percent of the population has seen their country's capital city would probably show Japan as having the highest percentage. In France, how many of its people have seen Paris? In the United States, how many have been to Washington? Some say there is no use in seeing Tokyo: it only tires the children; but children do not tire from trips like this. Far more valuable than what they actually see, in any case, is the chance to let the mind stretch and explore beyond the confines of school and home. One of these days I intend to do a proper study of the school excursion, for nothing irks me more than the view that everything that does not originate abroad is second-rate.

Japanese coffee shops are also unique. First, they are ubiquitous, cropping up in every corner of a city or town. The coffee is inexpensive and often quite good, and one is permitted to sit and think, study, or talk for as long as he likes. This is Japanese culture. It is beside the point to argue whether such institutions are worthless or not. The weekly magazine is another uniquely Japanese invention, whether or not it represents the culture. The first mass circulation weekly in the world was started by a Japanese newspaper company. After the Meiji Restoration and again after World War II, Japan underwent drastic changes, and in the process, all manner of amazing things were created, some purely Japanese and some improvisations and improvements on imports from overseas. I would simply say that to consider Japanese culture without attention to these is an empty exercise. The school excursion is one example, but in scholarship, the same principle applies.

Yukawa Hideki did not invent modern physics. Using the work of Western physicists, he moved forward, pioneering new horizons in the field. His achievements are not to be downgraded because they draw on ideas originating elsewhere. In the same way, Japanese beer, said by some to be among the best anywhere, is no less delicious because a European made beer first. Clever and imaginative Japanese have been busily at work in practically every creative pursuit since the Meiji era began. We can learn a lot from these people, from studying the intelligent and sometimes blundering directions they took, and once we have a perspective on their achievements, it may be possible to identify the nature of Japanese culture in the post-Meiji era.

I have offered some of my own ideas, with no particular conclusions in mind. I have intentionally tried to be impartial, or at least to balance positive and negative comments about Japan's culture. I have stressed my view of Japanese as being especially skillful at adapting to realities, or lacking stubbornness, but I hope I have not conveyed a judgment. There is good in the bad and bad in the good, a quality that is an inevitable consequence of Japan's cultural revolution. Finally, let me repeat that Japanese culture can be better understood by knowing, for example, that the rate of television viewing here is greater than that of France or England and second only to that in the United States, than by having the most intimate acquaintance with the hoary antiquities of Hōryūji or Katsura Detached Palace.

# 6

# Europe and Japan

FOR Japanese, to talk about Europe together with Japan is to
think of their own country in relation to the several Western
countries that became its models at one time or another during
an important part of the modernization period. China and Japan
and the United States and Japan, referred to in pairs, also recall
the special relationship of model and emulator.

Until the late nineteenth century, most Japanese looked to
China as the model. For centuries, a cultured life required
thorough grounding in the doctrines of Confucius and Mencius
and the ability to appreciate the poetry of Tu Fu and Li Po.
Then, beginning after the Meiji Restoration, Japanese turned to
Europe for their models, and after the second world war, to the
United States. But it was Europeans from whom modern
Japanese learned the most, and Europe's models have stood up
for more than a century. For that reason, I think the relations
between Japan and Europe and the kind of understanding that
has existed between them constitute an interesting study.

With the Meiji Restoration of 1868 came the rise of a new, in
some respects uncomfortable, consciousness among Japanese. As
the Tokugawa period drew to a close, the belief that Japan must
enter the world grew stronger, but intellectuals and political
leaders knew the nation could not hold its own without radical
change. They believed it had to be completely remodelled along
European lines. The conviction sparked the cultural revolution
of the Meiji era. It was grim. Very quickly the Japanese-style

Originally delivered as a lecture, entitled "Yōroppa to Nihon," at Iwanami Bunka
Kōenkai, Morioka, August 22, 1967.

painter had no patrons; the only work worth its salt was Western oil painting. The contemporary masters of the Japanese-style schools were driven nearly to starvation. If the plight of these artists can suggest what happened to the rest of Japanese culture at the time, it is probably clear that this cultural revolution was one of the most thorough ever to occur anywhere.

Our grandparents toiled to absorb and apply what Europe had to teach them, and they made Japan into the country it is today. During the century since 1868, Japanese endured misery in many forms, but the result of their work is the nation today, which has one of the most advanced, highly refined cultures in the world. When I visited the United States this year (1967), people told me that even if Japan was still lagging behind England and West Germany, in twenty years it would surpass both to become one of the three top industrialized nations, flanked by the United States and the Soviet Union. A recent newspaper noted that almost all the organs played in Europe were made in Hamamatsu, a city lying between Nagoya and Tokyo. Japan's cameras have outstripped those made anywhere else. It is said that the French auto industry would be crushed by Japanese companies in a few years if the French government removed its tariffs on cars. The list goes on, but the signs are all there that Japan will fulfill the Americans' prediction.

Books published in eighteenth- and nineteenth-century Europe, when Japan was still in isolation from the world, talk about the conservatism of Asians and Africans, people they describe as unable or unwilling to modify their traditions and customs. We Europeans are progressive, they brag, while Asians are reclusive. They paint Orientals as preferring to withdraw and chant sutras, burn incense, prepare tea, and gaze upon flower arrangements instead of taking their chances in the world. The image these books project is entirely alien to Japan today. The tea ceremony and flower arranging, for example, are flourishing industries; they have become so organized and commercially successful that the head of a school can make an extra several hundred million yen just by a little tax evasion. A piece of driftwood swept ashore in a storm with artistic potential for a flower arrangement is snatched off the beach, squabbled over, and finally sold for a good price. It is stocked and resold at a better price to become an element in an exhibit piece the following year, or later. But some Europeans, who have not been keeping up, still believe that ikebana is a reclusive art.

Despite such illusions, there is some truth in the impression that Asians are usually more conservative and enjoy seclusion more than the generally progressive, aggressive Europeans. An Indian, for example, notwithstanding food shortages so severe that Indira Gandhi is prompted to have only two meals a day, will never kill a monkey, no matter how much food he steals. If all the monkeys were deported from India, I think there is a good chance the Indians at least could subsist without importing food. But the monkey is a sacred animal, just as cows are. In Japan, when an animal grows old, it is killed and its bones are put to assorted uses. But a bull in India, even after he has lost all usefulness, is allowed to live until he dies naturally. A little more realism about monkeys and cows and a shift in priorities to human health and survival would go a long way to resolving the food shortage in India. There are statistics to support that claim, but for now, at least, no amount of statistics is going to make a dent in this particular situation.

It is such stubborn, impractical traditions that cause Europeans to see themselves as progressive and positive in comparison with conservative, reclusive Asians. Indeed, that image was probably valid once, but it no longer applies to Asians across the board. Japan broke the established Asian pattern decisively and permanently. The changes in Japan since the 1920s have been so progressive, aggressive, and rapid as to leave Europeans gaping in amazement. It is all the more remarkable, then, that so many of the old misconceptions remain.

In France in the 1930s, I remember talking with an elderly woman who was impressed that someone from such a faraway land should have come to France to study. "Does your country have trains?" she asked me. I replied that my country's trains were a lot faster and more efficient than France's, and she laughed. "Stop your joking," she scoffed. In June this year in England, I happened to look through a brand new children's book entitled *Locomotives and Airplanes*. The illustrations were beautiful, presenting the trains and planes of various countries. There were examples of the American Northern Pacific trains,

Germany's Rheingold, and others, with captions explaining
that these trains were very fast, some running at a good 175
kilometers per hour. As I came to the end, I realized something
was wrong. There was no mention nor any illustration of Japan's
210-kph bullet train.

Such ignorance reveals one of the reasons for England's decline.
If the book had been published two years ago or earlier, the
omission might have been excused, but last year, in 1966, at
the recommendation of the Science Council of Japan, the bullet
train won the Christopher Columbus Award for superior design
and performance, and it has already made quite a name for
itself. It seemed utterly foolish to ignore—or pretend to ignore—
the bullet train and boast about the 175 kph that some European
trains can manage. The airplane section showed Soviet MiGs
and French Mirage fighters, among others, each with a careful
commentary. Japan was mentioned, but only in connection
with its use of American jet fighters. If an English kindergartner
reads this book, he will probably get the impression, if he thinks
about this country at all, that Japan imports locomotives from
America or England, that they probably run at about 130 kph,
and that Japan has a full-fledged military equipped with fighters
from the United States.

Let me recount something else that happened in 1966 on a visit
to Strasbourg. The town was holding a small exhibition, and
one of the halls was devoted to sanitation. There was a large
world map hanging on a wall, with a sign "Wipe Out Starvation." The nations were color-coded according to the daily
caloric intake per person. The United States, France, and a few
others were deep red, indicating 3,000 or more calories consumed per person each day. The less the caloric intake, the
lighter the color on the map. India and Africa were among the
pale-colored regions. Strange to say, Japan was colored as a
"hungry zone," too. I lodged a protest, insisting that we were
a very well-fed nation, but I was informed that their statistics
were based on reliable sources, and they could make no changes.
Japanese may not eat 3,000 calories a day—that much is not
necessary for most people anyway—but we are certainly not
a hungry people. Apart from such misrepresentations, to claim
that Japan's postwar economic growth came about through

social dumping or similar statements reflects an unwillingness to be outdone, more than anything else.

Japan was a backward nation until the beginning of the Meiji era. It took a bona fide cultural revolution to let it catch up with Europe, but Westerners find that revolution difficult to understand. Since the Renaissance, Europeans have led the world, and never in that time have they found it necessary to uproot their ways of thinking or lifestyles. They never felt compelled suddenly to cast away their clothing and start wearing a foreign costume, as Japanese did when they forsook the kimono and changed into suits and dresses. For the most part, Europeans have not had to question their traditions, ways of life, or basic assumptions, but in my view they face a situation now that requires a change in attitudes.

Since Japan learned so much from Europe, it is only natural that many things produced in this country today originate there. Interestingly, some Japanese are embarrassed being so successful at imitation and improvement. They point out that the camera, now one of Japan's important exports, was invented by a Frenchman named Daguerre, and in any case, producing good cameras is nothing to brag about. But such thinking is negative, and really not to the point. It would be more useful to think out why the camera industry failed to grow in France.

In addition, Japan is not all imitation, to begin with. Of the many things that originated in Japan, the school excursion is one of the most interesting. Actually, the idea itself came from the European custom of sending five or ten children off on a tour with a priest. In Japan, trips for schoolchildren have been commercialized and mass organized to take on truly vast proportions. Buses, trains, boats, and entire inns are chartered for the hundreds of students in each group. I do not think any other country has such an institution. The sheer scale of the undertaking puts many people off by its evocations of animals being herded along, but it has admirers, too. A Soviet scholar once commented that he was very impressed with the school excursions in Japan. He said that his country did not have boats that could be chartered for such trips, but that they could learn much from Japan.

Some Japanese protest that such group undertakings, which

are ubiquitous, prevent the growth of individualism, or that a visit to Tokyo is a waste of time, as the group members see nothing but the national Diet building, department stores, and drinking places and taste sundry other vices. Still, if individuality can be worn down over the course of a three-day group tour, it cannot be very deep to begin with. In any case, there is little to support the argument that group activities per se inhibit individualism. And Japanese love group tours. One runs into them all over Europe, coming by chartered flights for language study, sightseeing, or other purposes. In summer, language groups are accompanied by college professors, and they can rent dormitories available during the vacation. It is an inexpensive way to earn a reputation back home for having studied at the Sorbonne. Many teachers participate in such programs, obtaining financial help from their local PTA groups. For many, the main attraction of such a tour lies in sightseeing; the chance to study a foreign language is secondary. Middle-aged women and others join language tours with the aim of seeing Europe, but I think it is all to the good. These trips give the ordinary person a way to stretch the mind and to experience and learn something in other countries.

Japan can also be proud of its department stores. They have been around longer in the West, but Japan has the most sophisticated department store technique anywhere in the world. I do not patronize department stores as a rule, because I find that if I stay too long I begin to feel dizzy from the mountains of goods and crowds of people, but once in a while I stop in out of academic curiosity. How many Europeans are aware of all the Japanese have done to make their department stores so much more efficient and attractive than their Western counterparts? Too many, I fear, assume that Japan remains basically unchanged from long ago. And too many Japanese still believe Europe is the bastion of progress and world power. They have not outgrown the sense of awe implanted during the decades when France, England, and Germany were models for Japan. This group clings to the notion that their country is still inferior to the West. Everything in England is "better," and every Englishman is a gentleman. To them, the Keeler-Profumo affair was probably an unthinkable aberration.

Some years ago, when the English leftist historian Christopher Hill came to Japan, I chaired a forum in which several Japanese scholars participated. One of them noted that while British capitalism had been built up from below, Japan's capitalism was imposed on the people from above, and from the outset it had supported imperialistic, militaristic, and aggressive tendencies. Hill replied that in his view, every kind of capitalism was evil; English capitalism, too, was aggressive in its own way and had been imperialistic from the beginning. Far from being just or constructive, English capitalism was as evil as any other, said Hill, to the chagrin of the Japanese scholar.

I sometimes think that when Japanese intellectuals harp on their country's "backwardness" and push England as a model, some of the guardian deities are working craftily behind the scenes. The effect of criticism by intellectuals—who align themselves with government thinking, even though they put up an antigovernment facade—that Japanese society needs more remodeling is to urge ordinary people to keep working diligently to catch up. Told that their country remains inferior, they become more determined than ever, and they work harder. This, I believe, is the clever working of the gods.

It is often said that England is the model par excellence of democracy. This, too, I doubt. Can a society where social status is emphasized so heavily be the best kind of democracy? Everyone may have equal rights, but I do not think the system is perfect, by any means. In England before the war, I questioned the justice of a society where a person's career was determined before he or she was old enough to make any choices. Whether one worked for a private company or a government agency, two paths were already set, I pointed out, one for executives and high officials, the other for clerks or low-ranking officials. Should not everyone be given a chance to rise through merit? I was immediately asked if I was a communist. Things are not so different in England now. If one made a statistical survey to find out what percentage of large company executives in England and in Japan come from what kind of family and educational background, the data would certainly show that in England family status is much more important than school education. Japanese, myself included, admire the English parliamentary

system, but I do not think we can talk about it in isolation
from the society upon which it is based. Channels for upward
mobility allowing individual successes in English society, regardless of class, are so limited that people get discouraged and their
will to work fades. Parliamentarianism, in this case, does not
represent the democratic ideal.

On a recent visit to England, I went with my friend, the
sociologist Katō Hidetoshi, to a pub in a small city. The place
had a single entrance, but inside it was divided into two rooms.
The one on the lefthand side had "Salon" written on the door,
and "Public Bar" appeared on the righthand door. In Japan,
"bar" would announce the presence of cute young hostesses
(another unique Japanese invention; even in European thinking
Japanese bar girls are fast replacing geisha in notoriety). Anyway,
since I had a necktie on, I went into the Salon and had a small-
size bottle of beer, which cost me one shilling and a half. Then
I learned that the same beer served by the same waiter cost less
in the bar. One would think that anyone would choose the bar.
Not in England. There, where social status is important, people
who can pay more sit in the Salon.

I visited a primary school in the same town. It was a Catholic
school for children from the middle class. Around the school-
yard was wire netting, and on the other side of the net was
a city school attended by children from the working class. That
would be impossible in Japan. Japan has its peers' school,
Gakushūin, which took only the children of the nobility before
the war, but today a grocer's child can enter if he can pass the
entrance exam and pay the fees. In England, children from the
upper reaches of society in regional cities do not go to local
schools; they study in London.

A pretty nineteen-year-old English college student helped us
with our research for a while. Once I asked her what English
people would do in a certain situation I described. Then she
asked me if I was talking about the middle class or the working
class. When I told her I was talking about the English people
as a whole, the girl said she could not answer me. So I had her
define the two classes. She gave an intriguing definition: working
class families eat supper together at the same table at around six
o'clock in the evening, while in middle and higher class families,

the children are fed separately at five or six, and their parents dine at eight o'clock with guests. Since I eat supper with my children at around seven, in England I would not qualify as a college professor in the upper echelons of society.

England's democracy, based as it is on a social status system, has a strong oligarchic tendency. But the British do not necessarily feel antipathy toward their clique of rulers. Sometimes I think that England could rule India for so long through only a small group of people simply because England has a caste system of its own. I am not entirely serious in this, for there are great differences between India's caste system and England's rigid class distinctions. But it seems to me that one aspect of English society is reminiscent of a caste system in the broad sense of the term. At any rate, Japan must be cautious in any attempt to use English democracy as a model.

Europeans have never experienced a cultural revolution on the same scale as Japanese. They have not even tried. Perhaps it is lack of curiosity for new things. They remind me of an old, wealthy family that repairs its buildings but would never consider tearing them down and replacing them with prefab structures. That attitude gives a quiet restfulness to European society. Unlike Japanese, Europeans do not move around nervously, out of breath, trying to get ahead even a little. If one prefers quietness, European society appeals for its elegance and dignity, but if you emphasize moving around and getting things done in your life, Europe would be frustrating. Long ago, the spirit of Japanese culture was symbolized by *wabi* and *shiori*, both of which mean something like "a taste for the simple and quiet." That spirit has been all but squeezed out in the restless Japan of today. Is there any *wabi* in the bullet train? You might find it in a local train meandering twice a day through the French countryside, or in a small town where you get off for a while, but rarely in Japan.

Wandering through towns in England and France often made me think of the Japan of the Meiji or Taishō eras. Some of the old remains in Japan, but it is vanishing far more rapidly than in Europe. In England and France, old things are used, and they are kept more carefully. Whether it is a centuries-old stone building or an ice-box or a radio, people have it repaired over and over again, and use it for many years. Their appliances or whatever are well built in the first place and are meant for long-time use. The manufacturer gives reliable after-sales service, as well. One cannot expect that in Japan. Once your machine gets old, that's the end of it. I have an old camera that still works all right, but if something goes wrong and it needs a new part, I can't get it. The camera shop clerk would protest, "But, Professor, your camera is a 1954 model. You must be out of your mind asking for a part to a camera made thirteen years ago!" English camera manufacturers seem very much more humane in comparison. Nonetheless, in terms of industrial development, Japan is much more progressive. Unlike agriculture, which goes on in the same old rut, modern industry tends to be unfriendly and quite unfeeling about making changes. It would be a heavy burden if the parts for all sorts of old models had to be produced for the company. It is far better—although unfriendly—to produce a constant stream of new models to keep technological progress moving rapidly.

England is facing an economic crisis now. Its per capita income is higher than Japan's, but Japan has more economic freedom. Japanese going abroad are allowed to take up to ¥180,000, for example, while British are limited to ¥50,000. This is only one indication of the more forward-looking, dynamic direction of Japan. England's economic plight is certainly related somehow to English conservative attitudes toward their lifestyles. Some Japanese intellectuals make a virtual fetish of Oxford and Cambridge, and their traditions are undoubtedly worthy and elegant. But the attitudes supporting the luxurious life of the colleges that was so thoroughly irritating to Natsume Sōseki, which demand professors to don a gown even to have a cup of coffee—these attitudes impede smooth industrialization and higher production.

My point is that industries in England and France are no longer more advanced than those in Japan. At this rate, Japan will move ahead very soon. Japan's industrialization has advanced by leaps and bounds since the end of World War II. Industrial progress is the single element that has pulled up the national standard of living, no matter what our more idealistic intellectuals would like to think. They may assert that Japan's progress in transistors has nothing to do with the fate of the nation, but they are not being honest. Actually, they should welcome the contribution industry has made. For one thing, with the bullet train, they can visit Kyoto as often as they wish.

At the same time, industrialization tends to encourage centralization and monopolization. And as a result, Tokyo receives way too much attention, to the detriment of life there and in the local regions. On a trip to France or England, in a small city of twenty or thirty thousand, or even a town of two or three thousand, one can find restaurants with food as good as that in Paris or London. On the other hand, when you think about it, you realize that because industrialization is slower, the distribution of goods is less efficient. The technology of sending fish to the big cities and keeping it fresh is more advanced in Japan; unless you are lucky, you can no longer eat the local *ayu* (sweetfish) in a restaurant on the Nagara River in Gifu. You have to go to a first-rate restaurant in Tokyo or Osaka for *ayu*. Once I was invited to Gifu to watch cormorants catching *ayu*, and I happily anticipated eating the fish on the spot. But when I got there I was embarrassed at my ignorance: of course, all the *ayu* caught there were sent to Tokyo, Osaka, or other major cities by the bullet train or by plane. All we did was watch. Even the local people can seldom eat the fish.

Another example is also related to food. Fruit in France tastes like it should taste—fresh, picked from the trees. Since it is the product of nature, it varies in size. But in Japan, *nijusseiki* pears, to name one, are almost all the same size, and they taste vaguely of chemicals. It is Japanese who began the artificial breeding of such fish as *ayu*, young yellow fish, and prawns. If we continue to see ourselves as a people who love nature and still do nothing to prove it, someday soon we will find ourselves living in a land that has the least nature in the world. This is obvious if you look at what development projects are doing to destroy the natural beauty of the mountain vistas in Nagano prefecture and other spots in Japan.

I do not conclude that industrialization is good or bad. Probably Japan has no other way to survive than to push forward in industrialization, moving ever further ahead of Europe. I neither criticize Europe nor praise Japan's industrialization.

Europe has a quiet and rich culture. At the same time Japanese must cease the attempt to model themselves after Europe. It would be far more interesting to study such questions as why Europeans have a less lively curiosity than Japanese do, than to go on imitating Europe.

# 7

## Cooperative Research in
## the Humanities

THE tendency for scholarship and research to branch off into ever-narrowing specialization on the one hand, and increasing joint, interdisciplinary, or cooperative efforts on the other, became an irreversible trend during the postwar period. The two kinds of endeavor need not be incompatible, for successful cooperative research needs the contributions of specialists, and specialists at some point must coordinate their achievements with others. It is the attitudes of scholars that sometimes make the divergence problematic. Cooperative research as an organized, conscious effort does not have a long history at Kyoto University, where I taught for many years. But when Kyoto's Research Institute for Humanistic Studies launched its first cooperative research venture after the Pacific War, we opened ourselves to attack and undisguised incredulity.

I am a historian—which should help my credibility when I dredge up details of events long past—and I clearly remember the lack of understanding or sympathy from Japan's academic community for what we in the Institute were trying to do. The thoughtless assaults we endured from scholars safely ensconced behind the disciplinary ramparts of their particular departments still irritate me. Even some of my old friends could not comprehend how I could let myself become "trapped" into cooperative research. They bewailed my wasted talents, imprisoned by such a "restricting" framework. I derive some satisfaction from having watched several of our harshest early critics become con-

Originally delivered as a farewell lecture, entitled "Jinbun kagaku ni okeru kyōdō kenkyū," at Kyoto University, March 21, 1968. Published in *Tenbō*, June 1968.

verts over the years. Some are now strong supporters of cooperative research. But our path was never smooth. We were like a ball bounding around wildly in a pin-ball machine instead of rolling straight downhill. This kind of joint effort means giving time and energy to something that may not be of direct personal interest, and I found that being director of the Institute was arduous work. But from the outset I enjoyed our venture into cooperative research immensely and relished the chance to play a role in it.

## Inception of the Idea

The building where we began cooperative research, which no longer stands, housed the Research Institute for Humanistic Studies. Many distinguished scholars contributed their efforts to the six projects we undertook, each of which produced a book: *Rusō kenkyū* [Studies on Rousseau] (1951), *Furansu hyakka zensho no kenkyū* [Studies on the French Encyclopedists] (1954), *Furansu kakumei no kenkyū* [Studies on the French Revolution] (1959), *Burujowa kakumei no hikaku kenkyū* [Comparative Studies on the Bourgeois Revolution] (1964), *Nakae Chōmin no kenkyū* [Studies on Nakae Chōmin], and *Bungaku riron no kenkyū* [Studies in Literary Theory] (1967). The people involved represented many areas and disciplines, including European, Chinese, and Japanese history, and also law, political science, economics, literature, sociology, and anthropology. Many participated in more than one of the six projects, but the numbers who worked on each one were 12 on the Rousseau work, 25 on the Encyclopedists, 18 on the French Revolution, 28 on the bourgeois revolution, 8 on Nakae Chōmin, and 19 on literary theory. I would like to say something about our methodology and the theory behind our approach, but first let me make a few comments about how we began and my thoughts on the significance of cooperative research in the humanities.

The term "humanities" is hard to pin down, but here I use it broadly, to include humanities and social sciences—everything that is *not* a natural science. Although the theoretical justification for cooperative research in the humanities is an interesting subject in itself, I would rather talk about the environment in which our diverse projects evolved and bore fruit. Because I was part of that environment from the outset, it is difficult for me to be completely objective. I also tend to wax sentimental when I recollect the past, but as the history of our cooperative research contains much that is autobiographical, perhaps my own experiences will round out the story of this endeavor at Kyoto University.

The predecessor to the Research Institute for Humanistic Studies was the Tōhō Bunka Kenkyūjo, Institute for Oriental Culture, established in 1929 at the same place. During World War II, I went to teach French literature at Tōhoku Imperial University, which is in Sendai, and I was too far removed to do more than watch the activities going on at the Institute. At that time it was engaged in a study of the Chinese classic *Shang shu cheng-i* [Correct Meaning of the Book of Documents] under the supervision of Yoshikawa Kōjirō. The study later produced a very substantial book. Another Institute project, led by Mizuno Seiichi and Nagahiro Toshio, was a study of the stone buddhas of Yünkang. Much later, after the war, this research was also published through the efforts of Kaizuka Shigeki, Chinese historian and then director of the Institute. I made my own small contribution earlier when René Grousset visited Japan. I gave the French scholar a guided tour of the Institute, and he was profoundly impressed when he learned about the work being done on the stone buddhas. As it turned out, Grousset was of real service to us. I knew that he had been invited to meet Prime Minister Yoshida Shigeru, and I asked him to put in a word on behalf of the Institute. Grousset did just that. He told the prime minister that he deeply admired Japan's achievements, but that any country which left unpublished such brilliant work as that being done at the Institute for Oriental Culture could certainly not be called culturally advanced. Angered that such an important project at a national university should have been so neglected, Yoshida issued strict orders to the Ministry of Education to remedy the situation. Still in Sendai at Tōhoku University, I ached to be involved in the kind of cooperative research the Institute was doing.

At Tōhoku I was coming into contact with people, ideas, and literature in areas other than my own, and I found it very stimulating. Just then I was reading John Dewey, Alfred North Whitehead, and many others whose works I might not have read until much later. The Faculty of Law and Letters, with which I was affiliated, held the literature, law, and economics departments, and they all got along quite well. In fact, the arrangement allowed maximum contact among specialists in different fields, and I wonder now whether the later separation of the three into independent faculties was a step forward or backward. Doi Kōchi, one of Japan's most distinguished literary scholars, had widely varying interests. If he was not engrossed in D. H. Lawrence, or some other writer, he was doing research on ancient Japanese and Chinese literature, literary theory, or using an oscilloscope to study phonetics. Professor Doi and I shared a house for a while after the war, and I learned a great deal from him.

I also learned from Yasui Takuma, the Keynesian economist, with whom I frequently played cards. During our card games, he managed to get across to me a vague notion of the concepts of econometrics. Nakamura Yoshiharu, an old friend from higher school who had become a respected scholar in Japanese economic history, and I used to ruminate on such questions as how the aristocratic ladies in the *Tale of Genji* blew their noses. We concluded that they must have used their fingers—it seemed simply not enough paper was produced in the Heian period to allow for such use as tissue. We tried to find ways to calculate how many calories the people of the Man'yō world (fourth to eighth centuries) consumed daily. We seemed to have a ready supply of eccentric problems. Another friend was Takayanagi Shinzō, whose specialty was the official circulars of the Tokugawa period. He and I had some illuminating talks on the Tokugawa feudal system.

Our diverse, sometimes random conversations later proved to have been valuable preparation for my involvement in cooperative research. When I came to Kyoto University I found that I could converse, after a fashion, with colleagues in law and economics. To my private delight, I discovered that occasionally I knew more than they did on certain points.

That is how, when I returned to my alma mater in 1948, I had developed a powerful urge to do cooperative research. We began the Rousseau project the following April. The person who played the leading role was the late Abe Takeo, the first director of the Institute. He deserves credit for the way the Research Institute for Humanistic Studies has developed. It was Abe who called me back from Sendai. Today the Institute has thirteen divisions, but when Abe made the initial plans, he insisted on sixty, which would have meant sixty full professors. The president of the university, Torigai Risaburō, was dumbfounded at the scale of his planning. Abe was determined that the Institute's work should be focused on cooperative research, and with the support of senior faculty members, he wrote a stipulation into the by-laws committing members of the Institute to obligatory participation in at least one cooperative research project in addition to their own individual work. If our Institute has achieved anything in cooperative research, it is because of the enlightened and farsighted ideals of Abe Takeo.

As with the other five projects, the first, the Rousseau project, fell naturally into the framework of cooperative research. No one scholar alone, using only the tools of his own discipline, could do justice to this towering figure in the intellectual history of the world. The study of this man embraced literature, economics, law, education, and many other fields, and was thus a most appropriate object for our first cooperative endeavor. Whether any or all of our six cooperative projects are valuable and may be considered successful, or whether they really have little to offer anyone except ourselves must be decided by others. But apart from our own achievements, or lack of them, there are good reasons to keep going. I believe the potential in cooperative research for contributions to scholarship is tremendous.

## Determining the Approach

The pursuit of learning has been going on since the beginning of human history, but until very recently its effects were gradual and cumulative. The huge leaps in scientific achievement, which have affected every area of our lives and our thinking, are the product of a relatively short period. I am speaking of natural science, but the term science can no longer be so narrowly confined. Because natural science led the way to modernity, subsequently it became the model for all branches of learning. Even history, an eminently literary discipline, has been cornered and tamed so that some people call it, too, a science. Ssu-ma Ch'ien's *Shih chi* [Historical Records] or the writings of Thucydides and Herodotus are magnificent, but they are not science. They are in fact little more than collections of anecdotes. That is why Descartes had only contempt for history. Today history is called historical studies or historical science. But regardless of the wisdom of dressing up history as "science," it illustrates what is happening in other areas of learning as well.

Cooperative research is affected by the same imperative to carry on in a scientific way. It is true that joint efforts in the natural sciences have been quite successful; many of the achievements of theoretical physics—a field to which Japan has made notable contributions—are products of cooperative research methods. But that type of cooperative endeavor takes place among scientists within a single discipline. What I am more interested in is interdisciplinary cooperation. Take the book by Norbert Wiener, *Cybernetics*. Nothing could be further from my own training and work than cybernetics, and in all honesty, I did not understand the book very well. But I think it is a great mistake to insist on full understanding or nothing. One can derive benefit from plunging into other worlds with the aim of understanding as much as one can.

For example, let me take the case of someone I don't know but like: Marilyn Monroe. When I see her on the screen I invariably respond by thinking how gorgeous she is, how elegant her walk, how I would love to invite her for tea. At this juncture I imagine an irrelevant intrusion: a scholar protests, "To what degree do you or can you really know the beauty of this movie star?" (In other words, "Why bother?") Granted, there is much I do not know about her, including her sex life, but I have seen her perform on the screen. My knowledge is incomplete but it is not without value. I am not a Freudian pansexualist, but I believe I can get some idea of the nature of her sex life by watching her actions, even if I am not in a position to conduct thorough research on the subject. At least I can enhance my esthetic sensibilities by appreciating her acting, and the way she walks.

I can also benefit from Wiener's book even if I do not understand it completely. Just as I have to leave sex out of my knowledge of Monroe, I have to leave mathematics out of my understanding of Wiener. Mathematical formulas may be the pillar of Wiener's world, but I can still understand some of what he says, and admire the brilliant way he quotes *The Divine Comedy*. And I can agree with him that in the classics, or whatever, one should not close oneself off from other stimuli and concentrate only on the classics, like putting blind kittens in a basket to protect them from the world. I prefer to remain open to all the beauty and ideas that the world can offer me.

Wiener's accomplishments are awesome; he opened up for research a no-man's land that had been passed over by others. Yet he conceived the ideas behind cybernetics through cooperative work with Arturo Rosenblueth and other scientists. The history is written elsewhere, but it remains that we will never again see a man like Leibniz or Darwin, people whose knowledge and analytic powers encompassed many branches of learning and who, as individuals, helped lay the groundwork for cybernetics, for all modern science. Lamenting the excessive compartmentalization of the modern academic world, Wiener writes:

> Today there are few scholars who can call themselves mathematicians or physicists or biologists without restriction. A man may be a topologist or an acoustician or a coleopterist. He will be filled with the jargon of his field and will know all its literature and all its ramifications, but, more frequently than not, he will regard the next subject as something belonging to his colleague three doors down the corridor and will consider any interest in it on his own part as an unwarrantable breach of privacy.

Wiener had to initiate cooperative research in order to open up a new field. He put together "a team of scientists, each a specialist in his own field, but each possessing a thoroughly sound and trained acquaintance with the fields of his neighbors. ..." A physiologist working with him was naturally an expert in his field, but he had to be willing and able to talk with physiologists in different areas of specialization and to be able to understand his colleagues in mathematics and other fields.

Wiener's idea of a good cooperative research team was one whose members developed familiarity with and understanding of each other's "intellectual customs" and recognized "the significance of a colleague's new suggestion before it has taken on a full formal expression." In other words, the "mathematician need not have the skill to conduct a physiological experiment, but he must have the skill to understand one, to criticize one, and to suggest one."

Wiener maintained that an effective team would not develop if it was under the thumb of a "great executive officer," nor would it work if fitted into a bureaucratic organization. It must pull together out of the free and common desire to cooperate, "joined by . . . spiritual necessity, to understand the region as a whole, and to lend one another the strength of that understanding." If one member publishes an article, the others will be familiar with it in advance and will be attuned to the patterns of perception that went into it. Above all, high-quality group research requires scholar-specialists who are curious about other fields. We at the Institute sought to form such a group.

The last chapter of Wiener's book, "Information, Language, and Society," holds the greatest interest and is fruitful reading even if one skips the rest. It is "all the great successes in precise science," he says, that allow man to control his material environment. "The main task of the immediate future is to extend to the fields of anthropology, of sociology, of economics, the methods of the natural sciences, in the hope of achieving a like measure of success in the social fields." Wiener warns that this attempt is born of "an excessive optimism, and a misunderstanding of the nature of all scientific achievement." The effort is doomed, because the "coupling" between observer and the observed, the way the researcher comes to a conclusion, is different in the sciences and the humanities. The humanities researcher is too closely identified with his object of study to be able to reproduce the kind of objective results demanded in the natural sciences. In the social sciences, "there is much which we must leave, whether we like it or not, to the un-'scientific,' narrative method of the professional historian." Wiener acknowledges the validity of cooperative research, but doubts its applicability in research in the humanities.

The Swiss psychologist, Jean Piaget, whom I met at a 1964 Unesco conference, also questioned the suitability of cooperative research in the humanities. Piaget wrote a report on "recherche interdisciplinaire" in which he explained why he thought cooperative research in the humanities would not be very constructive. First, he said, there is no hierarchy of disciplines within the humanities and social sciences. The natural sciences, in contrast, are arranged with mathematics on top, and move down through physics, chemistry, biology, psychology, and so on. The absence of such a developmental hierarchy in the social sciences and humanities makes reduction of one field into another impossible. Hence an important channel of cooperation is missing. Second, Piaget cited the parochial nature of training within academic departments as a practical barrier to cooperation. Abuse of the departmental system of education has led to overly strong sectionalism among scholars, and that can generate enough competition and self-consciousness to prevent cooperation between an economist and a specialist in law, for example. People in the natural sciences feel more interdependent and have a positive need to cooperate across departmental boundaries. In the humanities it is harder to carry off.

Piaget added that, antiquated as it is, the idea remains that the synthesis of disciplines is the function of philosophy, and this also constitutes a block to cooperative efforts among the humanities disciplines on an equal footing. When we began our cooperative research we had not grappled with the theoretical problems I have outlined above. Piaget's report came out in 1967, and the Japanese translation of Wiener's book was not available until after our research on the French Revolution was completed. In our case experience came first; theory followed much later.

It is conventional wisdom to methodically probe a given project, determine its feasibility, and find out as much as possible about it before launching it, but I think overcaution or exhaustive preparation can be the Achilles' heel of the scholar. In any case, I myself am too impatient to plough through all the initial material usually deemed necessary. If I were to do a study on India, for example, I would have to go there, get the feel of the throngs of Calcutta, walk around a few villages, stay with families here and there. Then, since I know so little about India, I would have to read as much as I could after returning to Japan. If, on the other hand, I had decided that some history was in order—to be thorough, that would mean studying the lot, from the Mohenjaro period through Nehru— it would be a good five years before I would get to India to start the research I had originally planned. I am simply not convinced all that is always necessary. Once I went to Indonesia on a business trip for about ten days. I went cold, knowing nothing about the place, but with some observation and talking with people while I was there, plus two or three books I read after my return, I felt satisfied that I had learned quite a lot. I like to think that I then understood Indonesia about as well as someone who had read twenty books on the country but had never been here. This is the way we began cooperative research. We just started and in the course of our endeavors came to believe that it was possible and valid.

Basically I have a feeling of trust, even affection, toward science, and it is that trust which sustains my pursuit of research. I cannot speak for everyone involved in our cooperative research, but I feel a sort of irrational affection for scientism. My study of the natural sciences and mathematics went no further than high school: a bit of algebra, plane geometry, and Newtonian physics. But I applied myself to those subjects with intensity and seldom got less than 100 on examinations. I think my subsequent progress in the natural sciences was almost zero; my understanding of science may actually have dropped. Yet, partially because of childish pride in my high school accomplishments, I have retained my original interest in and respect for the natural sciences. Galileo's statement that he wants "to measure everything that is measurable, and make measurable that which cannot yet be measured" was to me an inspirational poem. While I could never have incorporated sophisticated methodology into work I did myself, it is a source of pride and satisfaction that our research team could apply the methods of the psychologist W. Sheldon in analyzing the character of Rousseau and Nakae Chōmin, and that one of our team is an expert in the Rorschach test. It may not be a very strong element, but the spirit of science has infiltrated our own studies.

Alfred North Whitehead defined the spirit of modern science as a combination of two elements: passionate interest in concrete detail and an equally passionate love for abstract generalization. Note that passionate interest in facts comes first. If facts were all that counted, then East Asians would certainly typify the spirit of modern science. China has an ancient tradition of reverence for facts, and essays written in the Tokugawa period in Japan contain an endless array of detail. But theory and abstract generalization are also fundamental to science. Love for both—and I think the word "love" is appropriate—is to Whitehead the spirit of modern science.

Our own team was fully imbued with that spirit of modern science. It is something that not only facilitates cooperative research but is actually a prerequisite. It may be that abstract generalization in the humanities is not precise by the standards of natural sciences, insofar as the humanities deal with problems that often do not lend themselves to rigorous analysis; they seem to require a less defined sort of thinking. Nonetheless, our team always worked with a modern scientific spirit, seeking universal trends, if not strict laws. It seemed to me, for example, that a work like *Tenkō* [Conversion], by Tsurumi Shunsuke and others, which was received so enthusiastically, would have benefited if the authors had considered the theory of Konrad Lorenz. As I understand it, Lorenz posits a change, a reduction in the length of things, in proportion to acceleration of their speed. While the authors of *Tenkō* wrote from the vantage point of a moderately paced social and economic milieu, the many political conversions that actually occurred throughout modern Japan (typically a recantation of Marxist beliefs under pressure by the prewar police) took place during a time of social change that was several times faster than anything England or France has ever experienced. Lorenz's theory also helps us understand why ideological conversion never became an issue in China after the 1949 revolution, given the slow pace of modernization in that country.

Research projects most often use a mathematics or physics-based model, but we tended toward biological models in our cooperative research. Our approach is in a way reminiscent of the spirit of Chinese science that Joseph Needham describes in his *Science and Civilisation in China*. Rather than purely abstract sciences, like mathematics or physics, we have found that sciences dealing in concrete phenomena like hormones and endocrines are much more useful in constructing our models.

Interdisciplinary endeavors are becoming more common, and those of us involved are finding that cooperative research itself needs certain types of training, just as the established disciplines do. Every one of us involved was required, for example, to read one or more given works, and study it intensively. Then we discussed the work(s) among ourselves. In that way, each single expression—the building blocks—of an important author, be it Rousseau, Ssu-ma Ch'ien, or whoever, was absorbed by many, who shared their responses and impressions. In that way we avoided the danger of arbitrary interpretation. To follow such a procedure helps people to develop an ability to learn from each other, which is now lacking among many young scholars in the humanities and social sciences.

## Unexpected Fruits of Cooperation

When we began the Rousseau project, we decided to translate *Social Contract*. The participants met once a week. Each of us prepared draft translations in advance and these became the basis for our final translation. Because this method proved so effective, I decided to use it in other projects as well. We also used the note card system to pool our knowledge. We recorded on cards important facts or noteworthy quotes uncovered in the process of research and made copies of the cards for each participant, plus a few extras. We sorted and classified the extra copies at the Institute. Because we could not always make enough copies, and because I was not the best of managers, I do not think we used the card system to the maximum, but I think the system has much potential.

Recently the French Marxist historian Henri Lefebvre participated in two or three discussion meetings at Kyoto University. One of his many interesting points was that, in his opinion, no single discipline should be allowed to completely dominate the others. It stifles the growth of learning. Marxism, for example, has fallen into an unfortunate preoccupation with economics. Physics, too, has a tendency to be "imperialistic," as I have suggested elsewhere. Lefebvre stated that there must be democracy among the social sciences. This point brings out an element that is essential in joint work. When specialists gather to do cooperative research, rather than trying to set up a status hierarchy among the disciplines they bring to the project, they should consider each field of equal standing and be encouraged to provide mutual stimulus.

One major problem in cooperative research concerns the ideological leanings of the team participants. About the time the Rousseau project was completed, I had given a lecture at a student government-sponsored meeting at which Ijiri Shōji was also a lecturer. Before the meeting began he gave me his business card, on which was printed "Ijiri Shōji, Member, The Japan Communist Party." I thought this was admirable: most academics kept their political affiliations strictly to themselves. His speech on New Guinea was very interesting, but then, referring to my talk, he said that cooperative research could not be effective unless the work conformed to a single ideology to which all participants subscribed. While I did not have a good counterargument at the time, I totally disagreed.

Ideological unity probably enables a cooperative research team to reach conclusions quickly, but it also limits intellectual freedom, which is vital to a researcher who needs all possible resources in grappling with problems. A demand for ideological conformity would impose a handicap on objective research, particularly in probing the nature of problems at hand and selecting an appropriate approach to them. Ideologically unified groups may have produced some excellent cooperative research, but I have never seen any. A few years ago I went to Czechoslovakia. I passed out some English-language abstracts of our work in Kyoto and then talked informally with scholars there. They found it very difficult to understand how our efforts could win acceptance, particularly since joint projects would leave little time for individual monographs. Assistant professors would have a hard time being promoted unless they produced their own work, the Czech scholars argued, and younger scholars probably would not want to participate. I was surprised that the citizens of a nation that was supposed to be ideologically united should find it so difficult to imagine voluntary participation in cooperative research.

Our own team, I think, represented an appropriately wide range of ideological commitment. None of us approached the French Revolution project with the attitude that the revolution had been a brutal, essentially wasted uprising, but we had complete freedom of interpretation. Naturally our opinions differed, and rivalries over points of view definitely emerged, but we managed to confine any confrontation to the conference room. Invariably we would go out drinking together when our meetings were over. We were united in our shared love of learning, and respected each other's viewpoints and the right to express them. How constricted and frustrated we would have been had we felt compelled to conform to a fixed ideological position.

Not all disciplines can be profitably combined in research efforts; if the fields are too disparate they do not reinforce each other but move at cross-purposes. Japanese can take satisfaction in their achievements in primate studies, but some efforts along the way have been wasted. I was once asked to chair a panel discussion on the language of apes. Participants represented linguistics, psychology, anthropology, and ecology, as well as primate studies. They met in open discussion a couple of times, and thereafter the individual work of Itani Junichirō progressed rapidly, but it owed nothing to the joint research discussions. The fields of linguistics, psychology, and primate studies were too far apart to be productive.

Progress in the natural sciences has far outpaced that in the humanities, and part of the reason, as Wiener suggested, is the gains that become possible as science develops through the inevitable, ever finer process of specialization. But in general I do not think the humanities need take the pattern of advancement in the natural sciences as a model. A historian would lose ground if he gradually confined his interest in Japanese history, to Muromachi history, to the history of Nō, to the history of drama as developed by Zeami, and finally down to the exile of Zeami to Sado Island. One cannot grasp the subtleties of Muromachi Nō without a general understanding of Japanese history and historiography. The fact that the humanities are less specialized than the natural sciences is not something to bemoan. The two are simply different in the kind of approach they demand.

The main objective of cooperative research is to produce results, but the process of research has an important side effect, which is to break down the walls that separate disciplines. In Japan research and higher learning are almost the exclusive preserve of the universities, which are strictly organized into departments and operate on the chair system. The system has many merits, but it tends to encourage fragmentation by isolating the disciplines from one another. Thus cooperative research can function to build links instead of walls. Japanese scholars are thorough, serious searchers, but they commonly work alone and are not accustomed to dialogue. Free and open dialogue not only can affect the thinking of the discussants, it can also produce new concepts. It is this kind of dialogue upon which cooperative research thrives, as long as the team members participate as equals. This is hard to achieve in Japan, where one is seldom allowed to forget the hierarchy of professor, assistant professor, lecturer, and assistant. Scholarship can hardly grow when full professors running on about nonsense are treated with deference.

Some activities of our research team have helped to cultivate a sense of equality. At the beginning we interspersed films, novels, and English- and French-language practice with our meetings. It became obvious then that the assistants knew a great deal more about films, for example, than the full professors. The psychological effect tended to carry over: an assistant, bolstered by some good saké, who had impressed everyone the night before with his erudition on films, retained much of his confidence the next day when the work moved round to Rousseau. While we were not politicians enough to make deliberate use of this tendency, its effects were very beneficial.

In our English sessions Tsurumi Shunsuke acted as our teacher, guiding us primarily in writing English. When I was preparing to retire from the university the other day, I came across an English essay I had written for Tsurumi, and it made me terribly nostalgic. I was the French language teacher for our team. I used an American army method: a short course involving one hour of study every day from exactly five to six in the evening. I gave homework nightly and posted grades daily. Nagao Gajin and Tsurumi Shunsuke were always on top. I think one month of study by this method was worth about a year in the undergraduate course.

Criticism tended to be directed more often at the way we conducted research than at the results we achieved. One complaint was that everyone seemed to enjoy the work so much. How typically Japanese, to begrudge such fulfillment. But obvious pleasure in study goes against the image of ascetic, painful striving that is supposed to dominate all scholarly endeavor, and it is resented. Actually, too much pain is only masochism. It is no way to pursue learning. We were also criticized for frittering away valuable hours with "mere talk." Many of us looked forward with great eagerness to our Friday meetings as the high point of the week and would make no apologies for our zeal.

A related complaint was that our work lacked depth because it was simply a compilation of learning "by ear." This raises an important point. To reject any knowledge that is not direct sounds noble, but it smacks of a punctiliousness that is vain, misdirected, and just not necessary. To insist on reading everything for oneself, ferreting out the meat, making the summaries, and saying nothing until one has read all the original documents to the last page is not a practical methodology for modern learning. I tend to advise young scholars to start early the practice of learning by ear. Just to grasp a general concept by ear you must use your head; it is all too easy to think you have understood whatever you hear. Most people grossly overestimate that capacity.

Learning, especially in the humanities, is based on common-sense experiences in everyday life, but it inevitably produces premises that run counter to common sense. Remember the old argument for movement of the sun and stars (a common-sense observation) vs. the argument that the earth itself moves. My point is that exactly those things that were criticized most—the salon atmosphere, the element of enjoyment, learning by ear, the non-specialized nature of our research—while they ground against the ingrained common sense of the typical academic, turned out to be our strongest assets.

Scholarly research involves theory and ideology, but in the long run it is relations among people that influence both. Learning, like any great theories that develop out of it, does not take place only in an ivory tower. Learning comes out of the world of people. At some point it must transcend that world if it is to endure, but its inception and growth are mundane. There is an inseparable relationship between scholarship and life. It is possible to come up with a learned theory in isolation, but it can only be given life through unrelenting hard work by many people. How to profitably combine the efforts of these people is the major problem we confront. There is no point in simply gathering a group of solitary geniuses and hoping they will meld. Imagine trying to get Louis Pasteur and Jean Henri Fabre together, or Goethe and Beethoven. To ignore the element of personal relations is to guarantee that the results of cooperative research will be worthless.

# 8

# Japan and European Civilization

WESTERN history as it used to be taught in Japanese schools described European civilization as an unbroken continuum that began with ancient Greece and extended to the modern age. Geographically, we learned, it blossomed in the region covered by the states of Europe as we see them on the map today. The courses began with Assyria and Egypt, but they lingered only briefly there, moving on quickly to Greek civilization. Greece nurtured the great philosophers—Socrates, Plato, and Aristotle—and it produced the great dramatic lyricists— Sophocles, Aeschylus, Euripides, and Aristophanes. Greece is the home of unsurpassed sculpture and architecture. This civilization was governed, we were told, by the spirit of "democracy" and "freedom." We learned only about the splendors of Greek civilization. No one ever even suggested to us that the culture of the polis was sustained by slave labor.

## Images of Europe

The civilization of Rome fell heir to the glory that was Greece, we were taught, but unlike Greece, it was politically strong. Under the Pax Romana, the Roman Empire unified Europe and established a tight political order. In the Middle Ages, Roman civilization became synonymous with the Christian world, and it provided the binding force for religious unification of Europe under the Pope. It is too simple, of course, to say that under

Originally delivered as a lecture, entitled "Yōroppa bunmei to Nihon," at Asahi Zemināru, April 6 and 13 and June 8, 1971.

papal rule Europe became a cohesive religious entity, as if Christian Europe merely took over where the Roman Empire left off, and so we were taught that the empire split between east and west. By then the West, in particular, had fallen largely to ruin.

Eventually, we then learned, the rule of the Catholic church over the Christian world grew corrupt, and toward the end of the medieval period it declined, weakening under the pressure of movements that triggered and sustained the Reformation, notably that of Martin Luther. Then came the Renaissance, and Europe turned back to a rediscovery of Greek civilization. In the centuries that followed, the contradictions lying deep in European society began to surface, leading to the French Revolution and the age of *liberté, equalité, et fraternité*. From the time of the Renaissance, science began to advance, and the glorious civilization that would lead the modern world was born.

This is basically what we were taught about Europe, and it was impressive. Today, however, European history does not seem to go quite that way. Geoffrey Barraclough interprets it rather differently. Professor Barraclough, one of the eminent historians of our time, believes, first of all, that European civilization cannot be described in terms of the unbroken continuity described to us in school. He says that we must be careful to distinguish between Europe as a geographical entity and European civilization. After all, what we now call Europe—the land mass between the Urals and the Straits of Gibraltar—was neither unified from ancient times nor completely dominated by European civilization as such. One should think of European civilization not as the product of a given geographical area, but as a particular type of civilization. Europe itself then may be defined as the region in which that civilization flourished. If we take the same approach to Japan, the culture that developed on the islands of Honshu, Shikoku, and Kyushu in the northwest Pacific should not be identified as Japanese culture. Rather, Japan is the place where a particular civilization prevailed, one distinguished by polytheism, a peculiar esthetic sensitivity, and Buddhist ideas of impermanence and nothingness. In terms of its cultural traits, the island of Hokkaido would not be included as part of Japan until the late Tokugawa period.

It is important to be clear about time when talking about

Europe in history. Europe did not cover the same area from the ancient period on through. It expanded and contracted many times in response to the currents of history. It is also erroneous to think of the Roman Empire and Europe as being directly connected, or being one and the same thing. At its peak, the Roman Empire included large portions of Africa and western Asia. It never went south of the Sahara, but it expanded into parts of the Maghreb (Algeria, Morocco, and Tunisia). The Orient meant what is now Turkey, Syria, Israel, and other lands in that region, not Persia and India. Because the Roman Empire embraced such important areas of Asia and Africa, it is wrong to think of it as an exclusively European entity. In A.D. 395, the empire split between east and west. It was an era of great tribal migrations, and the Western Empire collapsed in 476. The Eastern Empire survived until 1453, but it was no longer Europe. So, while Europe, along with parts of Africa and Asia, was indeed a part of the Roman Empire, it was by no means the sole successor to Roman civilization.

Generally it is thought that Europeans began to be conscious of Europe as a region beginning in the eleventh century. It emerged not as an outgrowth of the ancient Mediterranean world but rather with an identity that developed around places far from Greece or Rome, long after the breakup of the Roman Empire. That identity must be established and Europe defined as the region where European civilization prevails, and then we can attempt to determine the characteristics of the civilization. Individualism, liberalism, materialism, and science and technology are usually considered foremost among them. These, however, are actually *products* of modern European civilization. Searching deeper, we can identify Christianity at the core of European civilization, and then we can define Europe as the region where this Christian civilization prevailed.

Europe has been the arena of frequent crises. Way back, the fifth-century invasion by Atilla the Hun placed even Paris in peril. The danger of attack from the East was constant from then on, but in the thirteenth century, Europe was truly in jeopardy, seriously threatened by rapacious Mongol tribes. Some of them invaded as far as today's Germany. From the north, there was pressure from the Vikings and the Normans, and in the south the forces of Islam battered Spain, penetrating up to central France. If the Muslims had been victorious in the Battle of Tours (732), who knows what European civilization would have become. As it was, Spain remained outside Europe until the fifteenth century. From the Middle East the ferocious Turks, also followers of Islam, pressed into the Balkan region. Ultimately the Eastern Roman Empire fell to the Turks, and until the nineteenth century the Balkan states also remained outside the European pale. Toughened by the unremitting onslaught and tempered by centuries of resistance and efforts to keep its enemies at bay, Europe gradually forged an identity of its own, and in the end, it turned the tables on the world. Emerging strong, it advanced to subjugate others all over the globe. Japan had its pirates and its seafaring adventurers, but for the most part it stood apart, its people remaining in the three islands, passive, but eagerly absorbing whatever came in from outside. That attitude was just the opposite of the way Europeans thought, which goes far in explaining why Japanese have difficulty understanding the occidental world.

Greek civilization is invariably called the forerunner of European civilization, and there can be little argument that Greece was a source of the European spirit. But the classical traditions of Greece and early Rome did not pass intact into modern European history. By around the third century B.C., Barraclough notes, the vigor of rationalism and the active spirit of inquiry that had been the hallmarks of Grecian culture began to fade, pushed back by mysticism and superstition. Contrary to the general notion that the art of medieval Europe was based on the classical thought of Greece and Rome, scholars now agree that it was actually nonclassical, even anticlassical in character. During the so-called Dark Ages, the light of Greek civilization was almost extinguished in Europe, and when, with the Renaissance, people turned back to study the great Greek philosophers, they had to seek the classical texts in the Islamic world. Greek thought and scholarship had been forgotten in Europe, but it survived in the Islamic Orient. The Muslim world possessed a formidable dynamism, which, until the beginning of European expansionism in the fifteenth century, made it the most advanced region in the world.

Again, we are accustomed to thinking of Christianity as Europe's own religion, but the earliest Christian activities took place in Africa. St. Augustine was born in Africa and was originally a follower of Manicheanism. Half of the popes of Rome, moreover, were born in areas outside Europe. In other words, it is not correct to assume that Europe, though unified through Christianity, became an established cultural or political entity during the Middle Ages. In fact, there was no period in European history in which a single clearly defined civilization prevailed, when the people spoke a common language, shared the same patterns of thought, and followed one religion. In addition, Europe was not only subject to continual assaults from outside but was severely divided from within. Its history is filled with recurrent power struggles between areas vying for dominance— Italy, France, England, Germany, and Spain. This gave the region great resilience and strength of character, but it only adds to the evidence that what we know today as Europe did not inherit one continuous civilization stretching from ancient to modern times.

The checkered progress of European civilization is all the more marked if we compare it with Chinese civilization. China's civilization expanded little by little, but it always represented the dominant culture of the Han tribes, which was passed down by that one ethnic group within a basically fixed territory. The state itself was frequently overwhelmed by "barbarian" invasions, when nomadic peoples from the northern steppes swept in and sometimes managed to set up their own ruling dynasties. The Northern dynasties, the Yuan, and the Ch'ing are all in that category. Yet every barbarian tribe that invaded the heart of China was eventually absorbed and assimilated by the Han civilization. China had no equal in Asia that could compete for cultural superiority, unlike Europe, where relations between England and France, and between Germany and France, were stimulated by rivalry that sometimes rent the entire region. When the long arm of Chinese sovereignty stretched out to the surrounding lands, to Korea, Annam, and central Asia, none could offer much resistance. The cultural traditions of China remained equally inviolate; one can hardly imagine the *Shih ching* or Confucius' *Analects* having to be translated back into Chinese from Sanskrit or Japanese after a period of anticlassicism. The very absence of such ethnic and cultural continuity and unity is one of the characteristics of European civilization.

## Colonial Frontiers and the Rise of Europe

The Europe under whose impact Japanese society was gradually transformed to what it is today was essentially modern. The first wave of influence came in about the sixteenth century, led by the Jesuit missionaries. These priests possessed the classical learning of Greece and Rome, but above all they represented a new Europe emerging out of the Renaissance. The second wave arrived with Perry's ships in 1853 and continued through the end of the Tokugawa and the Meiji eras.

Modern Europe is defined alternatively as beginning with the Renaissance or arising out of the French Revolution. The French Revolution had not yet occurred when the first Christian fathers came to Japan. In the mid-nineteenth century it was over, and while Europe was still in its early modern period, in many ways it was a different Europe from that of pre-Revolution times. Portuguese sailors landed on Tanegashima in 1543 with the first guns Japan had ever seen, and Francis Xavier, upon learning about Japan, set sail and arrived at Kagoshima in 1549 to propagate Christianity. Those sixteenth-century missionaries represented an age when the Renaissance and the Reformation were events of the past. Their appearance itself in Japan was evidence that Europe had finally broken out of its long period of stagnation. It was a new age of explosive, outward expansion. The new Europe had already come to India and to China; it came to Japan last, bringing a far more dynamic but still not overwhelmingly stronger civilization.

Europe was not always the supreme, most civilized, dominant region of the world. Looking at literature, for example, if a line is placed at the Renaissance and the number of books published before then is counted, they are extremely numerous in Asia and a mere trickle in Europe. After the Renaissance, Europe was the most prolific in publications and Asia fell far behind. The beginning of the sixteenth century is a turning point in European history. Previously weak and divided, Europe gradually began to assert itself in a more coherent way: gaining strength, it expanded, foisting hegemony on much of the world.

Until the beginning of the sixteenth century the Islamic lands and China were the most advanced civilizations. Science and technology thrived among Arabs and Chinese. Their quest for knowledge was vigorous, while Europe remained in the thrall of old ideas that led nowhere. Thus, not only the works of Aristotle and the other giants of Greek learning, but much other knowledge, especially scientific, was eventually brought from the Islamic countries. The French scholar André Siegfried, for one, notes that the civilization of the Arab peoples was much more advanced than that of premodern Europe and that their thinking was freer and more creative. Why, then, did the Islamic world not go on to develop its learning into modern science, as Europe did? This question still puzzles scholars. All we can say is that by its nature the Koran dominates thought, and it inhibited the kind of freedom that scientific and scholarly pursuits require. In Europe, once knowledge of science had taken root, it overcame hurdles and developed rapidly. It advanced steadily from the Renaissance period until it blossomed into modern science.

Such progress was possible partly because of the Reformation movements that broke the monopoly of the Catholic church on religious and intellectual life. As the authority of God ceased to be absolute, the idea of freedom of thought and speech flourished and the scientific knowledge introduced from the Islamic world spread rapidly. Still there were obstacles. Galileo and countless others continued to be persecuted as the old ideas hung on. For some time, Europe, not always the rational, enlightened world we think of now, held on to medieval remnants. The Inquisition continued in Spain until 1781, and the witch hunts in England were still going on in 1836. People charged with sorcery were burned in town squares.

We also think of Europe as being wealthy and prosperous, but it was not always that way. Ancient Europe was a poor region. Compared to Japan, the land was infertile, and food was perennially scarce. Famine was rampant until the twelfth and thirteenth centuries. It is said that in northern France one person out of four died of starvation. They could not get through the cold winters. In pre-Renaissance Europe, for every kernel of wheat sowed, the harvest might be only a few more kernels. In Japan, one seed of rice reproduced itself ten times over, and today the yield is much greater. For this reason the population density of Japan and China has been much higher than that of Europe since the ancient period.

During the eleventh century, vast expanses of reclaimed land in Europe were put under cultivation, and agricultural productivity greatly improved. Methods were found to keep domestic animals alive through the cold winters. Bolstered by the better standards of living that resulted from such techniques, fifteenth- and sixteenth-century Europe at last began to prosper. It was during that time, in 1498, that Vasco da Gama set forth on his expedition around Africa, ultimately reaching India. Before da Gama, communication between Asia and the West had been largely in the hands of the peoples of Islam. When Vasco da Gama rounded the cape, seeking a way to India, he hired Arabian pilots, for their navigation and maritime knowledge was unsurpassed.

Until very recently, Japanese tended to include only Westerners—Columbus, Livingstone, and so on—among the great world explorers. China's emissary Chang Ch'ien (d. A.D. 114), Morocco's Ibn Battuta (1302–77) and Japan's own adventurer Mamiya Rinzō (1775–1844) were entirely neglected. It is often forgotten that a giant among navigators, although he was not a trader, was the adventurer of Ming China, Cheng Ho (c. 1371–1434). I have met many Japanese scholars who know the West well enough but have never heard of this great explorer. Between 1405 and 1433 Cheng Ho commanded the largest fleet in world history, sailing through the Straits of Malacca, across the Indian Ocean, and north from Madagascar into the Arabian Sea, traveling all the way to Mecca. Cheng was a follower of Islam and a eunuch. The pressures of being a Muslim in a country dominated by Confucianism and being castrated might have been sufficient to drive a man to extraordinary deeds. But in addition it is said that Cheng's parents and brothers and sisters were all murdered. All this could certainly have generated the energy that led Cheng to attempt that epochal journey, made on the order of the Ming emperor Yung-lo (1360–1424). In the next century, however, China and Arabia would begin to fall back as a new force emerged in the world.

Around 1500, Europe began its outward expansion. At first it did not have an absolute advantage, as is illustrated in the cotton industry. When England first established the India trade, Indian cotton was cheap, produced from an ancient industry, and this cotton cloth poured into the English market. The local textile industry had such a hard time competing that finally in 1695, the British Parliament passed a law restricting Indian cotton. But protectionist measures, however strict, do not keep cheaper goods from finding their way into a market. By the eighteenth century, efforts to raise the efficiency and volume of cotton cloth production in England finally bore fruit, and by the nineteenth century, India was itself forced to purchase cotton cloth woven in Lancashire. In the end, the Indian cotton industry was completely ruined.

In other ways the incipient indigenous industries of India also were cruelly destroyed by Britain. The typical, perhaps natural, pattern of development of an economy is to proceed from agriculture to industry, but the statistics on India show that the proportion of the agricultural population was greater in the nineteenth century than it had been at the beginning of British rule.

Based on careful study of such phenomena, the American historian Walter Prescott Webb, in his book *The Great Frontier*, has developed an interesting theory concerning the emergence of modern Europe. Webb asserts that the prosperity of modern Europe was made possible by its expansion into "frontiers" abroad. He suggests that the accumulation of capital that made the industrial revolution possible derived from the wealth of the frontiers—the resources that European adventurers and explorers grabbed up practically for free. On this point, I sense in Webb an ally in the interpretation of European industrialization. The industrial revolution occurred first in England, generated and fueled by exploitation that reduced India's industry to helplessness.

In about 1500, the total population of Europe was somewhere around 100 million, with a density of roughly 26 people per square mile. From the time of Columbus on, as Europeans plundered the wealth of the world, they acquired territories more than five times the area of their own lands, and Webb estimates that the population density fell to under five persons per square mile. Europeans also acquired five times the freedom of action, and they grew rich upon it. Wealth included not just material goods, but also slaves. Trade in slaves was extremely lucrative, and in England of the seventeenth century, the slave trade brought the greatest profit. It is not my purpose to abuse Europeans, but simply to note that the "ancient tradition" of humanism that Japanese habitually attribute to Europeans is not as deep as they might think.

How much did Europeans profit from bleeding their colonies? Probably it was somewhere in the neighborhood of 10,000 percent. Invested capital multiplied one hundred times annually. Moreover, Webb ascribes the emergence of individualism, equality, democracy, the ethic of hard work, unbounded optimism— as well as arrogance—to the possession of those frontiers. Until that time, European society cultivated courtesy and politeness, but in the colonies Europeans grew crude and vulgar. It is clear, in any case, that the pursuit of profit and the growth of capitalism were made possible only by expansion to regions outside.

## Diffusion of Civilization

We would be fortunate indeed if civilization always spread peacefully and intelligently, but like it or not, it is usually diffused irrationally, through the exercise of power. Yet civilization, or culture for that matter, is by definition antagonistic to force; they are considered to be antithetical. A peaceful country like Japan, which was never invaded by an alien people—a blessing in the history of any country—does not provide a very good illustration, but civilization manifestly does not spread on the strength of its own dynamic.

During the time of Louis XIV, French civilization reached out to cover the European continent. The extent of its influence can be partly explained by the inherent greatness of French culture, but the fact that Louis XIV's France was the most powerful country in Europe at that time certainly cannot be discounted. Later, in the wake of Napoleon's rampages, French civilization again spread rapidly. In the aftermath of its great revolution, France was the most advanced nation in the world, and it had a great deal to offer that was new and superior: revolutionary thought, blossoming patriotism, as well as the Napoleonic Code and the metric system. But the incentive to adopt aspects of French civilization in other countries was given an irresistible boost by the presence of Napoleon's armies.

Today American civilization is a conspicuous presence all over the world. While it has some intrinsically superior qualities, its spread has been propelled by the important psychological factor of America's position as a leading world power. It is the civilization of the strong and forceful that can expand outward. European ideals and concepts, including rationalism, freedom, and democracy, were widely accepted throughout the world because, aside from their instrinsic value, they were introduced by the most powerful countries at the time, namely England, France, and Germany.

Today in Japan one seldom sees people dressed in traditional attire on a university campus or in a business district. Everyone wears European-style clothing. This is not because Western clothing is particularly attractive or esthetically appealing. Today it is primarily convenience that determines our attire, but we must not overlook the compulsion among Japanese since the Meiji era to wear what the people of the strong and advanced countries of Europe are wearing. As individuals, we are not conscious of being "Western" in such habits. They are the product of a general mood that governs our society.

The mood of the country had some bearing on the mutual response when Christianity was introduced to Japan. On this period of contact and the whole relation between Japan and Europe, I recommend the work of G. B. Sansom, *The Western World and Japan*.[1] The English historian writes, "The intrusion of this disruptive, challenging element into the sequestered and conservative life of Asia must be a dominant theme in the modern history of any Asiatic state." Indeed, this sentence aptly describes what was about to happen in Asia in the sixteenth century. The Christian fathers came to Japan and to China, and they wrote copiously about what they saw for their brothers in Europe. Among them is the work of Luis Frois, a Portugese missionary who arrived in 1562 and died in Nagasaki in 1597. This admirable priest labored in Japan to propagate his faith for about thirty-five years and he wrote a book entitled *Historia do Japaõ*, which offers many insights into the Japan of his day.

Most of the missionaries, from Francis Xavier on, held the Japanese in high regard, finding them intelligent and culturally sophisticated, and their reports uniformly reflected their conviction that Japan was the most fertile ground in all of Asia for the propagation of the Gospel. Some aspects of these reports sent back to Europe seem deliberately propagandistic and calculated to elicit financial support from the Vatican. Because of that, we must judge these reports with discretion, but overall, they contain much accurate and penetrating observation.

The missionaries talked about a strong sense of duty and responsibility among Japanese, their courage, strong intellectual curiosity, and sophisticated skills (although not necessarily in science and technology). Luis Frois commented that "Japanese are sagacious and possess a lively spirit." He also noted their perceptiveness, courtesy, and kindness. One quality that often was described with particular stress was strict obedience to persons of higher status. Frois observed that Japanese bowed their heads and spoke modestly and humbly when speaking to superiors.

These observations stimulate one's historical curiosity, but they do more. Because they provide a realistic portrayal of Japanese culture, the notes made by the European missionaries of the sixteenth century are a rich source for reference. Despite the Meiji Restoration and all the changes it brought, the portrait can still be recognized today.

The adjective "obedient" may seem objectionable, but to Europeans, the behavior of Japanese workers and company employees cannot be described otherwise. One Japanese reporter posted in Italy writes of his amazement when asked by Italians whether Japan was in fact a democratic country or still a totalitarian regime. They had observed Japanese employees reciting the company code and singing the company song each morning, and they found it curious. The missionary reports also point out that while most Japanese, the samurai class in particular, believed they could learn much from the Europeans, they did not become servile.

Christian missionaries in China failed to make many converts among members of the imperial court or high-ranking bureaucrats. The fact that so few were converted, despite the priests' access to the most powerful leaders of that vast nation, is closely related to the total, absolute confidence that the intelligentsia and leadership class had in the status quo of Chinese culture. In Japan, on the other hand, particularly after the Meiji Restoration, those who became Christians were almost all members of the upper classes and intelligentsia.

The difference in responses toward Western civilization when it began to filter into Japan and China was the most pronounced regarding weapons. China paid little attention to most aspects of European culture, including its military implements or weapons. Chinese reserved their greatest concern for the astrological knowledge and calendar brought by the Christians. The Japanese, on the contrary, were fascinated by the guns that were brought to Tanegashima, the first to appear in their country. The timing may explain their interest—the appearance of those guns coincided with a period of widespread internal strife that tore at the country. In no time firearms were being imported, studied, and manufactured in Japan. Only thirty-two years after the arrival of the first Portuguese gun, it became the decisive weapon in the Battle of Nagashino in 1575, which brought an end to the Sengoku period. The gun enabled Oda Nobunaga to destroy the greatest calvary force in all Japan, that of Takeda Katsuyori, completely destroying a rival whose constant attempts to gain more power had prevented unification of the country.

Seventeen years later, when Toyotomi Hideyoshi launched his notorious invasion of Korea, he was able to install an army to occupy the territory, and eventually he forced the Ming army sent to rescue Korea to capitulate. Both feats were accomplished by virtue of the advantage afforded by the gun. The Chinese invented gunpowder, but it was the Mongols who first used it in weaponry and introduced the notion of firearms to Europe. The gun was improved in Europe and later brought to Japan. Japan, in turn, used the gun to persecute China. It is an ironic twist of history that in this case, something one culture invented and had little use for was transported to other lands, only to return in diabolic form to persecute the people of its birthplace. The example of guns also illustrates Japanese foresight and talent for adopting things with potential for practical use.

In some stages of history, elements that are reactionary in one culture can be progressive in another. In Europe, the Jesuits represented a reactionary force that suppressed freedom of thought, but in Japan they played a progressive role. The Catholic priests had a way of speaking on equal terms with daimyo and commoners alike that shocked the people of the day, and when one thinks of the cultural influences they introduced—egalitarianism, equal treatment of men and women, parliamentarianism, the seminaries, books printed by Christians (*Amakusa-bon*)—the Christians clearly represented a very progressive civilization.

Christianity encountered severe persecution by the authorities and was finally banned, but it was not suppressed without the most tenacious resistance. Many were martyred because of the ban, perhaps more at one time than ever before, anywhere, and the climax came in the Shimabara Rebellion of 1637. The direct cause of the rebellion was resistance by local farmers to a crushing tax burden imposed by their provincial lord, but the uprising had the characteristics of a holy war—a battle to preserve freedom of thought—as the rural people sought to retain their religious faith. The resistance of 30,000 farmers against a force of 120,000 government soldiers ended in a massacre of the desperate peasant army. This was, incidentally, one of the most inspired cases of resistance to oppression in Japan's history. Two years after the Shimabara revolt, the bakufu clamped down in a policy of total national seclusion, and contact between Europe and Japan was virtually severed.

It is often said that all trace of the European culture that came to Japan with Christianity in the sixteenth century was wiped out. But certain things remained. Take for example, the Hakone waterway. It was built in 1670 by the Edo townsman Tomono Yoemon, as recounted in a novel by Takakura Teru. It was a large-scale project to build a canal extending from Lake Ashi into Shizuoka prefecture. This engineering feat must have required very precise surveying and mathematical skills, and these are believed to have been derived from the European scientific techniques brought by the Christian missionaries. Aside from a few similar cases, however, contact with Europe was largely cut off and Japan was isolated from the time of the seclusion edicts to the arrival of Commodore Perry's ships in 1853. A trickle of trade was maintained with Holland through the port at Nagasaki, which provided a closely controlled peephole on the West. Knowledge of European civilization made its way into Japan through the Dutch factory there, and, appropriately, it became known as Rangaku—Dutch Studies. This tiny stream of knowledge was vitally important, for it kept alive the tradition of curiosity about Europe.

The case of Dutch Studies also illustrates the difference between Chinese and Japanese attitudes toward foreign civilizations. China, the world's most ancient civilization, had been invaded time and again by nomadic peoples, but it had never confronted another people that represented a real threat to its civilization. Perhaps partly because of their unassailable conviction of the superiority of their own civilization, Chinese felt no urge or need to pay serious attention to such things.

Today in Japan, Chinese literature and language are standard subjects in university curricula throughout the country, and scholars of Chinese civilization abound. In China, specialized study of Japanese culture is almost nonexistent, and even Shakespeare, Leonardo da Vinci, and Rodin appear to hold far less fascination for Chinese than they do for Japanese. In the arts and in philosophy, Chinese are content with what they already have. Marxism, oddly enough, seems to be an exception, but it has been considerably sinified.

China's response to the civilization of Europe that came with Christianity was also different from Japan's. Chinese respected the knowledge of astronomy and technology of cannon-building brought by Matteo Ricci and Adam Schall, and they did deign to make use of what these men had to teach. Still, they showed no serious desire to acquire for themselves the learning of the West. Japanese, on the other hand, were literally frantic to learn about European culture, and they continued to seek out Western knowledge even after the country was officially closed. That attitude, however, was not something new, stimulated by the coming of the Christian fathers; avid curiosity and a willingness to embrace new ideas and things were characteristic of Japanese even in the ancient period.

Considering the gap of two or three thousand years separating the rise of Japanese and Chinese civilizations, the Japanese eagerness begins to make sense. Around the time of Confucius, when, as the *Analects* tell us, the sage gathered disciples about him for profound discussion on philosophical questions, Japan had still not advanced even to the stage of an agricultural society. Ancient Japan was a late developer, but as soon as it started moving, it was quick to overcome its backwardness. Agriculture began in China about 4000 B.C. and in Japan, about the third century B.C. By the second century A.D.—only about 500 years after the beginning of agriculture—the early Japanese states emerged. The early states in parts of western Asia, on the other hand, although agriculture had been practiced there since the seventh millennium B.C., did not develop until well into the third millennium. Thus, even 2,000 years ago, Japan was already demonstrating a rare ability to catch up quickly.

The interest, or lack of it, among Japanese and Chinese in study of the West was indicative of the difference in their attitudes toward foreign cultures, particularly as they influenced modernization. In the mid-nineteenth century Japan already had a long tradition of Dutch Studies, but China had not made the effort to learn from the European powers and found itself unable to mount any effective resistance to their encroachments. It is true that conditions in general in the two countries were very different, which makes it impossible to assess with any precision the relative weight of Western studies in the response to the West. In Japan's case, however, it is absolutely clear that efforts of individual Japanese both before and after the Meiji Restoration were instrumental in the relative smoothness with which Western civilization was introduced to Japan in the latter part of the nineteenth century. Important above all was the groundwork laid during the Tokugawa period.

## Learning from the West

Despite the seventeenth-century ban on Christianity and the seclusion edicts, Western learning developed early in the eighteenth century, led by the great pioneer in Dutch Studies, Arai Hakuseki (1657–1725). Under the eighth shogun, Yoshimune, Dutch Studies were encouraged officially beginning in 1740—that would never have happened in China—and this policy brought forth a number of distinguished scholars. Among the most prominent were Sugita Genpaku (1732–1817), Honda Toshiaki (1744–1821), Ōtsuki Gentaku (1757–1827), Watanabe Kazan (1793–1841), Takano Chōei (1804–50), Yamamura Saisuke (1820–47), Hashimoto Sōkichi (1763–1836), Shiba Kōkan (1747–1818), and Hiraga Gennai (1726–79). They pursued their studies under very trying conditions. Books were extremely hard to come by, and the Dutch language was difficult to master. Then, too, one ran the risk of being mistaken for a Christian and persecuted.

All in all, these scholars produced commendable work, but not one advocated the overturn of the established system or the Tokugawa regime. Shiba Kōkan, writing long before Fukuzawa Yukichi, said, "From the emperor and the shogun above, to the samurai, peasants, artisans, and merchants and even to the beggers and untouchables below, all alike are human beings." Under the strictly defined social hierarchy of the Tokugawa period, to risk even mentioning the idea of human equality was courageous, no matter how commonplace his observation may seem today, for it represented dangerous thought. Yet Kōkan went only so far as to suggest that all men are equal; he did not advocate that the shogun or the daimyo be pushed out of their positions of authority. Others such as Andō Shōeki were even more radical in their agrarian socialist type of thinking, but Andō remained unknown until the Meiji era.

The scholars of Dutch Studies may not have been revolutionary, but it must be remembered that they were members of the samurai class and part of the established system. As such, they functioned to awaken Japanese awareness of the existence of other lands, other civilizations in the West greater even than

China. Some of them were urban entrepreneurs. Hashimoto
Sōkichi was an umbrella maker of Osaka who had studied
the Dutch language and had become a Rangaku scholar.
He was only one of a group of scholars who emerged among
the Osaka townspeople, but they were active and strong enough
to found a center for some of their work, the Kaitokudō academy.

Other Dutch Studies scholars, including Watanabe Kazan and
Takano Chōei, lost their lives as a result of their pursuit of
Western learning. Kazan was forced to commit ritual suicide
(*seppuku*), and Chōei killed himself after being surrounded by
police. Chōei had an antiestablishmentarian side to him. He was
arrested and jailed, but he managed to escape; using a chemical,
probably hydrochloric acid, he disfigured his face and went
underground. Actually, although his evasion of the authorities
may mark him as an opponent of the establishment, he was not
so by preference. In many ways, he was forced into that position
by circumstances beyond his control. The reason Chōei could
survive underground was that provincial daimyo protected him,
seeking to make use of his knowledge of Europe. It was historical
phenomena such as these—the emergence of Western learning
among the townspeople and the protection of a man like Chōei
by the Uwajima domain—that laid the social and psychological
foundations for the smooth and massive introduction of European
civilization in the Meiji era.

What is significant about these Western studies scholars is
that they concentrated on practical knowledge, not on matters
of ideology. They sought knowledge that they could apply
directly, not theory or doctrine. This emphasis, for better or
worse, remained strong in scholarship in Japan during the Meiji
era and afterward. It derived from the same attitude that caused
Japanese to turn their attention first toward firearms, among
all the curiosities of European culture brought by the Catholic
priests in the sixteenth century.

The subjects these men studied were mainly medicine, astronomy, geography, and, above all, military science. Honda
Toshiaki was an enlightened scholar who believed, among other
things, that Chinese characters should be abolished from the
written language and replaced with the Latin alphabet, but
at the same time he was a militarist and supported external

conquest. He advocated the colonization of the islands near Japan, including the Ogasawaras, and suggested that the shogun establish a seat of government in Kamchatka. I do not know whether he had any idea how cold it is in Kamchatka, but it is interesting to note the extent of his thinking.

The salient characteristic of the Dutch Studies scholars, one that immediately identified them with the Meiji era, was their preoccupation with national power. Rather than concerning themselves with the "people's happiness," or such ideas as democracy, as a whole they were predominantly interested in how to make Japan a strong world power, and how to exert control over neighboring territories. Takano Chōei was highly respected for his thorough knowledge of Western military strategies. Yoshida Shōin, though not a Rangaku scholar, was one of the most brilliant personalities of the Bakumatsu period, and his thinking, too, was strongly oriented toward expansionist and military objectives. As mentor to many of the Meiji Restoration leaders, Shōin was at least indirectly responsible for the expansion policy adopted by the Meiji leadership. George Sansom's *The Western World and Japan* and Donald Keene's *The Japanese Discovery of Europe, 1720–1830*[2] both discuss the Rangaku scholars in detail. Keene's work is basically a study of Honda Toshiaki, but it includes many interesting accounts of other Rangaku scholars as well.

Dutch Studies certainly helped to diffuse a degree of knowledge about the West, but the actual appearance of Europeans and Americans at the end of the Tokugawa period nonetheless was a great shock to Japanese. In the sixteenth century, if the Portuguese and the Dutch had attempted to invade Japan, its military strength would have been sufficient to resist them: Japan had just undergone the grilling military experience of the Sengoku period and was prepared to hold its own. In the nineteenth century, when Perry sailed into Tokyo Bay, there was no way Japan could have resisted his forces. The visitors—from Russia, England, France, and the United States—were all from modern states where the industrial revolution and advances in science and technology had transformed the nature of military power. They represented a force that could not be turned away by a divine wind or any other "miracle."

Japan watched while England presented the Ch'ing dynasty with a list of impossible demands and then proceeded to overcome the great resistance of the nation of China in a single battle. Takasugi Shinsaku (1839–67) and others who went to Shanghai to see these events for themselves warned that Japan could not afford to wait any longer; like it or not, Japan must introduce Western technology or it would be doomed.

Many, especially conservatives, feared that to take such a step would destroy Japan's treasured traditions. The slogan devised to assuage their anxiety was *wakon yōsai*, "Japanese spirit, Western learning," an adaptation of the ancient phrase *wakon kansai* (Japanese spirit, Chinese learning). Later the great Bakumatsu scholar Sakuma Shōzan (1811–64) was to broaden the expression to read: "Eastern morality and Western technology." The West might excel in science and technology, but the East was superior in its ethical teachings. No matter how much "foreign" technology was brought in, it could not possibly destroy the ancient ethical heritage of the East. It was a political slogan that allowed Japanese to proceed with a clear conscience as they sought to acquire every possible appurtenance of European civilization.

## Japan's Cultural Revolution

There is considerable controversy about how the Meiji Restoration should be described. I like to call it a cultural revolution. The German physician Erwin von Baelz (1849–1913), who came to teach in Japan in the early Meiji era, wrote in his diary that what was happening in Japan was a kind of grand cultural revolution. In a cultural revolution, the people discard everything in their traditional culture and attempt to replace it with a revolutionary new and totally different culture. There are many theories about the Meiji Restoration: some claim it was a bourgeois revolution, and others argue that it was simply a change of regimes. I think it was more than a change of regimes. The Restoration was without doubt an extremely thorough cultural revolution, aimed at eliminating all trace of Japan's traditional culture.

Baelz describes the sentiments of intellectuals of the early

Meiji era as follows: "They insisted that they did not want to know anything about their own past; in fact, they declared that any cultivated person could only be embarrassed by it. . . . 'Everything in our past is completely barbaric. . . . We have no history, for our history is just about to begin.'" These words, spoken in 1876, reflect the intensity of the age. Japanese cut off the traditional topknots that symbolized samurai status, donned Western clothing, and began to eat beef for the first time.

The imperial edict issued by Emperor Meiji in 1871 gives some idea of the resolution that was behind these changes: "It is our firm wish that you, our subjects, change your way of dress and your manners, and enhance the national polity, with its martial tradition, that has continued since the time of our founding fathers." With this the emperor himself took the lead in eating the new dish made with beef, *sukiyaki*, and set the example by cutting off his topknot. It is not hard to imagine the supreme effort that required. Contemporary Westerners often wondered why the emperor invariably dressed in Western clothing; deliberately choosing to dress in a Western suit represented the determination to bring change to all the people.

I think it is symbolic of the difference between Japan and India that Nehru, Gandhi, and the other leaders of modern India, by contrast, consistently have worn traditional Indian attire, even after their country regained its independence. Japanese attempted to change everything, including their ways of eating and dressing. The Kabuki theater, sumo, many things we now associate with traditional culture, all temporarily vanished after the Meiji Restoration. Traditions that arose in the Tokugawa period all but disappeared for a time and were restored only after the Meiji government became firmly entrenched around the late 1880s. The fact that they were removed so completely is testimony to the drastic nature of the Meiji cultural revolution.

In retrospect, these things may seem trivial, but a time of transition is inevitably accompanied by all sorts of excesses. From the perspective of the calm and rational reformism of later years, it might seem that the change of the Meiji years could have been approached more slowly and cautiously. But when an entire nation or society is in transition, change has to be abrupt and explosive or it will not be permanent. After traveling around India for about a month once, I came away with the strong sense that the reason independent India has remained sluggish for so long is that there have never been any true radicals like Mori Arinori in positions of authority.

The Japanese did away with tradition on a massive scale, without hesitation, and they replaced it with European civilization. On the whole, their cultural revolution was successful, and today Japan is the third strongest industrial power in the world. I do not mean to bypass all the problems industrialization has wrought, but the point is that Japan was a backward nation in Asia, and it became a leading industrial power within the span of one hundred years. This is one of the wonders of world history, and people everywhere want to know how Japanese did it. During a recent visit to Japan by a delegation from the British Royal Society, the main question the members asked was how Japan industrialized so quickly.

The rapid progress of industrialization in Meiji Japan depended heavily on the introduction of new, European-style factory systems. We might call that process acceleration of existing industry. In the Tokugawa period, manufacturing was already going on at a certain level, providing fertile ground for the transition to the modern era. Indigenous industry kept on developing slowly but steadily during the nearly 270 years of continuous peace.

Japan was cut off from the mainstream of world history, and in many respects it lagged behind other countries. In its peaceful isolation, it tended to grow sluggish and stagnant. But among the positive results of the seclusion policy under the Tokugawa, the era gave birth to an extremely sensitive culture that was shared by all Japanese. George Sansom writes of eighteenth-century Japan that "perhaps no European society of that day was more civilized or more refined." The population of the city of Edo had passed one million, making it for a time the largest city in the world. This great city of one million consumers nurtured a unique urban culture that gave Japan its striking *ukiyoe* prints, the popular literature of Takizawa Bakin (1767–1848) and others,and so much more. Considering the vast readership of Edo, Bakin may well have been the best-selling writer in the world at that time.

Perhaps the most important factor in the Meiji Restoration was literacy. Many scholars tend to focus on the social structure and class relations, but literacy must not be ignored. It is a crucial factor in understanding the mentality that swayed both society and the social strata.

While there are no reliable statistics for the Restoration years, Ronald Dore has estimated that the proportion of people in 1868 who could read and write was roughly 43 percent for men.[3] This is a very high literacy rate for any country at that time. It may have been a result of the *terakoya* (lit., temple schools), which were found all over the country in the late Tokugawa period. There are no statistics on France before the revolution, for example, but it is thought that literacy among French men at that time was less than 30 percent. At the time of Lenin's revolution it stood somewhere around 15 percent for men in Russia. In 1949, the year Mao Tse-tung's revolution succeeded, literacy in China also is estimated to have been about 15 percent. Literacy appears to have been higher during Japan's Meiji Restoration than in Russia or China during comparable times of great social upheaval, despite the fact that their revolutions took place in much later periods. To be able to rely on a large number of literate people made matters much simpler when the Meiji reforms were carried out. It was not necessary to send out town criers for every notice the government issued; the people could read them for themselves.

Though they started with that basic advantage, the people of the Meiji era still had to exert tremendous efforts, but it bore fruit. As early as 1872, the new government managed to set up a compulsory elementary education system. In England, compulsory education was established only in 1870. France followed in 1882, the United States in 1918, and Germany in 1919. Japan's elementary school system was aimed at accommodating all the social classes in a unitary system, unlike England and France, where schools for the rich and the poor were different. This remains true even today in England. Intermediate schools were also separated. In Japan, there is no segregation on the basis of class or wealth. Japan stood in the vanguard at least as far as elementary education was concerned. The rate of enrollment rapidly increased until it was one of the highest in the world.

During the Tokugawa period, society was rigidly divided into four classes—samurai, peasants, artisans, and merchants, but this system was abolished in the Meiji era, as the schools and other institutions testify. In England and France today, the old class distinctions are still alive. In sum, the very radical nature of Japan's revolution had the effect of augmenting and releasing the energy of its people.

In the Tokugawa period Japan was divided into about 300 provincial domains, and yet it was a centralized state. In the *sankin-kōtai* (alternate attendance) system, the provincial lords were required to reside in Edo for fixed periods and to leave their families in the capital as virtual hostages. In that way, the shogunate kept a tight rein on power. It held close control over thought and the arts, and all aspects of society, right down to the daily life of the people. Yet because the homogeneity that had prevailed on the Japanese islands for millennia was combined with an organic, kinship-based society, official intervention in the personal lives of individuals was not coercive but relatively benign. This tradition of strong state leadership continued throughout the Meiji era, helping to propel Japan's modernization effort.

In the postwar period many Japanese are repelled by the idea of the state and the possibility that it played a positive role in their history, but to be objective, the achievements of the government cannot be ignored. We must appreciate the fact that by taking advantage of the well-integrated population, the strong leadership of the Meiji state was effective in speeding the introduction of European civilization and modernization of the country. Japan's capitalist system was also created and imposed from above. Its universities were set up not by private funds but by the government, again from above. The tendency for the government to take the lead has left a strong imprint on thinking today, as well.

George Sansom praised much about Japan, but he observed an unfortunate lack of "universalism." From ancient times until Meiji, he says, Japan's culture had no elements that could apply anywhere in the world, on a universal plane; Japan's traditions applied only to itself and its people. This is definitely a weakness, but in a closed society perhaps it was inevitable. At the same time, when these unique people were suddenly released from their isolation and sought to establish bonds with the outside world, the very absence of universalism in their culture may have generated the energy behind the drastic change and rapid modernization of the Meiji era.

## Realistic View of Europe

In his *History in a Changing World*, Geoffrey Barraclough draws a portrait of Europe at the close of World War II, beginning with a chapter entitled "Inquest on Europe."

In 1945, when the mists of battle cleared, a corpse was found lying, naked and despoiled, in a corner of the field. It was the old familiar Europe we knew so well—the Europe of the Congresses, the urbane Europe, well-nourished and prospering, which tasted with equal zest French wine and Gallic wit; which laughed at itself as it grew fat, but which grew fat and laughed; civilized, humanist Europe, for which the pleasures of youth were as nothing compared with the pleasures of middle age; self-satisfied, self-sufficient, with God discreetly in reserve, but its own world, the world it had contrived in its own image to its own liking, never out of view; sometimes with twinges of conscience, which may often have disguised spasms of indigestion, but never without ready cash to assuage conscience in the name of charity; tolerant, in its affluence and security, of cranks and heretics and doleful Jeremiahs, whose admonitions flattered and amused without endangering its anchored stability. We knew, before 1945, that it was getting short in the wind, this Europe of ours, that it suffered from occasional bouts of arthritis; we suspected that its teeth were false, and that round its middle it wore a masculine body-belt. But we cherished it, not least for the occasional grey hair; and it was an unpleasant shock to find the dishevelled corpse lying in the dirt, and two youthful giants disputing the spoils.[4]

Japanese historians, who are all terribly serious, are rarely capable of writing with comparable wit and irony. Europe was the center of the world, "the Europe of the Congresses." And the wonderful line, "for the pleasures of youth were as nothing compared with the pleasures of middle age . . ." captures so eloquently the sentiment of my generation. Europe had committed many sins, not the least among them the forced colonization of vast territories around the globe, and, to salve its conscience, it engaged in generous philanthropy. But well before 1945, old man Europe's health had begun to fail. Two great oafs had begun to strip him of his valuables—even the gold fillings from his teeth. The two, of course, are the Soviet Union and the United States. (Later, we see Japan sneaking up on the side to get its share of the spoils, but Barraclough does not go that far.)

This searing description of war-weary Europe was written by one of Europe's most erudite scholars, who makes his point in a memorable way. Still it is an exaggeration to say that Europe is dead; rather, it is debilitated, and the Soviet and American "youthful giants" are the successors to its fortunes. They represent the inheritors of Western civilization, and that civilization is as alive and prosperous as ever.

In some ways Europe has declined. Consider the population, for example. If the total world population in 1965 is divided between the so-called advanced industrial nations and the developing nations, that of the advanced nations makes up 31.5 percent, while that of the developing nations is 68.5 percent. In the year 2000, how will the balance be? According to the calculations of an American demographer, the population of the advanced countries will fall to about 22.5 percent, while that of the developing countries will rise to 77.5 percent. This means that by 2000, the population of Western Europe, whose countries are all advanced, will make up only 8 percent of the world's total. Although I do not have exact figures, I believe Europe's population today is about 13 percent of the total. That will decrease to 8 percent, and, by the year 2018, some 47 years from now, it will fall even further to 6.7 percent. No matter how competent, educated, or skilled the people of Europe may be, such figures can only mean that its power in the world will decrease.

Europe's prosperity began with its expansion in the sixteenth century. It thrived on conquest, bringing European civilization even to the hinterlands of Asia and Africa, creating for the first time in history something resembling "one world" in the space of a little more than four hundred years. But it is finally becoming clear that its age of prosperity is now a thing of the past. And Japanese, at long last, are growing out of the idolatry of Europe that has blinded us for so many years and are beginning to see it more realistically.

Before World War II and just after, Europe was for Japanese the object of awed admiration. In many ways our vision was blurred by the very radiance of the object. Our view of Europe in the past was distorted because it came across for the most part through books. Our impression of its people was formed also through the image of the missionaries, mainly Protestant, in Japan after the beginning of the Meiji era. Missionaries are usually upright, serious people not given to violence. We were inclined to think that Europeans are capable of doing no wrong, certainly not large-scale killing.

Actually, Europeans have committed acts far more reprehensible than most things even Japanese have done. One example is the pitiful fate of the people of Haiti. Once the Europeans had established control there, the population was reduced to one-twentieth its original level in only twenty years. Even when they did not actually kill, Europeans were capable of exploiting colonial peoples to the point of near exhaustion, as the English did in India, weakening and bleeding a country of its resources until it was almost beyond recovery. It is said that more than twenty million people died of starvation in India during the period of British rule. This was not a case of outright execution, but slow death caused by the evils perpetrated under British rule. It was an unqualified atrocity. Recently, when French troops tortured a young Algerian girl by tearing out her nails, this was nothing new; it was a method long in practice. But it came as an eye-opener for Japanese. Japanese, Africans, Americans,

Europeans—we are all human; we all want to eat well and enjoy the pleasures of life. There is no way to justify such treatment, but without the ability to be objective in our evaluations of each other, there is often little way to stop it.

In our youth, we believed that Japanese were a deplorable lot, sunk in prostitution, cruelty, and other shameful customs and practices, while the people of the advanced civilization of Europe were all of the most upright character. While there is no denying the superb achievements and qualities of the culture of Europe, England included, that culture nonetheless is not perfect, and never has been. Japanese must wean themselves from the notion that Europe is the sacrosanct cradle of higher civilization from ancient times and, as such, has some kind of ascribed superiority. It must be remembered that even in the brilliant age of Louis XIV, the era of Racine and Molière, most people, except aristocrats, ate with their hands. Japanese and Chinese have been using chopsticks for fifteen hundred years or longer.

Japan may be ahead of Europe in terms of social development, too. The Meiji leaders took the idea of equality seriously. A century ago they completely abolished the feudal class system, while class distinctions remain strong and deeply institutionalized in Europe. Officer ranks in the European military are still held by members of the nobility or wealthy classes, and the poor or lower classes make up the rank and file. A work by Aida Yūji, *Aaron shūyōjo*[5] describes the system very well. Even though problems remain in certain areas, such as the status of *burakumin* (outcasts), on the whole the class system has been eliminated far more effectively here than in Europe. It can be argued that a status hierarchy serves a useful purpose, but I think the people as a whole are much better off and happier without it. A class system, in any case, does not lighten the demands of bureaucracy for anyone. Japanese are apt to think that bureaucratic red tape plagues their society with particular virulence, but my own experience makes me think the bureaucratic mentality is strongest in French government offices. There is indeed an overload of civil servants in Japan, but in France the proportion is even greater. If Japanese wish fewer civil servants, any reduction will have to be initiated by themselves, without reference to European models.

Japanese have a habit of complaining that facilities in their universities are inferior, but relatively speaking, that is not true at all. The highest number of university-owned electron microscopes in the world are in Japan, to cite only one of our advantages. Japanese have an obsession with becoming the best and having the best. When they consider which universities to emulate, Harvard, the University of Paris, or the University of Moscow immediately come to mind. But the facilities themselves of the University of Tokyo are already excellent, much better than those of the University of Paris, for example. Japanese have an ingrained tendency to deprecate themselves and to idealize the big universities and other institutions of the West at the expense of objectivity. Such mental habits die hard.

One scholar launched an argument by writing that Europeans have never felt a sense of threat or competition from Japanese. He had not done his homework. Today Europeans regard us with great anxiety, mainly because Japanese industrial productivity has far outstripped theirs and is challenging them in almost every field. The same writer goes on to say from his ivory tower that Japanese industrial development is not a matter of serious concern for Europeans; they are too preoccupied with their own problems. Yet we find increasing numbers of Europeans coming to Japan not to pay tribute to haiku or Kabuki, but to find out how Japanese can make good cars and other products so cheaply that they are driving Europe's own industries into a corner. All Europeans are by no means unaware of the challenge from Japan, but it is true that many have little knowledge about this country. A recent survey made in England asked, "What kind of government does Japan have?" Of 1,855 respondents over sixteen years of age, about 11 percent answered "dictatorship," 35 percent "democratic," 18 percent "communist," and 37 percent had no idea.

Some Japanese think we should ignore the West and be satisfied without trying to compete. We should relax about ourselves, accept our strengths and weaknesses, and avoid the ugliness of competition. That is difficult, however. Aside from economic reality, when you feel poor and your neighbor looks rich, it is difficult to remain impassive, convincing yourself that he is just another human being and you should be content to be what you are. That lack of confidence is what drove Japanese of the Meiji era to their intensive effort to catch up with the West. It is an impulse that cannot be denigrated or easily quelled, and it keeps driving Japanese further. They still do not consider their standard of living to be particularly high even though it has already surpassed that of Italy and is approaching that of England.

Nonetheless Japan's social scientists, leftists included, still insist that Japan is a poor country, as if to drive people to work even harder. They cite figures: the GNP may be the third highest in the world, but per capita income in Japan ranks nineteenth. To me, the argument is spurious. To say that Japan is poor, only nineteenth in the per capita income range, is to be fooled by statistics. The measure of wealth may be not how much money one *has* but how much money one *uses*; the difference between Europe and Japan is the difference between stock and flow.

Take, for example, overseas travel. Among all the world's peoples, Japanese are second only to Americans in the distances and frequency of their travels. Statistics on air passengers around the world show that while 50 percent are Americans, roughly half the remainder, or 25 percent, are Japanese, the rest being English, French, Canadian, and others. Three times as many Japanese travel abroad at any one time as French or English, and they spend an average of $3,000 per trip. English travelers spend an average of about $130.

The relation between Japan and Europe has entered a new phase, along with the change in the Japanese perception of the West. Japanese are finally beginning to see the world with greater objectivity and realism. Nakae Chōmin, an outstanding thinker of the early Meiji era and a leader in the Freedom and Popular Rights Movement, described Japan's goal as the creation of a Europeanized nation in Asia. Today, this goal has been attained at least superficially. I say "superficially," but perhaps one should say "institutionally," for Japan has not totally absorbed European values. It is interesting, nonetheless, that although westernization and modernization have been achieved at least in the quantifiable aspects, Europe continues to exert strong influence.

For example, "horizontal writing" (as opposed to Japanese writing, which traditionally is written vertically) retains its fascination for Japanese. A political slogan, an advertising poster, a popular magazine cover page, is far more alluring if it can flash some English words or phrases. Foreign names, too, seem to scintillate, prompting singers and film stars to adopt stage names like George, Pinky, Peggy, and so forth. Market research shows that products sell better if the brand name is foreign-sounding. Foreign words have a mystique that over-shadows opposition to borrowing, and they excite interest, a phenomena I find immensely thought-provoking.

Tada Michitarō once pointed out that while the base of es-thetic sensitivity in the West is in the senses of sight and hearing, a strong sense of taste, smell, and touch seem to determine Japanese esthetic responses. Pursuing that intriguing observation, we find that sight and hearing can be measured scientifically. When it comes to smell, however, we can say that fluorine smells like rotten eggs, but we cannot chart its value in numbers. We can say that something feels like a raw egg or a half-boiled egg, but it is impossible to gauge such a sensation in objective measurement. The same is true of taste. If, indeed, the esthetic sense of Japanese is oriented to perceptions that cannot be mea-sured, this is unnerving. Since unmeasurable senses can only be acquired by habit and long familiarity, it would mean that traditional esthetic sensitivities may not survive the rapid advance of industrial society. In some ways, they seem to be fading al-ready. Senses that are acquired not through a process of famil-iarization but through esthetic "intuition" are in even greater peril.

Influenced by European civilization, Japanese preferences with regard to art are undergoing profound change. In the March 1970 issue of *Bungei shunjū* there appeared an article by Shirozaki Hideo entitled "Kobijitsu ryūshutsu shite kuni horobu" [The Drain of Classical Japanese Art and the Ruin of the Country]. The title is hyperbolic, but the article accurately describes the strong appeal of Western art to Japanese and the extent to which attachment to their own art is weakening. They are undiscriminating in their enthusiasm for Western works, happily paying tens of millions of yen even for an inferior work if it happens to be by Picasso, Renoir, or another great master. Meanwhile a truly outstanding Buddhist image from the twelfth century may sell for a fraction of such prices. That is one reason, says Shirozaki, that such statues are being bought not by Japanese but by foreigners and are rapidly being exported to the United States and Europe. Japanese department stores and banks customarily put out promotional calendars at the end of the year, and the illustrations that grace these glossy sheets are invariably from paintings by Cézanne, Renoir, Degas. I have never seen one with reproductions of Japan's great literati painter, Ike no Taiga, or of the *ukiyoe* artist Suzuki Harunobu.

A year ago a Japanese department store bought up three hundred paintings by an obscure painter in Paris and proceeded to retail three-fourths of them in Tokyo. The rest were handed over to local branches of the store, and they sold immediately. That could never happen in Europe. Ever since the Meiji Restoration, Japan's intelligentsia have been afflicted with an avid preference for all things Western, and after World War II, this intriguing ailment spread to the masses as well, in just one indication of the kind of reorientation the entire nation has undergone.

## Strengths of Japan's Mass Society

European values have been introduced, either directly or by way of the United States, to Japan, but it is difficult to argue that they have been transplanted thoroughly or properly. More basically, it is debatable whether the values created in one country can be exported at all to another with a different culture. Take the concept of rationalism. Most of us immediately associate rationalism with Europe. There is a kind of rationalism in Chinese thought and in other traditions, but Chinese or Confucian rationalism is not necessarily connected with science. Modern rationalism almost always is associated with the spirit of science, and hence with Europe. If we think of the sciences as consisting of mathematical and physical sciences on the one hand, and the life sciences on the other, we usually associate China with the biological sciences. But the kind of rationalism that characterized Chinese thought is not based on modern scientific principles. Scientifically-based, modern European rationalism has been transplanted to Japan, but its roots may not go very deep. In one sense, the reaction against it set in well before it fully penetrated Japanese thinking patterns.

I believe Japanese society would benefit by a greater degree of rationalism, but not everyone would agree. Today even in Europe the value of rationalism in thought and action is questioned. Japan has always had irrational elements, which we tried to cover with European rationalism, but now we are beginning to see strong irrational trends emerging even in Europe. Still, they are distinct from Japan's traditional irrationalism. Japan has no direct counterpart to existentialism, for example. On the other hand, European irrationalism suggests approaches to save Japan's indigenous irrationalism. On that level, the two become relative, and what Europeans think of as irrational becomes very rational in Japanese thinking.

Individualism is also strong in European values. Sakuta Keiichi, talking about the "proto-organization," has made some interesting observations on "respect for the individual." Sakuta refers to the kind of homogeneity and solidarity that has developed in Japan as "wholeness," which is the basis of Japan's cultural unity. Brought up in such a kinship-oriented, isolated, and static social milieu, Japanese experience little that encourages a strong consciousness of the individual. Many Japanese have had very distinctive individual character: Ogyū Sorai and Sen no Rikyū were definitely unique, but far from the "rugged individualists" of the Western world.

Few Japanese, no matter how intelligent, have managed to develop a high degree of personal independence and nonconformism. Some European observers doubt that true individualism is possible in Japan. Lafcadio Hearn, who lived a long time in this country, wrote in *The Japanese Spirit* that psychological theories of limited—or lacking—individualism notwithstanding, Japan as a nation and culture has a far stronger individuality than any European country. At that point Lafcadio Hearn was completely won over by Japan and its culture, and eventually he even became naturalized. His statements may not be completely objective, but in pointing out the uniqueness of the nation as a unit I think he has identified one source of Japanese character.

To Japanese, individualism is associated with the portrayal of the country as "Japan, Inc." Most Japanese are embarrassed by this label, but it is irrefutable that the society tends to present a wholeness, an organic unity. Public opinion on certain matters does not emerge in the form of some widely accepted theory; attitudes form on the basis of a consensus of sorts, and all tacitly observe certain taboos. For example, it is universally understood that one does not derogate the Ise Grand Shrine. I do not object to the shrine, but once I wrote a short article opposing its nationalization, and every day for a week I received threatening telephone calls from a sinister source that shook my family considerably. In Japan the observance of taboos seems to be particularly easy to achieve.

Individualism may not be fully developed in Japan, but even in the West today, nineteenth-century individualism is increasingly less secure. European society, like Japan, is becoming a mass society, with all the painful results. At one extreme, people are alienated and the society atomized, and at the other, they are organized into sharp, institutional patterns. Alone in an organization governed by the state or by big enterprise, a person is reduced to a little cog whirled about by a management society.

There are all kinds of people in Japan: some like the theater and some like films. Some like Chinese food, and some will not eat raw fish. The diversity, however, is on the surface. No matter where they go, the ticking computers of railway companies take no notice of whether they like plays or movies—the only concern is how many units have paid their fares. There is no place for the "dignity for the individual."

No matter how clever you think you are, without a corporation or a government agency or a place to work, you would not eat. No matter what you join, you are curbed by institutions, and if you hope to resist, there is no way to win out as an individual. If you intend to fight, you are forced to join a labor union, and once in the union, you must follow rules and established policy. The expression of individualism is extremely difficult, and is growing just as difficult in Europe.

The same thing is happening to "freedom." I believe that the concept of freedom was born out of the life of the metropolis, not in the conservative village. One thinks of Athens, but that polis did not survive. The real wellspring of freedom was in the post-medieval commercial cities of Venice and Florence. In Japan, only Sakai can be likened to the free cities of Renaissance Italy. In a sense, the idea of freedom did not exist in Japan. Yanagita Kunio (1875–1962) once told me that when he was young the word *jiyū* [freedom] was used in the sense of *jiyū katte* or "do as one pleases," which was equivalent to *wagamama* [egotism].[6]

Perhaps a word like "freedom" does not emerge unless there is also a word like "slavery." There is some debate about whether there were in fact slaves in Japan in the Nara period (7th–8th centuries), but in any case they no longer existed by the medieval period. Even if there were slaves, I suspect the system was much more moderate than the European system of slavery because of the relatively stronger homogeneity. In Europe, it was common to take alien peoples when slaves were wanted and use them for forced labor. It is believed that there was no such practice in Japan. Without it, I am inclined to think, freedom as an abstract concept was less meaningful, which may explain why it has been so difficult for Japanese to grasp.

Has freedom been fully realized even in Europe? That is a difficult question under any circumstances, but the development of the values and institutions of mass society in Europe today blurs the issue even more. As a study of the literature now emerging in Europe shows, there is freedom, but its bounds are narrower than they once were. Perhaps our society is like the meals on airplanes. You have little choice, but you do have the freedom to order either tea or coffee.

Honda Katsuichi has said that American blacks deny the existence of any freedom or equality in the United States. Our different historical experience may make it difficult for Japanese to fully understand the meaning of freedom, but that does not necessarily mean that their society is therefore deprived, or lagging behind. Certain freedoms are shrinking in the West, also, to the point that intellectuals are beginning to doubt whether their own society is really free.

The same goes for democracy. Recently in Japan, postwar democracy has been subjected to increasing criticism. There are specific reasons for that, but it coincides with a debate on democracy now going on throughout the world. A large segment of Japanese opinion claims that their democracy is not functioning properly. Indeed, it is not perfect, yet it seems to me that for a country which had no tradition of political democracy, where even the word "democracy" was unmentionable for years until after World War II, Japan has achieved in culture and daily life a working democracy that is actually more genuine even than that in Europe.

One of the characteristics of the European mentality is clarity and thoroughness. This thoroughness, in contrast to the Japanese habit of leaving everything ambiguous, made the West very appealing to Nakae Chōmin. Presently it would appear that more and more people are beginning to believe that thoroughness is necessary, and the historical figures that people currently idolize reflect this. Today one of the most popular is Oda Nobunaga. Japanese are famous for their tendency to seek unanimity and consensus. Yet that is not always true. The period when consensus and unanimity were most clearly out of favor, when demonstrated ability became more important, was the period of wars in the fourteenth and fifteenth centuries. The representative figure of this period is Oda Nobunaga. In many ways, Nobunaga was like a "Westerner." He had many characteristics that were typical of a Christian mentality, and the fact that Nobunaga was relatively generous with the Christian missionaries from Europe is somehow not surprising. But Christianity itself was intolerant. One pope even issued an edict condoning the killing of anyone who did not believe in it, as we are told in the stories of Komatsu Sakyō.

Takeyama Michio has written that "Christianity is a doctrine of proud victory. Its God is the one and the only God and a jealous God. No other gods are permitted. But the Christian God would save only those who worship him and destroy all others. In times past, followers of other religions were not considered human, but servants of the devil. The suppression of the devil's followers was not considered antithetical to humanism, but rather supportive of humanism." Modern Christianity is not that harsh, but for a long time that spirit dominated the religion in Europe.

By comparison, Shintō, in which the roots of Japanese society lie, and even Buddhism are extremely ambiguous faiths, definitely lacking in clarity and thoroughness. When we were young, we believed that Japan could never "improve" unless Buddhism were wiped out. But now it seems that the monotheistic religions, either Christianity or Islam, in their pursuit of clear distinctions between black and white, enemy and ally, may bring us to the brink of exchanging atom bombs or worse. If such a threat emerges, once more we will need the capacity to recognize other gods, gods of openheartedness and peaceful coexistence. And there the thinking of Asian cultures has potential as an alternative.

Individuals need a well-developed self-awareness, a sense of responsibility, but I do not think we can say categorically that individualism ought to be more thoroughly implanted in Japan. For example, in the case of old people—now I am one of them—life is easiest and most generous in China and Japan. The United States and Europe may be wealthier, but how many grandmothers and grandfathers are virtually abandoned in those countries? Perfectly well-to-do Western families often place their elderly members in old people's homes, where they are visited by their families on fixed days. This kind of situation, with all its "independence," could not possibly be the happiest way to live. Since wholeness—not totalitarianism—is what characterizes Japanese society, people are not expected to go off on their own at will. It is not desirable for an individual to break away from the norm, which is an extremely convenient principle when it is necessary to undertake a collective task. Of the many factors that help explain how Japan managed to modernize as quickly as it did, I think the element of wholeness was a major one. Aside from Nobunaga, there have been few dictators in Japanese history, and there has been little need for them because the country was relatively easy to unite under reasonable leadership, without massive use of force. For that reason, absolutism of the Louis XIV type or the repressive variety of Marxist absolutism never had a parallel here. That is why there are no massive monuments in Japan like Versailles Palace, the Winter Palace in Moscow, or the Forbidden City in Peking. After the great tombs which are even bigger than the pyramids were erected for Japan's emperors Nintoku and Ōjin, the absolutism they represented gradually faded, permanently.

I have shown many foreign visitors around the Kyoto imperial palace, and they are invariably surprised by its simplicity and modesty. "*This* is the palace of Japan's emperors?" they ask incredulously. But for more than two hundred years in the classical Heian period when Kyoto flourished, there was not even capital punishment; it was an extremely humane, congenial society that might have made Western society seem cold and formal in comparison.

It was that kind of warm, congenial society which gave the tendency toward *amae* [mutual dependence] ample space to develop. In the studies of psychiatrist Doi Takeo on *amae*, or dependence, in Japanese culture,[7] Doi does not actually affirm the value of *amae*, which really describes a way of leaning on someone in the expectation of support and sympathy, but says that it must be conquered. Indeed, the penchant for dependence will not help to cope with the severities of the modern world. But we need not disallow the fine sensitivities that are connected with this psychology of dependence; the task is to find a way to harmonize it with rational thinking.

After World War II, Japanese pushed through three massive reforms—revision of the Constitution, reform of agricultural lands, and reform of the national language. Except for China, no other country undertook such fundamental reform in the postwar period. Many Japanese still feel a particular fondness for the old phonetic writing system, and many large landowners grieve the loss of their lands. Some people wish the emperor had remained cloaked in the myth of divinity. Opponents of the reforms in particular complain that many of them were pushed through by the American Occupation forces. But such major reforms would never have been achieved without the youthful vitality for survival of the Japanese people, and it is to this quality that we owe their success. We must consider Japan's future with full appreciation for this vitality, and at the same time recognize the new realities of our mass society, which has taken root almost in spite of itself. Yet, for a mass society, Japan is quite a sophisticated one. Outstanding writers like Inoue Yasushi, Matsumoto Seichō, and Shiba Ryōtarō are all authors of so-called mass literature. There may be no other country where such high-quality writers have such an enormous reading public.

Those who find mass society distasteful and wish for a return to the society of aristocratic, high culture might find Japanese society repelling, but I think this country has built an outstanding mass society that can be respected for the quality it has achieved. One of the things that surprised American sociologist David Riesman when he visited Japan was the way the culture is shared, from top to bottom. University professors and top bureaucrats all watch the same television shows and read the same best-selling popular novels. This apparently caught him by surprise. In the United States, it would seem, a first-class university professor would probably not be caught reading popular literature. When I visited the United States, I talked with many professors, but whenever I tried to bring up the subject of movies like *High Noon*, I received no response. They had never seen it. And yet, they are connoisseurs of things foreign. They have seen films like *Rashomon*, but they have not seen *The Great West*, with Jean Simmons. The American intelligentsia are cut off from the masses. In Japanese society there is no such barrier, or if there is, it is thin. That is what stimulated Riesman's admiration. Japanese society has its faults, but nothing can be improved by simply importing intact the appurtenances of European culture, without taking into account the reality of our mass society.

# Notes

1.  G. B. Sansom, *The Western World and Japan* (New York: Knopf, 1951).
2.  Donald Keene, *The Japanese Discovery of Europe, 1720–1830* (Stanford: Stanford University Press, 1969).
3.  Ronald Dore, *Education in Tokugawa Japan* (London: Routledge and Kegan Paul, 1965).
4.  Geoffrey Barraclough, *History in a Changing World* (Norman: University of Oklahoma Press, 1955), p. 154.
5.  Aida Yūji, *Aaron Shūyōjo* [POW Camp at Aaron] (Tokyo: Chūōkōronsha, 1962).
6.  Yanagita Kunio, *Kokyō nanajū-nen* [My Hometown of Seventy Years] (Kobe: Nojigiku Bunko, 1959), p. 5.
7.  Doi Takeo, *The Anatomy of Dependence* (Tokyo: Kōdansha International, 1973).

# 9

# The Meiji Revolution and Nationalism

ALL peoples, races, or tribes, as long as they live collectively within a certain area, have their own culture. This is true no matter how primitive the group, for, in the case of man, the continuance of life is to have a culture. Among the many stimuli to cultural development, one is the transformation that occurs when the culture of a certain area is affected by another as the result of conscious or unconscious learning from it. I call this process "acculturation." American anthropologists first used the term in dealing with cultural change in the societies of American Indians, but here I use it to mean the kind of transformation that entire cultures undergo.

Acculturation does not occur between any two cultures whenever they meet, but when it does occur, it tends to follow certain patterns. It takes place during the process of development of civilization (here, culture and society together), and its direction is generally from advanced toward less advanced cultures. Thus, acculturation proceeds within the development matrix of human civilization, a series of stages characterized by progress from hunting and gathering to agricultural society, then industrial society.

Sometimes a culture adopts and imitates a selected part of another culture. This is not acculturation but partial borrowing. For example, people in some of the more advanced countries of Europe in the early nineteenth century were fascinated by the

Originally delivered as a lecture, entitled "Acculturation, Modernization, and Nationalism," at the East-West Center, Honolulu, February 12, 1973.

*ukiyoe* paintings of Japan, at that time an underdeveloped country. The late Impressionist painters absorbed much from the vivid, fresh color and the bold composition of the *ukiyoe* style, but that was by no means a case of acculturation on the part of French culture. During the T'ang period, cultural artifacts from Western Asia and the Middle East were much in vogue in Ch'angan, the capital, but they were never more than an accessory to Chinese culture. The penetration of outside influence cannot be called acculturation unless it brings about systemic change in the entire culture.

## Forced vs. Selected Acculturation

Contacts between China and Japan had already begun long before the third century A.D., when Japan's early states emerged. The continued and strong influence of the more advanced Chinese culture is sometimes likened to fertilizer, the necessary input that helped Japan's culture grow from a sapling to a full-grown tree. Naitō Konan (1866–1934), sinologist and cultural historian, preferred to think of Chinese influence as the brine that causes soybean curd to congeal; Chinese culture served to integrate and give definition to Japan's still amorphous culture elements. To me his metaphor makes good sense.

Chinese civilization is thought to have assumed clear outlines about two thousand years earlier than Japan's. The earliest known agriculture in China dates back to about 4,000 B.C., and China's first states arose two and a half millennia later in about 1,500 B.C. In Japan's case, agriculture is not known before about 300 B.C., but its first states emerged only five or six centuries after that, about A.D. 300. Thus the speed of development was much more rapid in Japan. Just as in the modern period, archaic Japan was bent on "catching up quickly," which has become a basic pattern in its cultural history.

A typical pattern of acculturation must have taken place at that time, but today it is impossible to describe exactly how it occurred. We do know that Japan continued to learn and benefit from Chinese culture, as attested by the missions to T'ang and the wealth of knowledge they brought back. Being an island country, an alien culture was never forced on the land by military conquest, as it was in Korea and Indochina. Japanese were free to assimilate what they wanted, right up until 1945 and the American Occupation. Thus, while they absorbed almost every aspect of the Chinese system, they could still be eclectic. They never introduced the punishing practice of castration, for example, and in Chinese literature, they ignored the political concerns and concentrated only on the esthetic aspects.

Adjacent cultures in other parts of the world also experienced relatively peaceful and gradual patterns of acculturation, but the tempo was accelerated beginning around 1500. The dawn of European expansion marked the turning point. Until then, acculturation took the form of influence from an advanced culture exerted over a less advanced culture. After 1500, however, it became, in many cases, a forced process of change imposed by the more powerful on the weak. One cannot contest the relation of power to culture as long as culture is rooted in the practical realities of human collectivities rather than in abstract ideas. French culture permeated Europe in medieval times and under Louis XIV and Napoleon I, but not simply because it was appealing: France was the strongest nation in Europe in those days. The thirteenth-century conquests of Genghis Khan did not bring about acculturation because the culture of the conquerors was less advanced than that of the conquered. In fact, the Mongols and other conquerors of China were themselves subject to acculturation by the more advanced Chinese culture, demonstrating a reverse pattern of influence exerted on the more powerful.

Japan's first direct contacts with European culture began in 1543 when a Portuguese vessel drifted into the islands. Shortly thereafter Jesuit missionaries began to arrive, bringing a wave of Western culture with them. At first the missionaries were welcomed by the Japanese people, but problems of doctrine and politics soon made the presence of Christians, whether priest or convert, untenable for the government. Evangelism was prohibited and believers forced to recant. There followed decades during which hundreds of Christians died as martyrs. Then in 1635, the military government enacted bans on foreign travel and intercourse with foreigners, effectively isolating the country. After the suppression of the Shimabara Rebellion in 1637, which ended in probably the largest-scale massacre that Japanese history has ever witnessed, European culture in Japan was virtually wiped out. The first wave from the West seemed to have left no traces. That was not quite true, however. The introduction of Portuguese firearms was to have a decisive effect on the history of Japan, beginning with the victories that enabled Oda Nobunaga and Toyotomi Hideyoshi to unify the country. The first Tokugawa shogun, Ieyasu, who followed Hideyoshi, established a dynasty that maintained peace for two hundred fifty years until its downfall in 1867. This unprecedented, long period of peace created an environment in which the unique culture could mature and permeate the nation, rising to its fullest potential, but at the price of national isolation and slow development.

Why did the Europeans, who destroyed the Inca Empire only ten years before the arrival of the Portuguese in Japan, not invade our islands? The basic reason is that there was no great disparity between the levels European and Japanese civilizations had achieved. The enormous geographic distance that separated Japan from Europe was also a factor. Both Spain and Portugal at that time were premodern, agricultural states. Modern science and technology were still in the offing, and the industrial revolution was three centuries away. Later on it would be different, but as Europeans learned when the Chinese drove the Dutch out of their settlements in Formosa in 1661, they did not have the power to conquer the old civilizations of East Asia.

Even though acculturation did not occur at that time in China or Japan, it did in other areas where the groundwork was being laid for the era of full-fledged colonialism. European influence, backed by guns, only grew stronger in the Americas, Africa, India, and Southeast Asia. With hindsight, we can see that eventually, when two cultures whose levels of development are significantly disparate sustain close contact, the stronger often exterminates the weaker, rather than stopping at transformation. The Tasmanians have vanished from the earth. Between 1519 and 1597, about three-fourths (roughly 8.5 million) of the population of Mexico was decimated. If measures had not been taken before it was too late, the aborigines of Australia and the Hottentots in Africa would have met the same fate, if not worse. There was no question of acculturation there. In other cases, like that of Japan's Ainu, the less powerful were—or are being—assimilated into the society and culture of the stronger. In fact, Ainu culture has almost died out.

Japanese of the mid-nineteenth century could not be expected to know the precise circumstances of the European forays into lands outside their own. But they were all too aware of the pressure on India and China exerted by the European powers. They also knew that China had suffered bitterly from the huge shipments of opium brought in and sold at great profit by Britain. When desperate Chinese finally resorted to violence, leading to the Opium Wars of 1840–41, Britain responded with greater force and clamped down harder than before.

The arrival of Commodore Perry in 1853 heightened the sense of crisis among the Japanese people. It is interesting that the effort to keep foreigners out was linked with a movement to topple the Tokugawa shogunate and restore the emperor to power. This movement reflected not only a nationalism focused on imperial authority, but also the view inherited from Chinese culture of foreigners as barbarians. Chinese culture in ancient times was so advanced that Confucius was able to state, "The barbarians of the East and North, with all their wise leaders, are still inferior to China without any wise leaders at all." It is doubtful that mid-nineteenth-century Japanese could have confronted the British, Russians, or Americans with such confidence, when all of them were pressing the bakufu to let them in. Having seen the power of the West demonstrated even within their own borders (e.g., in 1863 during the armed clash between Satsuma and the British navy), patriotic revolutionary factions made a quick about-face to push for the opening of the country. We will discuss the propensity of modern Japanese for conversion later. In any event, Japan opened its doors in the mid-nineteenth century, signalling the start of rapid westernization. The groundwork had been laid for a bold cultural revolution, unprecedented in world history.

The Meiji Restoration, at once the beginning of the cultural revolution and the reinstatement of the emperor in the seat of authority, took place in 1867. While it is euphemistically rendered as "restoration," it was a revolution. Since the term "revolution" was taboo in a nation-state where the emperor was sovereign, the conservatives emphasized the emperor's return to power and used the term meaning "restoration of imperial rule." I remember once getting a good scolding from one of my middle school teachers after using "Meiji Revolution" in an essay. On the other hand, Marxists regard the Meiji Restoration merely as a shift of power from the shogunate to the emperor: they deny that the event was a revolution, for there was no class struggle in which the ruled became rulers, nor was the exploitation by landowners rectified. Because Marxists are committed to the idea that they must bring about a social revolution in the future, they refuse to recognize that a revolution was achieved at that time. Thus, for different reasons, Marxists and conservatives alike shied away from the term "revolution"; instead, they talked about the "restoration of imperial rule" and substituted euphemism for honesty.

The revolutions in England, France, Russia, and China achieved much, but they were all exceedingly violent. During the Meiji Restoration, no ruler and relatively few citizens were slain. Although land reform was attempted in the revolutions in England and France, the landowner class remained intact in both. Japan was much more thorough in abolishing the feudal status system. If France's July Revolution (1830) or February Revolution (1848) were genuine revolutions, we are certainly justified in calling the Meiji Restoration a revolution, specifically, a bourgeois revolution typical of underdeveloped societies.

A bourgeois revolution "typical of underdeveloped societies" should be distinguished from a bourgeois revolution carried out after the bourgeoisie have attained considerable maturity. The former type is initiated with the purpose of pushing the bourgeoisie to maturity. Hans Kohn, for one, argues that revolutions in developing countries are most often concerned only with independence and nationalism, as opposed to individual liberties and civil rights, which were the focus of European revolutionary thought. That is not a fair judgment, however, and it reveals a lack of understanding of developing countries. It is completely natural that the people of a country which has lost its independence to a colonial power or is threatened by

more advanced countries should first seek independence, unification, and economic development. Success needs the support of
the masses, but it may be impractical to proceed with nation-
building through democratic discussion when the civil society
is still immature. In order that the nation gain freedom, it may
be necessary at first for the leaders to exert strong political
control. Individual liberties and rights may have to wait until
national liberty is achieved, but they are nonetheless important
goals.

Western scholars generally credit the Meiji Restoration with
much greater achievements than do Japanese scholars. The
more critical stance of Japanese intellectuals, ironically, stems
partly from their tendency to judge Japan by Western standards. Many regard the Meiji Restoration as a half-baked
reform, with the implication that it came nowhere near being
a socialist revolution. If anything, they say, it was a bourgeois
revolution. It seems, however, that the real achievement of
the Meiji Restoration lies in its thoroughness as a cultural,
more than a social or political, revolution. For Japan, which
had looked to China as the highest civilization and now sought
to rank with the European powers, the cultural revolution of
the Meiji era was an attempt to discard the old culture all
at once and assimilate the new culture of the West. Erwin von
Baelz (1849–1913), a German physician teaching in Japan,
recorded in a diary entry for 1877 the sentiment of early Meiji
intellectuals: "Everything in our past is completely barbaric. . . .
We have no history, for our history is just about to begin."
The eminent Japanologist, G. B. Sansom, observed in *The Western
World and Japan* that "two masters of classical Japanese painting,
Kano Hogai and Hashimoto Gaho, were almost starving ten
years after the Restoration, and their works were sold . . . for
a few pence."[1] Whether or not "almost starving" was an exaggeration, the fact is that while countless superbly endowed
artists suffered poverty in Europe because their work was too
progressive to achieve due recognition, it was the classical
artists in Meiji Japan, those refusing to abandon tradition,
who had a hard time.

Japanese attitudes in the early Meiji era toward the traditional culture may seem frivolous to us today, but a cultural

revolution is a question of all or nothing. China's well-known revolutionary writer, Lu Hsun, exclaimed "Youth of China! Refrain from reading the Chinese classics. Avoid them completely, if you can!" Could they not have preserved what was worthwhile in the society and improved or reformed that which was not? Such an attempt to be selective cannot be a revolution. A revolution does not mean improvement of what already exists, but the overthrow at one stroke of all that has been established.

In 1871, the Meiji emperor issued an edict to encourage the consumption of meat, Western-style haircuts, and Western clothing: "It is our firm wish that you, our subjects, change your way of dress and your manners, and enhance the national polity, with its martial tradition, that has continued since the time of our founding fathers." Although he speaks of "our founding fathers," what he is saying is that Japanese should switch from kimono to Western-style clothes. Today this message seems incongruous. But what is called revolution is inevitably attended by overdoing. Modernization needs its radical destroyers of tradition. Mori Arinori, a minister of education, exemplified this spirit in Japan. Actually, he went too far and was assassinated for lifting up a bamboo blind with the tip of his stick at the Grand Shrine of Ise, the most revered of all sacred places. Nonetheless Japan and India in modern times are exact opposites; Japan has a fear of unchangeability, whereas India shrinks from change.

Leaders in the early Meiji era often spoke of "Eastern morality and Western technology" and "Japanese spirit and Western learning," as they sought to introduce Western scientific and intellectual achievements while encouraging respect for traditional values. Regardless of principle, however, they aimed at thorough and rapid westernization. Their slogans were political, meant to alleviate the shock. The Meiji government intentionally carried out a national program of Western acculturation. What made acculturation possible and sped up its progress was not just the political demand for a powerful nation-state. It was a deep-rooted aspiration among Japanese to know, to be equal to, even to be part of the West. This provided a stimulus that is still active today. The symptoms of Western acculturation first began to appear among the upper classes and intellectuals, but as modernization and economic development advanced, acculturation gradually spread until even the most ordinary people were affected.

Acculturation can be seen in such areas as taste, which is determined more by emotional than by rational factors. A survey I made in 1954 of male preferences in women revealed that males even in the rural districts have gradually shifted from a predilection for traditional Japanese norms in feminine beauty to modern, Western types.[2] Buildings also reveal a penchant for Western styles. In rural areas where farmers have been able to get large sums by selling off their land to industry, one sees numerous new homes built in or near the villages from the proceeds of their sales. Almost all of them are in Western styles. The number of artists and intellectuals who retain the traditional Japanese esthetic sense is decreasing, and tastes in food, clothing, architecture, and decor are fast becoming westernized throughout the population. The number of Japanese string players in European orchestras is rising, and Japanese win more prizes in international music competitions than contestants from the countries where Western music was born. These are social phenomena whose roots are in the Meiji cultural revolution.

The westernization policy of the Meiji government was initiated by the upper class, and it had wide popular support. Even Nakae Chōmin (1847–1901), one of the leading ideologues of the Freedom and Popular Rights Movement, accepted the idea of westernization. But Chōmin, who was sometimes called the "Rousseau of the East," criticized the government for its failure to go far enough. He believed the whole political system should be overhauled and democratic institutions introduced. His ultimate goal, in fact, was to remake Japan in the image of Europe, "to create a solidly European island-state in the East."

There was some opposition to the government's westernization policy on the part of Shintō priests and other conservative-reactionary groups, but it was remarkably little. Generally, anything Western—because it was Western—was considered to have status, and that helped palliate antagonism. Acculturation in the Meiji era was synonymous with westernization, and westernization was synonymous with modernization.

## Necessity of Revolution

In essay three, "Tradition Versus Modernization," we noted six factors in successful modernization: (1) democracy in political system; (2) capitalism in economy; (3) shift from handicraft to factory production in industry, accompanied by advances in science and technology; (4) universal compulsory education; (5) national military force; and (6) psychological liberation from communal life and the growth of individualism. These six factors are not exhaustive, and they are so closely interrelated that it is hard to separate them. The understanding of modernization can vary, depending on which index one emphasizes, and so I will comment briefly on each.

(1)  For our purposes, I will describe democracy in government simply as something that is not autocratic rule by a privileged class or elite group. That qualifies the Soviet Union, China, and other countries with socialist systems as democratic countries. Leftist-oriented critics generally regard prewar Japan as a semifeudal and semimodernized nation whose "autocratic" imperial institution dominated the political system, while "parasitic" landowners exploited the predominantly rural population. But the abolition of the system of social ranks in Japan and the achievement of considerable social equality are accomplishments that perhaps surpass what even the modern democracies of England, France, and others were able to do. It is debatable whether or not Japan has fully modernized in the sense of building a democratic political system, but we can say with assurance that this country has one of the most highly advanced mass societies in the world.

(2)  What I called "capitalism" in my earlier essay should probably have been rendered as "national concentration of capital," or "capital accumulation on a national scale," for the term was meant to include the state capitalism of the U.S.S.R., or of any country, apart from political system. Japanese capitalism may have been distorted by having been instituted from the top by the government, rather than from among the people, as in England, but that was inevitable as Japan was still an underdeveloped country. Japanese capitalism is still closely

bound to state authority, but today the same is true of many other countries.

(3)   Manufacturing made huge strides during the Tokugawa period, and as the division of labor grew more sophisticated, it worked to the advantage of industrialization. One reason many Asian countries have had difficulty in industrializing may be that long years under colonial rule interrupted the development of feudal systems which could have served as a base for commercialization and industrialization.

(4), (5)   Regarding education and a national military force, the abolition of the old social class system in Japan had an inestimable impact on the type of social equality that now prevails. Unlike England today, where the children of the rich and poor still attend different grade schools, in Japan no discrimination has been practiced since the founding of the grade-school system. Primary education became compulsory in 1870 in England and in 1872 in Japan, considerably before the United States (1918) or Germany (1919). Japanese may be the most enthusiastic people in the world about education. In the Meiji era Japan already had grade schools virtually wherever there were children, and those schools were as good or better than European grade schools. The principle of equality dominated the military, as well; it was possible even for the son of a farmer to become a general.

(6)   It is fair to say that Japan failed in cultivating individualism. It did not grow during the Meiji era, and it has not fully developed today. This is one of the indexes of how much modernization has achieved, but individualism is not necessarily a desirable goal for late-starters trying to modernize. When industrialization and national education have reached a certain point and when the standard of living has gone beyond hand-to-mouth subsistence, then there may arise a new concern for the dignity and freedom of the individual. Walter Prescott Webb, author of *The Great Frontier*, claims that in Europe individualism, democracy, and the principle of equality remained no more than ideas, or ideals, until long after 1500 when territorial expansion had brought power and great wealth to Europeans. European capitalism eventually yielded dividends on capital investment at the rate of 10,000 percent. An average population density of twenty-six people per square mile dropped to less

than five with the huge increase in colonial lands. Webb argues that the growth of liberalism demanded that materialistic base. But once an industrial society develops beyond a certain point, the freedom of the individual becomes more tenuous. According to Webb, the advanced countries have reached this point: "The individual is compelled to answer many of these questions in a way that adds little to his ego. He is curbed on all sides by corporations or government agencies or labor unions, or associations, and the chief choice left to him is a choice of curbers." For Japan, a poor and underdeveloped country, planning for modernization with the aim of fostering individualism would have been counterproductive.

Let us think once more about what modernization means. Using objective standards, could we not define modernization as synonymous with industrialization? The other five indexes may be applied within the broad area of industrialization. If the process of industrializing is not to be the exclusive sphere of a privileged class but is to be supported by the people as a whole, the abolition of social classes and diffusion of education are necessary conditions. And if we agree with British economist Joan Robinson that a socialist revolution is the most effective means for an underdeveloped country to catch up, then the democratization of government and state concentration of capital are also necessary for industrialization.

In the end, however, if modernization is synonymous only with a higher degree of industrialization, one wonders about the quality of the objective. More advanced industrialization might only accelerate the tempo of life and further destroy our peace of mind, threatening us with worse and more widespread pollution and other instruments of sickness and death. Yet because industrialization elevates the material standard of living and can satisfy certain desires for comfort, it continues to be a primary goal for those who have not achieved it. Now that industrialization dominates the main currents of contemporary history, no single country or nation can avoid its influence. There are no more unknown and isolated lands. Even primitive tribes have been forced into a money economy and are compelled to purchase industrial products. In our time, just to survive, industrialization is unavoidable. The men who led the

Meiji Restoration and their contemporaries also recognized that their survival lay in development, and development meant modernization. Their attitude served the needs of that particular era well, and their attempt at modernization, though it inevitably brought distortions, can be called successful on the whole.

What are the reasons for that success? I do not wish to downplay the efforts of our grandfathers, but I think luck was the primary factor. The geographic and historic conditions of mid-nineteenth-century Japan were favorable, including the very important fact that it remained an independent sovereign state. Because of that, the country was never drained of its resources by a colonial power and it never had to go through the agony of a nationalistic independence movement inevitably ending in confrontation with the metropolitan country. When such confrontation does occur, the antagonist is likely to be modern and capitalistic. The leaders of the opposition movement invoke tradition as the symbol and inspiration of their resistance, and so they are very likely to have antimodern and anticapitalist sentiments. The position taken by Mahatma Gandhi, for example, was useful in the struggle for India's independence, but in the end such attitudes undercut the essential premises of modernization.

In contrast, Japan was an independent state when it embarked on the road to modernization. That is one reason that Japan never clung intractably to tradition and why very few Japanese were ever seriously repelled by westernization or modernization. In a sense, they had been prepared by the small but steady trickle of European knowledge that continued to seep into Japan through Nagasaki via the Dutch language, even after Christianity was banned. Certainly their knowledge of the West was unsophisticated and incomplete; while they fully appreciated the military genius of Napoleon, for example, they regarded the French Revolution as an uprising of bandits who slaughtered their own king. "Liberty, equality, fraternity" had no meaning for pre-Meiji Japanese. But Japanese kept in touch with world affairs in their own way, unlike Chinese, and that later proved to be a strong advantage when they set out to modernize their country.

The reactions by Japan and China to the arrival of Catholic missionaries in the sixteenth century were quite different, revealing divergent attitudes toward Western culture. Both were confident of the merits, even superiority, of their own culture and institutions, and neither was inclined to defer to Europeans in the slightest. Sansom observes that "the Japanese felt themselves in no sense inferior to Europeans, while the Chinese professed to feel themselves in every sense superior." To this day Chinese retain the same strong confidence in their culture. China, Asia's most advanced culture, remained bound to its tradition, but that attitude prevented Chinese from looking outside and it dampened their curiosity. Ultimately it caused China to fall behind while Japan surged forward in modernization. On the other hand, Japanese, until recent times backward and perennially on the lookout for what foreign peoples and cultures had to offer them, were more open to the possibility of new things and techniques even when these would supplant traditional ones. China's late nineteenth- and early twentieth-century pioneers in modernization toiled in vain. China became a semicolonial state; the ruling class turned into compradors. The contradictions that had weakened imperial China from within became so pronounced that men like Lu Hsun felt forced to cry out to Chinese youth to sever themselves from tradition. The tumult of events and ideas led to a fusion of nationalism and radical social revolution, and finally to the Great Cultural Revolution. I think there were defensible reasons for China's attitude toward Western culture, but I do not agree with Takeuchi Yoshimi that modernization which proceeds without resistance to westernization is corrupt.[3] He is correct that Japan's modernization was basically superficial, but if every modernizing nation, including those without well-established traditions, had the rigid, idealistic standards of Takeuchi, they would probably never get anywhere.

## One Chance for Nationalism

Even more important for Japan than the so-called Dutch Studies was the spread of education during the two and one-half centuries of peace under the Tokugawa. During the mid-Tokugawa period, private schools called *terakoya* ("temple schools") became very widespread. Ronald Dore surmises that by about 1868 the literacy rate was 43 percent for men and 15 percent for women.[4] No statistics regarding literacy in France at the time of the French Revolution are available, but according to F. Brunot the number of French people who were able to sign their names when they got married is estimated at 47 percent for men and 27 percent for women.[5] At least they could write their names, but literacy in France at that time is thought to have been lower than in Japan at the mid-nineteenth century. Literacy in Russia in 1917 was 15 percent. It was about that level in China in 1949, and in India on the eve of independence in 1948 it was approximately 10 percent. A relatively high rate of literacy in Japan was undeniably important in 1867 and 1868 and later in minimizing bloodshed during the Meiji Restoration, and it greatly facilitated the process of modernization thereafter.

Notwithstanding favorable conditions to begin with, the driving force behind Japan's successful modernization was nationalism. Lafcadio Hearn once commented that no matter how psychologists strain to generalize about the lack of individuality among Japanese, there can be no question that Japan as a nation-state has a much stronger individuality than Western nations. He seems to have observed accurately the efficiency of Japanese nationalism, as well as its uniqueness.

The term "nationalism" was first used in the nineteenth century. It did not occur in French until 1812, but "patriotism" had long been in use. Patriotism connotes the attachment of a group or society to the place where they live and the love for that place that inspires them to protect it. Thus patriotic sentiment is universal, and it runs through all human history. But nationalism is the extension of sentiment and awareness from the local area to the entire sphere called "nation" and the channeling of the people's sense of solidarity to become a source of energy. This is a modern idea. Nationalism in Western Europe arose on the base provided by the emergence of absolute monarchy and the bourgeoisie. Patriotism was transformed when the French Revolution destroyed the old class system and opened new intellectual horizons. As the idea of popular sovereignty grew stronger and spread, more and more people began to identify with the nation. They sought the independence, integration, and development of the state, as well as their own civil freedoms, for the first time placing loyalty to the state above other loyalties. Nationalism tends to dissolve class consciousness rather than strengthen it, but in the West, it was inspired by the rise of the bourgeoisie and grew side by side with capitalism.

Pre-Meiji Japanese feudalism was stabilized in a system of shogunate government under which were about three hundred clans, whose lords were called daimyo. Some historians identify the kind of nationalism that emerged from the feudal system as an immature "early nationalism," but such a distinction seems gratuitous. The Japanese are a relatively homogeneous people whose national culture has spread throughout their islands. Industry had already reached the manufacturing stage by the Meiji era, and there was a standard language, although dialects were still in use. The methods of agriculture were the same throughout the country. Japan's national unity was probably stronger than in France before the revolution. Agriculture in southern France, for example, was quite different from that in the north, and written law prevailed in southern France while northern France followed common law. Furthermore the whole country was sprinkled with *octroi*, toll-houses that marked the borders between provinces.

In Tokugawa Japan, on the other hand, relatively good communication and common ways of life among the regions encouraged similar responses. The people began to chafe at the political divisions, finding the clan divisions increasingly unnatural. When Japan's modern nationalism did arise, it was given momentum by the sense of crisis generated by the impact of the West.

Japanese nationalism did not just naturally emerge, however. The leaders of the Meiji Revolution deliberately set about to create a united front by carefully fashioning a new imperial system from the fabric of national tradition over a thousand years old. I will not go into the unique political and social system that was the Japanese imperial institution, but one point is worth noting. Because the emperor was the commander-in-chief of the military and the pivotal figure in Japanese militarism until 1945, he is often identified as the final locus of responsibility for the developments that led to the Pacific War. Apart from the political and ideological effects of the imperial system, however, it proved to be a built-in vehicle of the nation's modernization. It provided an instrument for national management whose value was proved in 1945 and after when the U.S. Occupation forces worked through the system to maintain peace and public order and get the economy back on its feet.

Given two factors, the unique institution of the imperial system and the reluctant, uneven development of civil liberties —despite precipitous modernization—Japanese nationalism cannot be seen in parallel with European. The character of European nationalism was conditioned by political history, by the unifying influence exerted by the Roman Empire over Western Europe long before the rise of nation-states, and it inherited the universalism already deeply implanted by the Roman Catholic church. Even when the nation-states of Europe became definite political entities and eventually confronted each other, they remained particular units within the context of a new universalism based on natural law and enlightenment thought, and they were held together by a conscious international solidarity. In contrast, Japan became a nation-state by integrating 300 feudal clans, whose memory died hard. In effect, Japan became one great clan. Unable to rid themselves of the patterns fostered under the clan system, Japanese could think only in terms of power relations when they looked toward other nations, other "clans" of the world. They lacked awareness of Japan as a member of an international society.

The culture of the Japanese people, living together in isolation from the rest of the world for two millennia, became highly refined, but it never crossed the seas to spread into other lands. That is probably the main reason it remained a particularistic culture. Most countries outside Western Europe lack a base in universalism. But if we discount any nationalism that is not grounded in universalism, we are rejecting virtually all Asian and African nationalism. Thanks largely to colonial domination, those peoples, except the Chinese, were never able to develop their own type of universalism. Europeans imposed their ideas on them as the only universalism. Today, however, European thinking and values are rapidly declining in influence, even in the West, and it has become abundantly clear that we cannot measure other parts of the world by Western standards alone.

An idea is invariably transformed as it spreads out from its birthplace. Sooner or later the original idea may be completely superseded by the variants and die out. This is what is happening to the classical nationalism of Europe. Japanese nationalism is probably one of the first of its variants, while the nationalism of the Soviet Union and China are more recent examples of this transformation. The Marxist formula posits dissolution of the state after the completion of revolution, but in both China and the Soviet Union, nationalism is still a very potent fact of life.

Attempts to modernize in the newly independent countries of Asia and Africa rely heavily on nationalism to mobilize the people, but often nationalism seems to accomplish little. It may be that in many cases the country failed to carry through a revolution that could completely liberate the people from their past. Marxist critics claim that the Meiji Restoration left nothing but a submissive populace servile to authority, but I believe that the sense of liberation it produced by wiping out the feudal status system, with all its ramifications, strengthened the nationalist consciousness and greatly facilitated modernization.

Japanese nationalism had some negative effects, also. For example, it reinforced the fickleness and frivolity of the Japanese people, of which Nakae Chōmin was so critical.[6] Modern Japanese tend to change their minds or course of action all too easily. The nineteenth-century patriots, having loudly clamored for everyone to "revere the emperor and expel the barbarians," suddenly turned around and started pushing for the opening of the country. The only way this seemingly illogical about-face can be explained is in terms of nationalism. Japan adopted the French military system, but suddenly converted to the Prussian when Napoleon III was imprisoned after the Franco-Prussian War (1870–71). Sakuta Keiichi, the sociologist, explains, "There is a deep-rooted tradition in Japan of accepting a given situation as fate and accommodating oneself to the prevailing circumstances."[7] This tradition encourages flexibility in a society whose forms are established and whose institutions demand conformity. This society, closed and homogeneous, is not fertile ground for the growth of logic, rhetoric, or abstract reasoning. A society such as Japan's, where abstract principles for their own sake are not particularly respected, does not encourage the determination that enables one to stick to a position no matter what the circumstances. The principle that matters most is the principle of adjustment and accommodation. Whether it is based on intellectual or emotional response, this is what underlies the art of living, as nature demonstrates in the life patterns of all creatures. Thus, at the source of Japanese thought and behavior, instead of abstract universals, we find a type of practical naturalism that emphasizes life itself; and as the basis for action, we find accommodation to changing situations.

By the mid-nineteenth century, the poor and backward country of Japan was determined to survive the blows aimed by a demanding world. Nationalism was born and grew more intense as the country mobilized to fend for itself. In the long run Japan succeeded, but I believe that nationalism can be effective only once in the life of a given people; for Japan, it has already carried out that function. For both Japan and the world, nationalism in this country has served its purpose and may never again be able to make a positive contribution, particularly when it can never again be strong enough to be effective. Rather, it is Japan's turn to help developing countries mobilize the energy of their nationalism for positive ends, suppressing the remnants of nationalism in Japan that would thwart such an effort.

# Notes

1.  G. B. Sansom, *The Western World and Japan* (New York: Knopf, 1951), p. 398.
2.  See essay two, "Seven Beauties and the Modernization of Rural Tastes."
3.  Takeuchi Yoshimi, "Chūgoku no kindai to Nihon no kindai" [Modernization in China and Japan] (Tokyo, 1948).
4.  Ronald Dore, *Education in Tokugawa Japan* (London: Routledge and Kegan Paul, 1965).
5.  Ferdinand Brunot, *Histoire de la Langue Française*, vol. 7 (Paris: Colin, 1926-34).
6.  Nakae Chōmin, *Ichinen Yūhan* [One and One-Half Years] (Tokyo: Hakubunkan, 1901).
7.  Sakuta Keiichi, "Jikkan shinkō no kōzō" [The Experiential Approach], *Tenbō*, June, 1965.

# 10

## Japan's Third Opening

IT may sound extraordinary to suggest that now, in the late twentieth century, Japan must open its doors to interchange with other nations. But that is exactly what a great many people in Japan, and even more elsewhere in the world, are doing. Have they all forgotten that Japan has already opened its doors twice, once in the Meiji era and again after World War II? Today's critics claim, however, that Japan's "openings" on the previous two occasions were never brought to completion. This time the effort must succeed and it must be spontaneous, stimulated from within. It must not be a reluctant effort, compelled by external pressure, as it was in the past. This demand seems to be based on sound common sense and on the recognition that Japan simply cannot afford to be isolated.

Isolationism is a broad term, but in the sense of cultural isolationism, it can have a heavy impact on the most basic attitudes. Cultural isolationism is strong in this country, yet few Japanese, even if they are conscious that it is a force in their relations with other peoples, would admit it. Most, if asked, would heartily endorse much greater interchange and communication with the world. Nonetheless I suspect that on a deeper level they are quite satisfied with their "small, sweet home" just as it is, and that few have little desire for the interference or change that might arise from more active mutual involvement with other peoples. One cultural anthropologist talks about cultural

Originally presented as a lecture, entitled "Kokusai komyunikeishon to Nihon bunka," at the Asahi International Symposium, 1979.

interchange in terms of a communications apparatus; he says that in Japan's case, while its receiving equipment is in perfectly good shape, the transmitters are not working.[1] Japan's Kyodo News Service, for example, is one of the few major international news agencies that does not transmit news; it only receives. The observations of this scholar drew wide attention, but despite their penetrating accuracy, very few Japanese have taken them seriously enough to try to initiate the long-term remedies that he warns are necessary.

## Barrier of Complacency

Perhaps, in fact, they do not want to. Japanese respect the principle of cultural interchange, and they readily acknowledge the objective need for more, but in reality they tolerate one-way traffic only. The mechanism for their traffic control is a set of assumptions. They take it for granted that the poet Rimbaud, being French, can be understood by anyone, even Japanese, but Bashō, their own master of haiku, is beyond the comprehension of non-Japanese. Contentment and a new kind of pride in Japanese culture seem to have become stronger recently, but these feelings do not necessarily generate the desire to make the culture more accessible to others. As more and more people experienced the benefits of economic growth beginning around 1960, the tendency to become complacent grew stronger. This is a disturbing development, but before we embark on a discussion of ways to improve cultural exchange between Japan and other countries, let me make some brief comments on the culture as a whole.

The philosophy or essence of culture is important, but here I am more interested in the sociological, practical aspects of culture as it affects daily life in Japan. I am not concerned with such traditional elements as simplicity, spare beauty, or profundity, or the ancient arts of Nō and classical dance; they are relevant in this context only if they can be identified in urban and rural life, right now. We can no longer pretend that Japan's ancient artistic traditions represent our contemporary culture, but it is important to know how and why the culture changed. For that, we need to review a little history.

An important fact to consider is that from the eighth century or earlier until 1945, Japan was never conquered by another people, race, or nation. Its people were able to develop a stable, racially homogeneous society in their own way, cut off by the sea from unwanted incursions from outside. During the two and one-half centuries of Tokugawa rule, which lasted from 1603 until 1868, much of the world was deep in the turmoil of burgeoning overseas trade, exploration, and colonization, while Japan kept its doors closed tight. Undisturbed, the government enforced peace and order throughout the nation. Deeper than political nationalism, a psychological commitment to "small, sweet home" was nurtured during that time, and it remains to this day. It is a commitment that makes sharing and exchange with outsiders difficult. Japan has been permanently changed in some respects by the influence of other cultures, but Japanese have always been eclectic with regard to what they import. This was true even after World War II, under the Occupation, which was a peaceful one, in any case. In return, excepting *ukiyoe*, perhaps, and judo or ikebana, this country has exerted little cultural influence on the world. Part of the reason is the Japanese inability to assert themselves and their culture in the same way that Westerners, especially the French, have done.

Thus, while we speak of an exclusive commitment to "home" on the one hand, we can also identify an uncertainty about that "home" which prevents strong self-assertion. Think back to 1868 and the years that followed, when Japanese performed a wholesale attic-cleaning. To prevent colonization by the West and to strengthen their ability to defend themselves and resist, they had to open up and receive an entirely new technology, a new set of ideas, and vast amounts of new information. The old precepts, strategies, and priorities, which derived in large part from Chinese culture, had been rooted in Japan since the beginning of the historical era. These had to be discarded. There is something fresh and youthful in the decision to modernize everything at once, completely. In Japan's case, it produced a genuine cultural revolution. But there is an element of flighty rashness, also, in abandoning traditions so abruptly. The effort did not abate, and the rapid development into the modern nation and super-economy we know today is the result of a cultural revolution that began almost a century ago. But perhaps because recent changes have been so rapid and so radical, they have left Japanese at a loss as to how to explain themselves.

The main significance of this cultural revolution lies in its unprecedented thoroughness, in both content and participation, and in the fact that what was discarded was replaced with something new. It was a constructive revolution. But in some ways it required an unusually long time. When I was studying in Paris just before the outbreak of the Pacific War, Fujiwara Yoshie, a Japanese opera singer, came to France. A public performance was out of the question, and so it was arranged that Fujiwara would sing before a small gathering of French intellectuals. The drift of reviews carried in two or three newspapers the next day was entirely negative. The critics taunted and ridiculed the Japanese singer for his poor performance; it was a pathetic imitation of Western singing, one quipped. Undoubtedly his technique and style were mediocre by French standards, but what the critics did not see was Fujiwara as a product of cultural revolution. Here was a young man, undaunted by the obstacles as he tried to absorb the sensitivity and technique of an art from a different culture, enthusiastically pushing on. His zeal and industriousness made no impression. The critics were blind to the possibility that, years later, one of Fujiwara's students would become a prima donna in Israel, and more Japanese than French would take the first prize at the Paris Conservatoire. Recently Japanese have been outdistancing others in many areas besides music, most notably in industrial production.

Western styles and tastes did not spread much beyond the upper classes and intelligentsia until after World War II, but during the postwar period they began to touch the lives of everyone. The change in lifestyles and thinking was accelerated after the beginning of rapid economic growth around 1960. It had taken about a century for the effects of Western culture to penetrate the whole country, but at that point we can say that the cultural revolution was complete. Then, interestingly, the nationwide popular acceptance of Western culture seemed in turn to generate a new desire to reassess Japan's indigenous culture. While virtually everyone had abandoned traditional dress, hairstyles, and ceremonies, there arose an intellectual

nativist movement whose ideas reflected a self-conscious awareness of Japan's new status as an economic giant. An implicit
given in this deliberate focus on the indigenous culture was
the new confidence among Japanese in their society. It was generated in part by the economy's spectacular successes, but also
by a more realistic understanding and appraisal of the West
gained through intensive firsthand study and observation.

It is easier to appreciate the impact of the nativist movement
when one considers that Western, not Japanese, ideologies were
the base for revolutionary, antiestablishment intellectuals from
the Meiji Restoration onward, most conspicuously in the 1920s
and early 1930s. The government consistently pushed westernization in the technical and industrial fields, but it remained
conservative in basic social philosophy and ethics. It was severely
antipathetic to Marxism and socialism. Pressed to search outside
their traditions for an underlying thought system, intellectuals
did not recognize the value in some of their own native systems of
ideas until after Western ideas had all but buried them. Just the
opposite occurred in the colonized countries of Asia, especially
in Islamic countries. One might say that Japanese woke up to
the strengths of their own traditions and ways of thought only
upon discovering that their old culture had almost disappeared.
The importance of that loss was underscored by the crumbling
dream of socialism, and disillusionment in the course of events
in the Soviet Union and other communist countries. Only then
did many Japanese begin to study popular culture and the works
of Yanagita Kunio and other nativist folklorists.

## Creating a Two-Way Flow

The very existence of a movement to reassess indigenous traditions is symptomatic of the dominance of Western elements in
popular culture today. Women's magazines, for example, all
seem to have Western titles—*Woman, Madame, Mademoiselle*—and
products like cosmetics must have names taken from French or
English in order to sell well. Few Japanese ever wear traditional
kimono and no one binds their hair in the old-fashioned topknot
or chignon, except for special occasions. Many foreigners believe
that the Shinto wedding ceremony conducted in the shrines is

an ancient Japanese tradition, but in fact it was introduced in quite recent times under the influence of Western-style wedding ceremonies.

But Japanese still tend to downplay the less exotic, newer elements in their culture when presenting it to others. The Nō drama, to use a classic example, is by no means dead, but it is neither contemporary nor popular. Nonetheless, foreign advertisements and travel brochures depict Nō masters and Nō literature, and films on the Nō are sent abroad, while few foreigners are told anything about the musical revues, modern plays, and Western dramas that most Japanese go to see. Hence we have the professor in the Southeast Asian country going to the Japanese consulate in his city, then on to Japanese firms, trying to find out more about Nō. Much to his surprise and disappointment, not one of the Japanese he talks with has ever even seen a Nō performance. At that point he gives up, and asks them instead to tell him about the arts that ordinary Japanese enjoy most. In this case, using the classical arts to publicize a culture only created an embarrassed, clumsy retreat by the representatives of that culture.

The failure to place Nō in realistic context when projecting an image of Japan creates nothing but frustration among people who want to understand the culture. The bewildered foreigner wonders why Japanese claim a super-sense of esthetics and delicacy, but instead of offering the beauty of their culture to the world, they send vast shipments of their industrial products and proceed to push mercilessly into the other fellow's economy. At least Japanese could help others to understand the link between the traditional arts and modern industry by explaining, for example, the hierarchical *iemoto* system in schools of tea ceremony, flower arrangement, and so forth, and pointing out the many parallels that exist between the structure of these vast organizations and the large corporations.

No matter how much the two types of organization share, however, modern institutions and corporations do not allow sacrifice for the sake of preserving tradition. Japan cannot always afford to preserve the good and the beautiful for their own sake. The rows of historic buildings in an ancient city may be replaced, bit by bit, by ugly, cheap high-rise apartments, and gaudy neon signs in the Hong Kong mode may invade the street. The result is a hodgepodge of new styles and old relics that coexist in a typical slice of present-day Japanese urban scenery.

Visitors to Japan a century ago could usually find something to criticize in the society if they wished to, but most were lavish in their praise of the understated esthetics and the simplicity of design and decor. Very few failed to notice the flower arrangement set in the alcove with a hanging scroll above it. Compared with such spare decoration, a modern living room is inevitably small, and it is often cluttered with knickknacks from trips abroad and reproductions of famous Western paintings hanging on the walls. Many contemporary visitors think the term "simplicity" has no place in a description of Japanese culture today. The same can be said of cooking. The Japanese who still gets most protein from fish or soybean products, for example, is a rarity. Japanese first tasted beef in the late nineteenth century, and meat consumption now is eight times the prewar level. It would be impossible for a people whose diet had changed so radically not to change in their outlook and sense of values. Here, too, it is clearly impossible to explain modern Japan in terms of its traditional aristocratic culture.

Another important side of Japan about which little direct information is offered the world is its mass culture. Japan's mass society is probably the most advanced in the world, but scholars and intellectuals do not emphasize this aspect, and the Japanese government actually seems to conceal it in films, publications, and other public relations efforts in other countries. Mass society is one of the premise of modern Japan and its culture; one must be aware of it to even begin to understand the country. It is also useful to know that this mass culture has centuries-old roots. Edo (now Tokyo) had a population of approximately one million during much of the Tokugawa period. At one time it was the largest city in the world. Although the society was feudalistic, even then an urban popular culture flourished and brought public entertainment in music, drama, and story-telling to greatly refined heights. An eighteenth-century best-selling writer could count on a readership smaller than that of Jean-Jacques Rousseau's *Julie, ou la nouvelle Héloïse,* but nonetheless one of the biggest in the world.

The popular culture of urban Japanese during the feudal era was indirectly supported by an absolutist government, on account of which Japan achieved a stability and national unity far stronger than that of prerevolutionary France. When the four-tiered rank system was abolished during the Meiji Revolution, national unity was already a fact. Removing class barriers paved the way for the achievement of one of the most egalitarian mass societies anywhere, and it was based on the belief that all people are equal. According to the results of a recent survey by the Organisation for Economic Co-operation and Development, the countries with the smallest gap between rich and poor are Japan and the Scandinavian countries. The country with the greatest gap is, ironically, France, the cradle of the idea of equality.

A commitment to social equality and the possibility—backed by economic growth—of mass education through college are important factors in Japan's mass culture. They provide the base for some remarkable institutions, one of which is the Japan Broadcasting Corporation (NHK). The scale of its broadcasting activities is probably larger than in any other country, and it maintains generally high quality. The big national newspapers have circulations of more than seven million. Largely because of the giant newspapers and the major television stations, the earnings of Dentsu are higher than any other advertising agency in Japan or abroad. In a society whose information flow is dominated by such organizations and whose people all receive virtually the same compulsory education through grade nine, cultural uniformity is bound to be extraordinarily high.

A fad in Japan does not just take hold among urban or regional groups, but sweeps through most of the nation, and quickly. Enthusiasm for certain sports is widely shared, too, especially baseball. This sport offers a good example of what can happen in such a society. Every August there is a senior high school baseball tournament. It is carefully organized to include virtually every school throughout the country. School teams representing the prefectures vie for a highly coveted national championship. Even though the competition is the project of one newspaper firm, all the rival newspapers give it the same coverage. Of course, wide coverage gives publicity to the teams' hometowns, but it is noteworthy that here, as in many other cases, it is considered more beneficial to share than to engage in competition that might undermine one's competitor.

If contemporary Japanese culture must be understood in terms of popular culture, the same is true for literature. Translations of and studies on classical Japanese literature, the works of Mori Ōgai, Natsume Sōseki, Tanizaki Jun'ichirō, Kawabata Yasunari, Mishima Yukio, Abe Kōbō, and other modern writers are most numerous, but these authors do not attract the largest readership in Japan. Books most widely read are those by Inoue Yasushi, Matsumoto Seichō, Shiba Ryōtarō, and others, yet studies on their works are relatively few, especially in other countries. The serious student of Japanese culture should also be aware of the large number of weekly magazines, many with vast circulations. A survey of these periodicals provides a very good overview of the seemingly limitless range of subjects Japanese read about and reveals a lot about one source of their knowledge and frivolous sophistication. For someone to become truly an "expert" on Japanese culture he must augment his knowledge of the classical culture, ancient or modern, with a realistic appreciation of the society of the masses. The modern era may seem to have played havoc with the Japan of pre-westernization times, but the energy it generated produced a vigorous new cultural milieu, and a people whose sensibilities are geared to that milieu.

Let me say a word about the term *shominteki*, which conveys a sense of the burgher, or townsman. It has the connotation of feeling completely at ease with the common people, of sharing their tastes and enjoying their company. It is naturally taken for granted that a small shopkeeper is *shominteki*, but when used in reference to a high official, professor, artist, or someone of noteworthy professional achievement, it amounts to respect and praise. The late Dr. Tomonaga Shin'ichirō, the Nobel Prize-winning physicist, was a well-loved figure in Japan because he had that quality of sharing popular tastes. He was fond of bawdy *rakugo* comedy and the cheap saké sold at the tiny, cheap *oden* (hotchpotch) night-stalls. There are differences in status according to profession, perhaps, or wealth, but the popular culture pervades all strata. David Riesman, the American sociologist, did not expect to find among Japanese university professors an avid interest in professional baseball, television or movies. He is undoubtedly not alone in having been unaware of the strength of Japan's popular culture and its mass base.

It may be that of all the important factors, the language barrier most directly hampers significant exchange between Japan and other countries. Edwin O. Reischauer has pointed out that foreign-language education in Japan is still not up to the task of erasing the image of Japan as a tongue-tied giant or a stranger loitering around the international community. It is true, for example, that only a handful of Japanese politicians can converse adequately in a foreign language. Japanese must do something about this, but the basic block is not an inability to learn languages. It is the isolationism that underlies their sense of culture. More immediately, it is the fact that writers, scholars, and critics have sufficient outlets and appreciative readers at home: they sense no need to produce work in foreign languages to sell abroad.

But there is a more basic problem. While Japanese struggle with foreign languages, there are very few intellectuals in other countries who can speak and read Japanese. How many non-Japanese in other countries are there who read Japanese-language newspapers published in Japan? Probably very few. One reason may be the difficulty of the written language, but more important is the lack of interest in Japanese culture. If so then we must think hard about what this means for the future of Japan's relations with other countries.

Personally, I support the policy of simplifying the Japanese language, which was recommended after World War II. If the language were made clearer and easier to understand, more people would learn it. But we are now running up against a new barrier of conservatism, a growing belief, rooted in new confidence, that Japanese culture should remain as it is, and this idea is being extended to the language, also.

There is no single way to improve the quality of communication Japan carries on with other countries. There may be, however, a precondition for a genuine two-way flow, and that is willingness by Japanese to leave aside the principles of the traditional culture and concentrate on the practical realities when they present their culture abroad. They would have to take new pride in the culture of today—not just the economy— and learn how to assert its character. Certain concrete measures would help a great deal. One is to simplify—or should I say internationalize—the national language. There is no longer any way for Japan to survive without close ties with many nations, and if we are concerned with our future, I think we must, before anything else, facilitate the means of communication.

# Note

1. See Umesao Tadao, "Escape from Cultural Isolation," *The Japan Interpreter*, vol. IX, No. 2, 1974.

# 11

# The Secondary Art of Modern Haiku

THE quality of Japanese creative writing since the Meiji era is mediocre. It may be that inadequate intellectual and social awareness on the part of the writers accounts for this, but a distinctly casual attitude toward creative writing prevails among Japanese,[1] and haiku is a prime example. Yet whenever I am invited to speak on this subject, I encounter vehement objections, especially regarding haiku. This never fails to impress me, for it reflects how deeply rooted haiku writing is in this country. Nonetheless, as we keep on working to rebuild our culture as well as our nation, now committed to peace, we will have to reappraise the entire tradition of haiku, going back to Matsuo Bashō.

Since the end of the Pacific War, as before, haiku by the leading modern poets has been appearing in journals and newspapers, but I never paid much attention to it until quite recently. Not long ago, however, my daughter came to me with some haiku reproduced in her primary-school Japanese-language text, asking for an explanation.

Yuki nokoru
itadaki hitotsu
kuni-zakai

Snow lingers
on the lone ridge
bordering the provinces
—Masaoka Shiki

Originally published as "Dai Ni Geijutsu ron" in *Sekai*, September 1946. The editor wishes to acknowledge the collaboration of Hiroaki Sato in the checking and revision of this translation.

Akai tsubaki                A red camellia
shiroi tsubaki to           has dropped, then
ochi ni keri                a white camellia
                                —Kawahigashi Hekigodō

And then, she brought a couple she had composed for a homework assignment for me to criticize:

Suna-bokori                 Dust billows
torakku tōru                as a truck passes
natsu no michi              the summer road

Yoku mireba                 Now I see it!
sora ni wa tsuki ga         there in the sky the moon
ukanderu                    floats

That aroused me to start reading the haiku by professionals
printed in the journals lying in my study. Most children take
little interest in "flowers, birds, the wind, and the moon." As
the second example of my daughter's work shows, they may notice
that there is a moon in the sky only when required to produce a
haiku for school, and so one can hardly expect much. Nevertheless, some children can put seventeen syllables together
quite cleverly, and if they are encouraged and become good
at it, they may take as models works of the modern poets.

After reading more of the recently published works by the
modern haiku poets and thinking about the indignant response
and questions my lectures had provoked, I was inspired to
attempt a little test. From the materials at hand, I selected one
haiku apiece by ten of the more prominent modern poets, as well
as five by unknown or amateur poets. I arranged them in random
order in a list without the authors' names. Undoubtedly one could
come up with all kinds of interesting results if one subjected
such a list to the kind of experiment I. A. Richards conducted
in *Practical Criticism: A Study of Literary Judgement*,[2] but for the
moment I simply showed my list to a few colleagues and students
of mine and asked their opinion of the poems on it. I invite
the reader also to examine the fifteen poems below, and (1) list

them in order of excellence, (2) guess which are by professional
haiku poets, and (3) distinguish the poems by professionals from
those of the amateurs. (The poets are identified at the end of
this essay.)

1. Megumu ka to        "So you're budding,"
   ōkina miki o         I say, caressing
   nadenagara          the great trunk

2. Hatsu chō no         A first butterfly
   ware o mawarite     has circled me,
   izuko ni ka          and now whereto?

3. Seku hipoku-         Coughing hypocrite:
   ritto Bētōben        Beethoven resounds
   hibiku asa           in the morning

4. Kayu-bara no         Without a solid meal
   obotsukanashi ya    I am weary
   hana no yama       climbing the hills in bloom

5. Yūnami no           The twilight waves
   kizami sometaru     are rippling, tinted
   yū suzushi           the evening cool

6. Taishiki ya          Above the undulating
   uneri no ue no      seine for bream,
   Awajishima          Awaji Island

7. Koko ni nete         "He used to sleep
   imashita to iu      here," she says,
   yamabuki iketearu ni  and there where kerria roses
   tomari               are arranged
                      I stay

8. Mugi fumu ya        Do they tread the wheat?
   tsumetaki kaze no    Days of cold winds
   hi no tsuzuku       continue

9.  Shūsen no                    After war's end
    yo no akeshiramu             the dawn comes white
    Amanogawa                    under the Milky Way

10. Isu ni ari                   I'm in the chair.
    fuyubi wa moete              The winter sun, burning,
    chikazuki-ku                 comes closer

11. Koshi tateshi                On the scorched earth,
    shōdo no mugi ni             the south wind harasses
    nanpū araki                  the young wheat sprouts

12. Saezuriya                    Warbling—
    kaze sukoshi aru             it's a bit windy
    tōge-michi                   on this pass

13. Bōfū no                      The angelica
    koko made suna ni            has been buried under the sand
    umoreshi to                  this far, they say

14. Ōibi no                      Slapping the face
    kawamo o uchite              of the Great Ibi River—
    hisame ka na                 the icy rain

15. Kaki hoshite                 Persimmons hung up to dry.
    kyō no hitori-i              Today I'm alone
    kumo mo nashi                without even a cloud

What is your impression? For someone like myself who has little
interest in haiku and utterly no experience in writing it, this
exercise reminds me of the time when, as a middle-school student,
I was taken to Hirakata to a chrysanthemum exhibition. The
plants had been trained with arduous care to grow into lantern
shapes, cascades, and so forth, by adherents of various schools
of chrysanthemum growers, but I could not have been less
interested in their relative merits; I was in fact thoroughly bored
by it all. As with the chrysanthemums, these poems move me
little esthetically. If anything, they provoke a certain sense of
irritation. I had no sympathy with the attempts to make cascades

and other fanciful shapes out of the chrysanthemums, but at least they were real flowers—artificially contorted perhaps, but reassuring in their concreteness. By comparison, several of the verses make no sense to me and convey no particular mental image. I find numbers 3, 7, 10, 11, and 13 verbally incomprehensible, to begin with, and my puzzlement was shared by several of the well-educated people I asked to evaluate the list. Unless one is told that these are the works of famous poets (Nakamura Kusatao, Ogiwara Seisensui, Matsumoto Takashi, Usuda Arō, and Takahama Kyoshi), who would bother even to try to understand them?

Of course, ease of understanding does not determine the value of a work of art, but how much meaning does art have if a work cannot evoke for others the experience of the creator? In this respect, modern haiku is sadly wanting. The vast volume of writing, some of it by the poets themselves, on the appreciation and interpretation of modern haiku poetry is ample testimony. Such explanatory material may be necessary for the work of the classical period, when manners and customs as well as language usage were quite different, but I find it jarring to think that we should need such reams of commentary as well as that most inartistic of all vehicles, the paraphrase, to make comprehensible the writing of people living in the same country, at the same time, as ourselves. To me this only means that the genre itself is in some way incomplete, unable to stand alone. Alain (Emile Chartier) provided commentaries on the poetry of Paul Valéry, but Valéry's poetry is extremely close to perfection; it is so completely and concretely alive that Alain could develop his thoughts on the basis of the poems. He did not have to explain, rescue, or—worse—complete them. As far as I know, French writers never produced the kind of self-serving commentaries on the poetry of Baudelaire or Verlaine that appears in Japan's world of haiku.

I may be asking for criticism by judging haiku this way without ever having tried to write any myself. Mizuhara Shūōshi once said that "unless one attempts to write it, he cannot understand what haiku is."[3] But this, coming from one of the most conscientious men of the haiku world, seems like a sentence of doom for haiku as a modern art. No Japanese novelist—and their work is hardly the most modern—has said, "Not until you have written one will you truly appreciate the novel." Rodin never protested that only those who had experience in sculpting should discuss sculpture; anyone told that he should refrain from criticizing *Casablanca* or other films because he had not already made two or three himself understandably would be indignant. Only in haiku does one encounter remarks like that of Shūōshi: "I do not think it is right for those who have not struggled to write haiku to take it upon themselves to advise those who have." (Ibid.) He can express himself in this way only because the world of haiku is a kind of exclusive guild of like-minded people who join and perform simply for their own enjoyment.

My colleagues and I next discovered that it is very difficult to determine the relative skill of a given author and distinguish a leading poet from an amateur only on the basis of a single example of his haiku. Certainly Kyoshi's *Bōfū no koko made suna ni umoreshi to* (13) does not strike one as much better than an amateur piece I found in a company magazine: *Saezuriya kaze sukoshi aru tōge-michi* (12). And the latter one is surely more poetic than Hino Sōjō's *Kayu-bara no obotsukanashi ya hana no yama* (4). Truly superior works of modern art would not present such problems. A comparison of the complete works of Leo Tolstoy and Kikuchi Kan would leave no question as to which was the superior novelist; just a look at only a single short story by each is enough to establish the difference. Even to suggest comparing a work by the master of the short story, Shiga Naoya, with something by an immature writer finally published in an obscure literary journal would be insulting to Mr. Shiga. I have seen in Paris many of the small sculptures of Rodin and Emile Bourdelle, and even the most diminutive stands apart from the finest works displayed at the Imperial Academy art exhibitions (now known as the Nitten Exhibition).

When it comes to haiku, one must know the author to be able to differentiate among works. Some are distinctive; only Seisensui self-righteously flouts the rules of form, e.g., *Koko ni nete imashita to iu yamabuki iketearu ni tomari* (7), and no one but Nakamura Kusatao would produce the awkward modernisms that appear in *Seku hipokuritto Bētōben hibiku asa* (3). But their distinctiveness does not derive from intrinsic artistic merit. Starting off an article entitled "The Dignity of Haiku," Kinbara Seigo quotes the all too familiar and all too frequently misunderstood words of Shiga Naoya: "When gazing at the Guze Kannon in the Yumedono of Hōryūji, one does not think to ask who made it. The statue itself is an existence so extraordinary that it transcends its creator." Kinbara goes on to philosophize about the dignity of haiku: "When a work is detached from time and space, and even from its author, what is it that emerges from it? It is the person of the author himself." Far from explaining its "dignity," this approach reduces haiku to absurdity.

When haiku began to be written independently, apart from *renga*, the longer, "linked verse" form composed jointly by several poets, it became a separate literary genre but an awkward one. In the case of modern haiku, in particular, the calibre of an author is extremely difficult to establish on the basis of single, isolated verses. It becomes necessary to determine the status of an artist according to some criteria other than his art. One must evaluate his influence on a more mundane level. Unlike artists in other media, whose reputations usually rest on the artistic value of their work, a haiku poet's reputation is sustained by the number of his students, the circulation of the journal he publishes, and even his personal social connections. Inevitably, therefore, the world of haiku is filled with numerous factions and schools.

Insofar as factions are a product of the struggle for supremacy, it is only natural for a poet, as he rises in importance, to break away from his group and establish a separate faction of his own. These self-styled haiku "bosses" have established themselves all over the country. Today there are no fewer than thirty haiku journals (*Haiku kenkyū*, 1946). A faction formed even around Bashō, but because his poetry is so outstanding, he is rarely thought of as a faction leader. (Takarai Kikaku, Nozawa Bonchō, and Ochi Etsujin are some of the better-known poets who broke away from Bashō in his later years.) In the centuries following Bashō's death, there appeared many haiku leaders who, wanting "credentials," claimed poetic lineage from the early masters (as is frequently the case in the performing arts). Modern haiku poets like Kyoshi and Arō are not often identified as independent artists; these two are known first and foremost as the leaders of the Hototogisu and Shakunage schools.

The world of fiction writing, too, once had its schools—the Ken'yūsha of the Japanese Romanticists, the Akamon school (Tokyo Imperial University), and the Mita school (Keio University) were prominent—although they have disappeared today. Ishikawa Jun and Sakaguchi Ango may be close friends, but as novelists they are recognized as independent authors. In contrast, the vast majority of haiku poets are associated with some faction or other. They are no longer identified in terms of the specific generation following a given master, but the spirit is the same. For example, in a recent issue of the *Yomiuri shinbun* I came across an announcement of a haiku lecture series, in which the speaker was described as "Ikeuchi Yūjirō-sensei, son of Takahama Kyoshi." About a novelist, for example Hirotsu Kazuo, no one would say that he is the "son of Hirotsu Ryūrō."

I use the term "faction" not in the current sense of political faction, but to convey something like the medieval *compagnonnage* or guild of artisans with its carefully nurtured mystique. Like the old guilds, modern haiku factions also need, in addition to a specific leader, some ancient authority through whom to derive the necessary esotericism, a patron saint, as it were. The patron saint of haiku is Bashō. The relevant scripture goes back to his concepts of *sabi, shiori, karumi*, and so on. Fortunately Bashō was kind enough not to define these words clearly. Declarations such as Arō's "I, haiku, and the spirit of Nature form a trinity" are still accepted among haiku poets.

In organizations held together by mystical bonds, leaders constantly preach to new members as a way of preserving their authority. In truth, I know of no group with such a penchant for guidance as haiku poets. They teach their followers to "absorb yourself in haiku," "seek after Truth," "learn about pines from the pines," "perfect your humanity," and so on. It was a practical impossibility, even in the feudal period, for anyone to devote all his waking hours to the art. By preaching ideals impossible to attain, the leaders won ever-increasing respect from others. Yet how often did they practice what they preached?

The world of haiku vaunts the ideal of "escaping from worldly cares": one should "recite poetry while gazing at the moon, admire the flowers, and let your heart roam free" (*Tsuki ni usobuki, hana o mede, kokoro o jinkan no soto ni asobashimu*). But haiku is also a mass art that uses mundane images and plain language, and so it contains two inherently contradictory inclinations. I am not familiar with his theoretical writing, so I cannot do more than speculate on how a genius like Bashō tried to overcome this contradiction. Perhaps, surrounded on all sides by the iron walls of feudal society, Bashō found he could not make even a crack in the walls and had no alternative but to seek freedom of the spirit as an artistic recluse. He discovered that the only thing capable of change is the human heart, and he turned to Saigyō and Tu Fu as models for expressing the lonely, yet ambitious burning of his mind. I believe that his famous phrase *ka-ro, tōsen* (lit., like the brazier in summer, the fan in winter) reflects his attitude.[4] But even the "flower of the heart" born of it ran into the feudal iron wall extending overhead as well, leaving no choice but to grovel on the ground. That probably accounts for the genre's use of the vernacular and its mass orientation. A haikai recluse was forced to seek support among the masses (wealthy men like Sanpū). Famous for being strict, Bashō was generous with the people who participated in haikai contests, saying that "although they do not really understand poetry, they help feed the families of the judges, who, in turn, enrich their landlords, so what they do cannot be all bad" (from letter known as "A Piece on 'Three Kinds' [of Attitudes toward Haikai]").

Bashō lived in a time of rising interest in the classical arts and scholarship, when the shogun himself gave lectures on the Four Confucian Classics—although, needless to say, the era was totally different in quality from the Renaissance. Even ordinary townspeople with no claim to scholarly knowledge were caught up in the classical tide. Inspired by the same enthusiasm, Bashō, with his keen eye, could look at nature through Saigyō's *waka* and Tu Fu's poetry, thereby managing to avoid becoming vulgar in his own work. (Bashō did not see nature as we do today, and we cannot see nature as he did because of our knowledge of natural science.) His travels, which exposed him to minor dangers, were probably intended to be a means of softening—if not transcending—the contradictions in his art. I think it is significant, incidentally, that the Meiji-era poet Masaoka Shiki (1867–1902) undertook the reform of haiku while suffering from a fatal illness.

After Bashō, haiku became even more popular among the masses, and the Tokugawa feudal system became deeply entrenched. Because they lived in a period of stability perhaps unsurpassed anywhere else in world history, it was natural that haiku poets should grow corrupt and their work begin to show signs of decline. It was not because they forgot the spirit of Bashō, or because they no longer sought what he had sought; rather, they degenerated precisely because they continued in narrow idolization of him. They declined because of the increasing mystification of Bashō's words as interpreted by his disciples and later generations of haiku masters, and more, because they would not give up Bashō.

In the arts, it is not possible simultaneously to master both the spirit and the forms of genius. To do so, one must assume that the spirit is embodied in the form, whereupon the spirit will inevitably become formalized. The result is academism or mannerism. Bashō is said to have learned from Saigyō and Tu Fu, but because the forms—*waka* and Chinese poetry—were different from haiku, he could only abstract and digest their essence, and while accepting the traditional spirit he could escape the pitfalls of mannerism. Bashō's successors clung to the same forms, and sought constantly to return to his teachings, so it was unavoidable that their work should grow hackneyed and stereotyped.

The fact that a single artistic form has managed to survive virtually unchanged for three hundred years is one indication of the stability—or stagnation—of Japanese society. Just as the spirit of the modern army established after the Meiji Restoration remained rooted in the traditional samurai ethos, the spirit of the haiku world stayed constant, despite the trappings of modernization: scores of new journals in printed form and offices ensconced in new Western-style buildings. Yet the contradictions inherent in the world of haiku became increasingly apparent in the glare of social progress. Even as the masters continued to chant the other-worldly liturgy of their genre, they had to survive in the new society. They had no choice but to give precedence to the instinctive and mundane in life. Declaring such sentiments as "the ultimate in human life is solitude," when faced with the rise of a powerful social force, they shrewdly deferred to it. Then, when its influence receded, they picked up their lofty ideals once more. The willow never breaks under the weight of snow. (This applies to all the traditional highbrow pursuits and performing arts in Japan. The tea ceremony was one organized cultural endeavor that served to give particularly enthusiastic support to the war effort.) I recall that when the Literary Patriots Association (Bungaku Hōkokukai) was formed, the number of applicants to the haiku division alone was so great that the association headquarters was forced to strictly limit the membership in that division.

Among writers of fiction, some were opportunists or apologists for militarism, but today those people are no longer capable of producing outstanding work. The novel as a modern genre does not permit such opportunism, and that is one of its strengths. But in haiku, some of the poets who were quickest to proffer dazzling public relations verses lauding patriotic efforts during the war, such as the Silver Collection Movement, are leaders in the genre even today. Haiku is a literary genre in which the work of artists seems to be absolutely unaffected by their activities in society. (When young men of literary bent took jobs with the government or business before the war, those who enjoyed haiku were well thought of by their superiors, while those who wrote fiction were usually frowned upon; I think there was good reason for that tendency.)

Insofar as haikai aspires to be an art, it must resist vulgarization. In an endeavor to do just that, Bashō turned to the classical literary traditions of Saigyō and Tu Fu. Yet today the classical traditions have been all but forgotten. At least they are no longer fashionable. Whether they really understand it or not, people prefer modern Western art. It might seem a good idea to incorporate its spirit in haiku, but that would never succeed. Although Saigyō and Tu Fu were far removed from Bashō in time, they were, like Bashō, flowers that bloomed on the ground, not blossoms that rose high. Modern Western art, though its roots may be in the soil, is like a towering tree, flowering in lofty idealism high above. The flowers of both may be beautiful but the difference

198 JAPAN AND WESTERN CIVILIZATION

between them is irreconcilable. If Western art were properly transplanted to haiku, it would burst the pot. The only reason the pot has not burst is that the cutting has not taken root. Quite apart from the success or failure of the attempt, if haiku had truly sought to learn from Western literature, it should have paid attention at least to nihilism, but haiku poets did not even notice it.

There is an effort to create something new in haiku by breathing into it the stuff of human life, but life itself is being modernized, and the realities of contemporary life simply cannot be expressed in haiku. It is all very well to declare that writing haiku disciplines and refines a person's character or that "haiku throws light on the human personality," but it is hardly likely that people who pretend to breezy transcendentalism today have much to illuminate for us. How accurately do the prominent haiku poets understand the world? We can learn something from Ogiwara Seisensui's attempt at an interpretation of freedom, in his essay "Kokoro Kisowazu" [Noncompetitive mind]:

> Freedom by definition depends on the self. The peach tree blossoms of itself and the wheat that grows at its feet sends forth heads of grain of itself, each according to its own nature. One does not interfere with, block, or compete with the other, but each simply and naturally expresses its own life. This is freedom in the true sense. Freedom is the noncompetitive state of mind. On a grand level this is the ideal of mankind; on a smaller level it is a principle of the art of linked verse (*renku*).

I need not go any further into the difficulties of introducing human life into modern haiku. Mizuhara Shūōshi, in his essay *Gendai haikuron* [On Modern Haiku], was correct in his open observation that "the materials for haiku are derived from natural phenomena and from everyday things that are affected by changes in nature." Shūōshi's conscientiousness, which I mentioned earlier, is reflected in this statement. He does not look to Bashō, and he believes that modern haiku should discard *sabi* and *wabishisa* and turn to brighter things. This, I would say, is a step in the right direction. But is even that step enough to rescue modern haiku as an art? The important thing is the work of art, how to produce a work of art. Shūōshi advises poets to learn from painting. "In writing haiku, it is wise to write as if drawing a small painting, about the size of a number four frame, if measured according to the size of Western paintings, and a little larger than a *shikishi* painting board if by Japanese standards. . . ."[5]

It is a rule in the arts that when one genre is drawn strongly by another and tries to adopt its methods, it provokes its own decline [Alain]. When the leaders of the genre begin to advocate such methods of writing haiku, I believe they are spelling out the doom of their own art. And what are they trying to portray? "Natural phenomena and everyday things that are affected by changes in nature"—expressed more bluntly, vegetable-like life. You will recall that Ogiwara Seisensui explained freedom, which may be the most important problem of life for modern man, by means of plants—peaches and wheat. If modern haiku tries to be conscientious, it ends up learning about a peach from a peach and about wheat from wheat, and reproducing a vegetable-like life as in a small painting.

This pursuit is well suited to be the pastime of old people without other occupations, or the sick, but can modern man truly devote his soul to such frivolity? Is it not perhaps careless to apply the term "art" [*geijutsu*], as we would in modern fiction or drama, to haiku? (In *Gendai haikuron*, I might note, Shūōshi does not use the word "art" [geijutsu], but only "craft" [*gei*].) In every age, man is permitted some diversions. No one can find fault if old men choose to devote themselves to cultivating chrysanthemums or bonsai, holding periodic exhibitions or contests and publishing a journal or two (although thirty is really too many!). Even if cultivating chrysanthemums does not have what one would call "contemporary significance," it has its own labors and its own pleasures, and no one would deny that. And haiku as an old man's pastime also satisfies, as expressed in Kyoshi's *Ku o tama to atatamete oru kotatsu kana!* [Snug in my foot warmer, I coddle a haiku as if it were a gem.]

But one hesitates to call cultivating chrysanthemums an art [*geijutsu*]. One might call it a craft [*gei*], or if the term "art" must be used, I would suggest "secondary art," in order to distinguish modern haiku from other arts. Once we accept it as a secondary art, there is no need for any theory or rationalization. A "return to Bashō" is all well and good, but it would be more constructive —and more fitting to the present state of the genre—simply to accept the frivolous aspect of haiku, as Nishiyama Sōin (1605– 82) did, and enjoy it for what it is. "Whether in the old style, the current style, or the in-between style, a good poet is a good poet, and a bad one is a bad one; there is no such thing as distinguishing which style is the correct one; the best thing is to amuse oneself by writing what one likes; it is a joke within a fantasy (*mugen no gigen*)."[6]

I have made my point, but, at the risk of repeating myself, I would like to add a few more remarks to address all the recent talk about becoming a "nation dedicated to culture." If we seriously aspire to build a cultural nation, we must think carefully about the stuff of which it is made. A secondary art, which is what we have decided haiku is, perhaps ought to be put under some restraint. In a cultural nation, it goes without saying that art must be respected and accessible to everyone. The new culture should not be designed to focus primarily on the arts, but there must be awareness of the artistic qualities that make a creation worthy of respect and wide appreciation. Everyone would like to see a country whose entire population understood and appreciated the arts, but we must not fall victim to the sophistry of a "nationwide character" in traditional Japanese civilization (see Hasegawa Nyozekan, *Nihonteki seikaku* [Japanese Character]). How far can we stretch the meaning of art—even by attaching some qualifier like "lowbrow"—just to embrace the haiku of your local barber or the earthy humor of *senryū*? Regarding haiku and *senryū*, Nyozekan claimed that "rather than disdaining them as lowbrow, we should disdain the fact that the villagers and townspeople [of the West] do not have even such lowbrow literature."

While in France, I noticed that words were used artistically even in the most casual of encounters, from the conversation of intellectuals to the prattle at my boarding-house dinner table. The French are especially fond of skilled repartee, but they would never call it an "art." They regard art as something much more noble, and art is very highly respected. Anyone who has ever lived in France is familiar with the great respect with which the French people utter the word *écrivain* [writer]. People savor the arts but do not suppose they can turn them out at will.

And in Japan? If the arts are taken lightly here, that may reflect the dearth of truly great artists. But I think a more important reason is the tremendous sway of certain genres, like haiku, in which just about anyone can easily acquire some skill. Art, in the popular notion, is something anyone can do with a little practice. The great poets are simply fortunate enough to be able to devote themselves wholly to haiku. Anyone, the idea goes, can be a great artist if he so chooses. It is simply a matter of some skill and the leisure to perfect it.

This kind of attitude will never earn for art the high respect that is commensurate with truly great achievement; and more, we will never produce great artists. I have no statistical evidence, but surely there is no other country with so many amateur artists as Japan. I suspect it is the "mass orientation" myth that is responsible for the proclivity of every young thing who has had an affair to sit down and write a novel (and even bring it to someone like myself to comment on). As long as there is no understanding that modern art is a serious pursuit requiring total dedication, and that the creation of a single work of art means the growth or the degradation of the creator, nothing of artistic importance will emerge. Moreover, as long as people casually assume that one has done creative work after he has written a few haiku, they will never be able to fully appreciate the great modern arts of Europe.

I have nothing against adults enjoying haiku as they please; I only hope that we might extricate the teaching of haiku from our schools, for it has no more place in the curriculum than instruction in old Edo samisen music has. Some think that haiku can serve as a guide in observing nature, but to me, that means they have no real understanding of the nature of modern science. Nothing could be more completely opposed to the scientific spirit than the haiku spirit, which casts aside all concern for the laws of nature or human society and seeks to capture nature in words as a photographer tries to freeze nature in a snapshot.

# Notes

The names of the professional haiku poets are: 1. Awano Seiho; 3. Nakamura Kusa-
tao; 4. Hino Sōjō; 5. Tomiyasu Fusei; 7. Ogiwara Seisensui; 8. Iida Dakotsu; 10.
Matsumoto Takashi; 11. Usuda Arō; 13. Takahama Kyoshi; and 15. Mizuhara
Shūōshi. The rest are amateurs or newcomers to the genre.

1.  Some of my observations appear in the February 1946 issue of *Ningen* and the
September 1946 issue of *Shinchō*.
2.  I. A. Richards, *Practical Criticism: A Study of Literary Judgement* (London: Paul &
C., 1929).
3.  Mizuhara Shūōshi, *Kibachi*, no. 2.
4.  Ebara Taizō does not interpret this phrase as expressing Bashō's belief in art
for art's sake, but rather in art for life (see *Bashō: Kyorai*, p. 120). Since art for art's
sake would not have been possible without the emergence of modern, individual
self-consciousness, it is probably not accurate to represent Bashō as an advocate of
that idea, but I am not satisfied with his explanation of the "art for life" thesis. If
it were "art for *my* life," it might make sense. I hope some day Mr. Ebara will
enlighten me on this.
5.  Mizuhara Shūōshi, *Kibachi*, no. 2.
6.  Translation by Donald Keene in *World Within Walls* (London: Secker & Warburg,
1976), pp. 48–49.

# Index

Abe Kōbō, 183
Abe Kōzō, 60
Abe Takeo, 101
Aida Yūji, 142
Akagi Kensuke, 48
Alain, 191
Andersen, Hans Christian, 20
Andō Shōeki, 131
Aoki Ichigorō, 58
Arai Hakuseki, 62, 131

Baelz, Erwin von, 134, 161
Barraclough, Geoffrey, 116, 139–40
Baudelaire, Charles, 73
Bourget, Paul, 17
Brunot, Ferdinand, 169
Bungaku Hōkokukai, 56, 197

Catholicism, 3, 67; missionaries, 125–28, 167–68
China, 51, 52–53; classics, 65–66; history, 156
Chang Ch'ien, 122
Cheng Ho, 122
Ch'eng Yen-ch'iu, 52
Ch'i Po-shih, 14
Chinese Communist party, 22
Columbus, Christopher, 122
Confucianism, 65–66

Daguerre, Louis Jacques Mandé, 76, 89
Descartes, René, 102
Dewey, John 4, 11
Doi Kōchi, 100
Doi Takeo, 152
Dore, Ronald, 137, 169

Einstein, Albert, 46
England, 91–92, 93–95, 96

Esenin, Sergei Aleksandrovich, 17
existentialists, 4

Franco, Francisco, 3, 14
Frois, Louis, 125–26
Fujiwara Ginjirō, 62
Fujiwara Yoshie, 178
Futabatei Shimei, 50, 55

Galileo, 106, 123
Galois, Evariste, 13
Gama, Vasco da, 122
Gandhi, Indira, 87
Gandhi, Mahatma, 167
Giroux, Yvette, 15
Goebbels, Joseph Paul, 3
Gorki, Maxim, 22, 23, 53
Grousset, René, 99

haiku, 47–48, 189–203
Halpern, Abraham, 43
Hasegawa Nyozekan, 200
Hashimoto Sōkichi, 131, 132
Hearn, Lafcadio, 147, 169
Hemingway, Ernest, 14
Higuchi Ichiyō, 56
Hill, Christopher, 91
Hino Sōjō, 192
Hiraga Gennai, 131
Hirotsu Kazuo, 196
Honda Katsuichi, 149
Honda Toshiaki, 131, 132, 133
Hugo, Victor, 18, 19

Ibn Battuta, 122
Ihara Saikaku, 55
Imanishi Kinji, 27
Impressionism, 156
Ino Kenji, 48

Inoue Yasushi, 152, 183
Ishikawa Takuboku, 39, 42, 50

Japan Communist party, 22, 43. *See also*
   Marxists

Kabuki, 48, 50, 51, 53, 59
Kaizuka Shigeki, 99
Kaneko Naokichi, 62
Katō Hidetoshi, 92
Kawabata Yasunari, 72, 183
Kawahigashi Hekigodō, 188
Kawamori Yoshizō, 54
Keene, Donald, 133
Ken'yūsha, 194
Kikuchi Kan, 55
Kinbara Seigo, 192–93
Kitamura Tōkoku, 39, 42
Kohn, Hans, 160
Komatsu Sakyō, 150
Kondō Takayoshi, 48, 49, 50
Kurahara Korehito, 55–56

Lefebvre, Henri, 22, 108, 109
Lenin, Nikolai, 51
Liberal party, 43
Livingstone, David, 122
Lorenz, Konrad, 107
Lu Hsun, 21, 52, 53, 162, 168
Lu Yu, 76
Luther, Martin, 116

Malraux, André, 14
Mamiya Rinzō, 122
Mao Tse-tung, 13, 21, 52
Masaoka Shiki, 187, 196
Maruki Iri, 14
Maruki Toshi, 14
Marxism, 13, 48, 50
Marxists, 3, 45–46
Matsumoto Seichō, 152, 183
Matsumoto Takashi, 191
Matsuo ¦Bashō, 187, 193, 194, 195–96,
   197
Mayakovski, Vladimir Vladimirovich,
   17
Mei Lan-fang, 52
Meiji era, 39–40, 79, 82–83, 87–88
Meiji revolution, 66–67, 134–36, 137–39,
   159–60
Mihashi Michiya, 15–16
Minami Hiroshi, 51
Mishima Yukio, 183
Miyoshi Tatsuji, 69
Mizuhara Shūōshi, 191, 192, 198–99
Mizuno Seiichi, 99

Mori Arinori, 136, 162
Mori Ōgai, 50, 183
Motoori Norinaga, 62
Murayama Tomoyoshi, 49
Murphy, Robert, 49
Mutō Sanji, 62

Nagahiro Toshio, 99
Nagao Gajin, 112
Naitō Konan, 75–76, 156
Nakae Chōmin, 77, 80–82, 144, 150, 163,
   172
Nakamura Kusatao, 191
Nakamura Yoshiharu, 100
Nakano Kiyomi, 32, 33
Nakano Yoshio, 68
Nakazato Kaizan, 54, 55, 56
Natsume Sōseki, 39, 55, 72, 94, 183
Needham, Joseph, 107
Nehru, Jawaharlal, 78, 106
Nihon Bungaku Kyōkai, 47, 48
Nishiyama Sōin, 200
Nō, 100, 180
Noma Hiroshi, 22, 55
Nozawa Bonchō, 193

Occupation, 42–44
Ochi Etsujin, 193
Oda Nobunaga, 127, 150, 151, 158
Odagiri Hideo, 47
Ogiwara Seisensui, 191, 192, 198, 199
Ogyū Sorai, 147
Osanai Kaoru, 50
Ōtsuki Gentaku, 131

Perry, Matthew Calbraith, 129, 159
Piaget, Jean, 9, 105
Picasso, Pablo, 14
Poe, Edgar Allan, 73

Reischauer, Edwin O., 184
Research Institute for Humanistic Stud-
   ies, 97–99, 101
Ricci, Mateo, 129
Richards, I. A., 189
Riesman, David, 153, 183
Robinson, Joan, 166
Rodin, Auguste, 14
Rosenblueth, Arturo, 103
Rousseau, Jean-Jacques, 8, 181

Saigyō, 195, 196, 197
Sakuma Shōzan, 134
Sakuta Keiichi, 147, 172
Sansom, G. B., 125, 133, 136, 138, 161,
   168

Sartre, Jean-Paul, 9
Schall, Adam, 129
Sen no Rikyū, 147
Sheldon, W., 106
Shiba Kōkan, 131
Shiba Ryōtarō, 152, 183
Shiga Naoya, 193
Shimabara Rebellion, 81, 128, 157
Shimazaki Tōson, 55
Shimizu Kon, 15
Shirozaki Hideo, 145
Sholokhov, Mikhail Aleksandrovich, 18
Siegfried, André, 121
Soviet Union, 3, 51, 52, 53
Spanish Civil War, 14
Stendhal, 19, 73
Stowe, Harriet Beecher, 18
Sugita Genpaku, 131

Tada Michitarō, 145
Takahama Kyoshi, 191, 192, 193, 199
Takakura Teru, 128
Takano Chōei, 131, 132, 133
Takasugi Shinsaku, 134
Takarai Kikaku, 193
Takayanagi Shinzō, 100
Takeda Katsuyori, 127
Takeuchi Yoshimi, 54, 168
Takeyama Michio, 150
Takizawa Bakin, 136
Tanizaki Jun'ichirō, 56, 72, 183
Tokuda Shūsei, 56
Tokugawa Yoshimune, 131
Tokutomi Roka, 20, 55
Tōma Seita, 50, 55
Tomonaga Shin'ichirō, 183

Tomono Yaemon, 128
Torigai Risaburō, 101
Toynbee, Arnold, 66
Toyotomi Hideyoshi, 127, 158
Ts'ai Yuan-p'ei, 52
Tsubouchi Shōyō, 50
Tsurumi Shunsuke, 107, 111, 112
Tu Fu, 194, 196, 197

Umehara Ryūzaburō, 15, 60
United Nations Educational, Scientific,
    and Cultural Organization, 65, 74
Usuda Arō, 191, 193, 194

Valéry, Paul, 9, 16

Watanabe Kazan, 131, 132
Webb, Walter Prescott, 123, 124, 165,
    166
Whitehead, Alfred North, 107
Wiener, Norbert, 69, 102, 103–4, 105

Xavier, Francis, 120, 126

Yamamura Saisuke, 131
Yanagita Kunio, 149, 179
Yasui Sōtarō, 15, 60
Yasui Takuma, 100
Yokoyama Taizō, 15
Yoshida Shōin, 133
Yoshikawa Eiji, 54, 55, 56
Yoshikawa Kōjirō, 69, 99
Yukawa Hideki, 84
Yung-lo, Emperor, 122

Zeami, 110